LOVE TODAY

LOVE

NEW YORK

TODAY

A NEW EXPLORATION

Edited by HERBERT A. OTTO

ASSOCIATION PRESS

LOVE TODAY: A NEW EXPLORATION

Copyright © 1972 by Herbert A. Otto

Association Press, 291 Broadway, New York, N.Y.   10007

International Standard Book Number: 0-8096-1839-7
Library of Congress Catalog Card Number: 70-167887

Printed in the United States of America

Contents

Preface

The word "love" is among the most often used words in the English-speaking countries. Innumerable novels, poems and songs have been written about love. Despite this literary profusion and the extensive use of the word, and despite the fact that love is a widely shared experience, especially among Western cultures, behavioral scientists and contemporary thinkers, with few exceptions, have avoided intensive study of the subject. This volume represents an effort to remedy that situation.

There is today a beginning realization that at this particular point in time, the nourishment and regeneration of love has never been more important. It is heartening to know that we are discovering a means to help man become a more loving and caring being. In that sense this volume brings both a message of hope and a call for action. Looking back to both recent and past history, we can clearly see that there has been a great deal of talk but little action in helping man to become a more loving being. We have been too busy "conquering nature" and developing the concepts and tools which today make man the artist of his own creation. *The functional application of love and caring to our daily living, our relationships with others, our institutional structures and our ecology represent our greatest challenge.*

I would like to express my appreciation to Henry Regnery Company of Chicago for their permission to publish excerpts from Chapters 1 and 2 of Pitirim Sorokin's *The Ways and Power of Love*. My thanks go, also, to colleagues and friends who have given advice and counsel. Finally, I would like to dedicate this book to my wife Roberta, whose sustaining love has been an inspiration.

H. A. O.

La Jolla, Calif.

1

The Prospects of Love:
An Introduction

Herbert A. Otto

Love is more important today than at any other time in man's history. The phenomenon of love has for a long time been one of the most neglected areas of research, shunned and avoided by most disciplines. It is very heartening that we are now on the threshold of a new and developing interest in this area, especially among humanistic psychologists and other behavioral scientists.

This volume represents the first comprehensive inquiry by a collection of Western behavioral scientists deeply interested in the study of love and its dimensions. All papers, with one exception, are original contributions, prepared specifically for this volume, an outgrowth of a symposium entitled "Love as a Growth Experience" presented at the annual meeting of the American Psychological Association in San Francisco, August 1968, of which the editor was the chairman.

Most of us are not sufficiently aware that to love and to be loved are a form of nurturing which we need throughout our lives. An infant dies without love. In an adult who is without love, there is often a withering away and dying of the tenderest and most sensitive parts of his being. Contemporary love and rock lyrics recognize our continuing need for love. Sweet love, we are assured, is the only thing of which this world has too little. Surprisingly, most so-called love songs deal with the painful aspects of love, such as longing, parting, etc. In a survey conducted over a two-week period (while driving to and from work when I was in Chicago) I found that roughly 70 per cent of the love songs either concentrated on the pain of love, or pleaded for love: "Please love me, don't leave me," another 5 per cent combined pleas with painful and positive elements. Only 25 per cent of the songs surveyed focused on love's positive elements (love is great, wonderful). If this is correct, then we must conclude that the so-called *love songs to which we listen tend to condition us against participating in the love experience and foster an attitude of caution and distrust toward loving a person of the opposite sex.*

Certainly, what emerges from this vest-pocket survey is a recognition that despite an obvious verbal preoccupation with love in our culture there is a great deal of ambivalence about the subject. Nor are we very clear about the role love *should* play in a society devoted to the development of man's possibilities. For these reasons the papers and research summaries prepared for this volume by pioneering scientists constitute a promising beginning effort toward a fuller understanding of love as a dynamic force in our lives, and in contemporary society.

We have reached a point in our development where the massive accumulation of destructive weaponry, if even fractionally used, will put an end to all mankind. For the first time in history, one key statesman's indifference or anger at a specific point in time can mean the destruction of the human race. The regeneration of love has never been more important, *for without love we shall not survive.*

This thesis is not new. It has been the main theme of wise men and saints from the earliest time since man recorded his thoughts—and possibly before then. What *is* new is that we are now on the brink of specie destruction, and that by and large, we are indifferent to this drastic state of affairs.

If indifference is the opposite of love, then the nature and depth of our indifference today is both the final warning and the clearest expression of our need for love. In a very real sense, then, everyone is engaged in the ultimate crisis of love. This is the crisis of our age—for without love man cannot endure on this earth.

Confronted with this overwhelming problem, we can, as always, each begin with himself. Key questions we must ask ourselves are: "How shall we overcome our indifference?" "How can we give more love to ourselves, thus enabling us to give more love to others?" If we have the strength to ask these questions, and the courage and compassion to seek the answers, we become participants in the regeneration of love.

Since we have been present at the demise of an ill-defined concept called "the great society," perhaps we can, with the utter naïvete of great wisdom, begin to build a Loving Society. *This Society emphasizes the development of love in man and devotes a considerable percentage of its energies and time to help its population become more loving and caring beings.* In this society there is a constant encouragement, nurturance and support, so that love can become a functional personal value; thus, love can proliferate and the enchantment, ecstasy and nourishment of love will be available to all who wish it. The Loving Society fosters caring, empathy, trust, openness, sharing and sensitivity to what the other person is feeling. It helps its members to develop an environment of warmth, security, affection, beauty and joy. This is the environment most conducive to the evolutionary unfoldment of the human spirit and the actualization of human potential; and this is the society which recognizes that *the more you let yourself love, the greater the wholeness you bring to yourself and others.* Perhaps we are at a state of readiness where a national, professional or other organization can call for a committee to formulate an action framework of "First Steps Toward a Master Plan for the Establishment of a Loving Society."

On becoming acquainted with the concept of the Loving Society, some people might react negatively. "You can't expect everyone to love everyone else." They miss the point. There are myriad forms, shades and dimensions of caring and of loving, and there are many more ways of *expressing* this caring and loving. (We may, for example, care enough for a person to share with him that, due to some action on his part, we are angry with him.) In the Loving Society the emphasis will be on the affective domain, the recognition and communication of feelings, on self-understanding and self-awareness, on our continuing development and growth as caring persons, and *on the recognition that our way of life can be an art form and that we can become the great artists of our own joyful becoming.* No one must "love" everyone else—but we can all develop that quality of caring for each other which is manifest by translating our values and beliefs into our daily actions and interactions.

With its emphasis on the reawakening of love, the Human Potentialities Movement is highly significant because it represents a vital force in the regeneration of our society. It is based on several hypotheses: (1) that the average healthy person functions at only 5 to 10 percent of his capacity; (2) that man's most exciting lifelong adventure is actualizing his potential; (3) that the group environment is the best setting in which to achieve growth; and (4) that personality growth can be achieved by anyone willing to invest himself in this process.

It is from this perspective that the emergence of over 175 so-called Growth Centers, such as Esalen Institute in California, Oasis in Chicago, and Aureon Institute in New York, is best understood. Nonprofit organizations, these institutes offer growth experiences under professional auspices for people who wish to actualize more of their potential. Those engaged in the search for personal growth by their participation in these group experiences express both their deep caring for themselves, as well as their fellow man. *This type of caring is essentially an expression of love, as well as the clear indication of man's thrust to become a more loving human being.*

For the person who cares enough about himself to become engaged in the risk-taking processes of personal growth, these institutes offer the excitement of self-discovery, the adventure of self-unfoldment, and the joyous realization that the capacity for love and caring will blossom in every man who wishes to nurture this facet of his being.

Many of the professionals in the Human Potentialities Movement clearly recognize that the actualization of personal potential is inseparable from the regeneration of our institutions. There is widespread acceptance that, to a much larger degree than we have previously recognized, personality is dependent for its functioning on environmental inputs. This includes both the interpersonal and physical environment as well as the institutions with which we come into contact.

For the most part, what surrounds us in our interpersonal environment is neither love nor caring. The physical environment in which we live is certainly neither one of beauty nor of cleanliness (of air, water, cities); nor do our institutions give us a sense of support, warmth and nurturance. (For example, in today's society the pressures, concerns, obligations and organizational demands shape marriage in such a way that it is difficult for love to occupy a vital and central place in the relationship.) Again, our educational institutions discriminate against the creative child, destroy intellectual curiosity, foster conformity and authority-centeredness, and "learning-in-order-to-make-a-grade." The key question here is, "To what extent do our institutions foster the realization of human potential?" If we take a clear look at our institutions, we cannot help reaching the conclusion that social regeneration has become a necessity. Our institutions are dysfunctional and operate at a fraction of their potential.

If, as a part of institutional renewal, we acknowledge that love should play a more central role, then inquiries into the nature and meaning of love need to be encouraged. If on the other hand we hold the position that the social status quo should be maintained and believe that love is an essential ingredient in today's social structures, then again deepening our understanding of this phenomenon becomes a necessity. From both perspectives enlarging our understanding of love and its unfoldment is desirable. In this light, the collection of original inquiries written for this volume represent a beginning step in the right direction.

What is gained by saying "I love you" or making a commitment of love to the sexual partner? Conversely, what is lost when there is no commitment of love, and sex is a momentary experience? In his contribution, "The Spiral of Growth: Love, Sex and Pleasure," Alexander Lowen answers these questions and evaluates the interrelationship between love, sex and pleasure vis-à-vis the process of continuing personal growth.

In a well-documented paper, Joe Adams argues that there is a "Hidden Taboo on Love." To be fully effective, a taboo must be hidden and indirect so that the population is unaware of its existence. People can be explicitly encouraged to "love" one another, but the conditions which lead to love are effectively stifled by our societal institutions which induce guilt, fear, cynicism and pretense in those who actually engage in loving. Conversely, the open recognition and acknowledgment of the taboo on love can lead to a social change and the enrichment of personal lives.

Sidney Jourard takes a subjective approach in "Some Dimensions of the Loving Experience." He discusses his own love relationships; how he feels about those he loves, what his love for others brings both to himself and to the others whom he loves and, above all, how the love experiences make life meaningful for both partners.

"Love as an Adventure in Mutual Freedom" by Colin Wilson is presented from the point of view of the phenomenologist. He deals positively and creatively with the subjects of love and of freedom from a phenomenological framework and shares some of his far-ranging thoughts on the subject.

In today's fast-moving society, increased skills in communication are considered to be very important and a great deal of research has been done in the field of human communication. In contrast, we generally neglect "Communication in Love." This area is little understood, even by lovers themselves. In this chapter Herbert Otto discusses the necessity for increased sensitivity to lovers' nonverbal communication. He also discusses some of the more important underlying principles which regulate nonverbal communication and the importance of symbolic communication in man-woman relationships.

In "Love and Women's Liberation," Rosalind Loring presents a succinct and challenging analysis of the changing role of love in the radical women's movement. She concludes that ". . . liberated women even more than women liberationists will change our notions and ways of love."

Clifford Swensen summarizes the results of his research in "The Behavior of Love." His studies are designed to measure the consequences of love: how people express their love to each other, what they say to each other, and how they *say* they feel about each other.

Henry Winthrop asks, "Why should we be concerned with the place of 'Love and Companionship' in human life?" He answers, "Because in their quest for community, these are precisely the two intangibles which men and women seek."

"Homosexual Love" by Del Martin and Paul Mariah, both for some time active in the homophile movement, is a provocative essay. Due to its frankly partisan viewpoint, it will disturb many people but should also stimulate a reassessment of widely held attitudes about the role of love in homosexual and lesbian unions.

In "Love Relationships in the Life Cycle," David Orlinsky, drawing on his extensive research experience, expands on the theme that different love experiences are regularly, rather than randomly, distributed over the life cycle from infancy through adulthood. Each stage of growth has its own proper form of love, and through participation in each love relationship one progresses to the next stage of psychological development in the life cycle.

Theodore Blau describes what he calls "The Love Effect"—an affective experience which "comes upon us" as a stirring, powerful experience, characterized by excitement, a heightened state of affect, warmth and sexualization. The love effect occurs when one's idealized self-concept is reflected by the attitudes of another and one believes he is being seen as he would like to be seen by this other. At this time, the fantasized ideal self is met in real life.

In "Melding of Personal and Spiritual Values in Love," Billy Sharp examines the cycle of mortal love and its three levels—the magic level, the black and white level, and the existential level. He then explores the relationship of personal and spiritual values in love. Lowell Colston's essay "Love and Creativity" presents a rich exploration of the many dimensions of creativity sparked by love.

In "Love, the Human Encounter," Everett L. Shostrom points out that love is an authentic human encounter wherein two persons grasp each other in emotional contact, have mutual concern for the welfare and fulfillment of each other, and experience each other with attitudes of honesty, awareness, freedom and trust. He discusses love as an experiential human encounter, the ways distortion of this encounter may take place, and the occurrence of these distortions in the various stages of growing up.

Al Lewis in "Love and the Youth Culture" finds that a specter haunts America and the postindustrial Western societies—young people who have been and are again becoming a major political factor and who are part of a youth culture in which love is a dominant and dynamic factor.

Carl Levett in "Function—A Dimension of Love," posits three vital forces in an interpersonal relationship: love, function and caring. He concludes that the totality of the relationship is dependent on these three dimensions; and that the quality of the relationship is finally dependent on the function—the performance—of each partner, one to the other.

David Jones finds that "Love and Life Goals" are inextricably woven together, in that life goals clarify for a man what he hopes to accomplish. Love for self gives him the self-knowledge to determine his goals realistically; love for others gives him the courage to act on them. Man can control much of his life, but the presence of love and life goals are a necessary condition for the development of an autonomous and meaningful life.

Next, Herbert Otto offers some reflections and thoughts with special emphasis on the idea of "Multiple Love Relationships." As a fitting conclusion, a method developed to enhance love is described—the Love Integration Experience.

No volume on love can stand without a contribution from the pioneering work of the late Pitirim Sorokin. In a letter written to the editor just prior to his death Sorokin noted that since "I am on my way to the 'exit' from Life" he wished that his contribution to this volume should consist of excerpts from the two first chapters of his book *The Ways and Power of Love*. The first part of Sorokin's contribution consists of an essay which isolates the important characteristics of love as a psychological experience. Also included is his unique description of a five-dimensional universe of love and his important study of the relationships between the love-dimension variables.

Finally, in "Epilogue: Love—The Alpha and Omega," the editor of this volume explores some of the next steps to bring about the regeneration of love.

The status of our psychological and psychiatric arts and sciences is such that we now have the means at hand so that those persons who wish to engage in this adventure can become artists in exploring the dimensions of self-creation. Many new ways of creating and re-creating ourselves will be discovered in the years to come.

In the not-too-distant future, we will be the participants in as many of our own rebirths as we wish to. We will discover that the ongoing formation of loving relationships is inseparable from man's development as a creative and loving being. We will find that an intricate relationship exists between love as a factor in man's personality and the quality and dimensions of his creativity. As man becomes more loving, he will devote more of himself to the endless, delicate, gentle unfolding and permutations possible in singular and multiple love relationships. This may become one of the major focal points around which we will build our existence. We shall finally recognize that life can and should become a festival of love and that the attainment of love is the prime catalyst of man's evolution.

2

The Spiral of Growth:
Love, Sex and Pleasure

Alexander Lowen

Human beings engage in sex primarily for pleasure. This is true even in those cases where sex directly serves the reproductive function. Since the striving for pleasure is biologically rooted in all animal organisms, it would seem that love is extraneous to sex. For love actually limits an individual's freedom to seek his sexual pleasure wherever he can find it, inasmuch as it binds two people in a personal relationship that excludes other sexual partners.

The idea that love and sex are independent and to some degree unrelated functions has been advanced by a number of psychoanalysts. Theodor Reik says, "I believe that love and sex are different in origin and nature." Sex, he says, is a biological function that aims at the release of physical tension. Love is a cultural phenomenon that aims at happiness through the establishment of a very personal relationship. Sexologists such as Albert Ellis hold the same view. Aside, then, from the question of children, what value is there in a force that leads to commitment and ties one person's welfare to another's? For love means caring and the person who cares looks beyond his immediate satisfaction to the needs and feelings of another being.

The advocacy of sex without love in the interest of pleasure gains some support from the feasibility of oral contraceptives on the one hand and the availability of antibiotics that reduce the dangers of venereal disease on the other. These technological achievements make it possible for sex to be a pleasurable experience largely unclouded by concern over "consequences." Finally, with the demise of the double standard, sex apparently emerges as an activity that seems to impose no obligations nor require any commitment from the participants.

In my book *Love and Orgasm*, I pointed out that love increases the pleasure of sex. It does this by singling out the love object as the focus of an individual's erotic desire and of his need for closeness and intimacy with another person. This focus upon a single individual raises the level of sexual tension, for it inhibits the tendency to discharge the tension indiscriminately. If the feeling of love could be fully expressed sexually, the resulting discharge would have a total quality. It would embrace the whole body and leave the individual with a deep sense of satisfaction and joy. It could, when the love feelings were sufficiently intense, lead to an ecstatic experience. Only with love is sex capable of producing this effect, for love is a feeling that emanates from the heart and extends through the blood to every cell of the body.

Sex and love are not distinct and unrelated feelings. Sex is an expression of love, the love of a man for a woman or a woman for a man. The question really is—how much love is experienced in the sexual act? Where the feeling of desire is limited to the genital organs, the sensation of a pleasure is similarly restricted and the feeling of love is reduced to a minimum. The converse of this statement is equally true. When the feeling of love is reduced to a minimum, the erotic desire is superficial and mostly confined to the genital organs. In this circumstance the pleasure of the discharge is low and neither satisfying nor fulfilling. With stronger love feelings, more of the body is actively involved in the physical and spiritual union with the sexual partner and greater pleasure is experienced in the fusion of orgasm. The total surrender to love and sex allows the head to be flooded with pleasurable sensation and the conscious mind to be overwhelmed by the ecstasy of this yielding to the most elemental force in our nature.

Love implies total commitment to the love object. It emerges from the infant's consciousness of its absolute dependence on its mother and grows through its awareness of the pleasure which this relationship can provide. It is insolubly linked to the feeling of joy that arises where the pleasure of contact between two individuals is mutually experienced. Love, therefore, links one person's welfare to another since it is based on the experience that their pleasure is interdependent. Unfortunately, any disturbance in the mother-child relationship creates ambivalent feelings of love and hate, affection and hostility, which will subsequently impair the child's ability to give himself fully in love when he reaches adulthood. Any disturbance in this ability also limits the depth of the person's physical involvement in the sexual act and reduces the pleasure he will experience in this activity.

There is another aspect, however, to the interrelationship between love, sex, and pleasure that is particularly relevant to the phenomenon of growth. The process of growth does not occur as a momentary phenomenon nor does it result from a single experience. Growth is a continuing development, in which time and security are the coordinates of its progress.

In the context of this concept of growth, it is relevant to ask what is gained by saying "I love you" or making a commitment of love to the sexual partner? It may be better, however, to phrase the question in the negative. What is lost when there is no commitment of love, and sex is a momentary experience?

Let us consider this question from the point of view of two adults who are strongly attracted to each other sexually and of whom one is a married person. They are informed by their feelings that a sexual relationship between them would be a pleasurable experience and yet, in most cases, they would hesitate to consummate such a relationship. If we leave moral and religious principles aside, we can best explain their hesitation by their knowledge or belief that one or both parties will inevitably be hurt through a liaison. If the man is married, the woman faces the prospect that a renewed desire for closeness and intimacy with him cannot easily be fulfilled. The same thing can be said of the man. The pain of this unfulfilled longing will be proportionate to the pleasure they experience; it is the nature of pleasure to seek a renewal of the situation in which it was experienced.

Love is the promise of continued pleasure on the part of the person who gives his love and the expectation of pleasure on the part of the person who shares the love. This is not the same thing as the promise *to love*. Love is a feeling and, as such, is not subject to one's volition. But it is a feeling of total commitment that embraces the future as well as the present. The feeling of love is one of loving with all one's being and for all time. It is unconditional in time or degree. Conditional love is a denial of love. Nevertheless, this feeling of love imposes no obligations. It cannot be understood as a promise to love tomorrow. It says simply,

"The way I feel now is that I love you with all my heart and forever." It is a statement of feeling representing a total commitment in the present, which also necessarily embraces the future.

For a human being the present cannot be divorced from the future, nor vice versa. Unlike the lower animals, man knows that his sexual desires will spring anew tomorrow and he can anticipate their fulfillment or their frustration. This consciousness of the future is part of his present and affects his behavior in the present. A woman cannot give herself fully to a man if she is conscious that the future holds a painful separation. Some part of her being will erect defenses against the anticipated pain and her sexual surrender will not be wholehearted. This is not to say that she will not give herself under this condition. If her desire is strong enough, she may yield to it but while her pleasure may be intense, it will also be poignant. It cannot be joyful.

The feeling of love is a commitment that allows the full surrender of the self to the sexual experiences and ensures, therefore, the pleasure that passes all bounds, the joy or ecstasy of total sexual fusion and discharge. In the absence of a commitment of love, the giving of one's self is conditional and limited, and the pleasure is correspondingly reduced. Our hearts yearn for love because our bodies long for joy. It must be that the advocacy of sex without love expresses the desperation of an individual who has not known joy and is willing, therefore, to settle for the lesser pleasure derived from the release of genital tension.

The person who has known joy as a child anticipates it as an adult. I believe that marriage (not necessarily a legal marriage but the union of a man and woman in love and sex) offers a continuum of affection, acceptance, and security that parallels the parent-child relationship. A woman who has a series of lovers or husbands is essentially like a child who has a series of parents. The basic continuum is broken and in place of inner growth she acquires the skills of adjustment. The same thing could be said of a man, for in this respect they are alike. These adjustments always contain an element of self-denial that often masquerades as sexual sophistication.

In the continuum of a child's world, love represents the eternal aspect of life. If a child does not sense that his mother's love is unconditional (that she will always love him), he feels threatened with abandonment and extinction. If he has cause to question her love, he will erect security defenses against the possibility of extinction. These defenses soon become structured, psychologically and physically, making him incapable of fully opening himself to the giving or receiving of love. He becomes a person with a closed heart. The sexual problems of such individuals are discussed in *Love and Orgasm*.

Love has the stabilizing element of the eternal. It is this quality in love that makes growth possible. A child cannot develop normally in the absence of such love (such security). Just as one has to build a house on a stable foundation, preferably rock or concrete, so one cannot build a life on the shifting sands of physical desire only. This is not to denigrate the importance of physical desire. Rocks, particularly sedimentary rocks, are composed of sand that has been compressed for seemingly endless time. Love also evolves from pleasure that has an endless quality. Without the prospect of continued pleasure, love crumbles into dust.

The adult does not outgrow his need for the security that love offers. The child needed that security for the creation of his individuality, the adult needs it for the creation of a family unit. The family founded on love can grow and this means both the growth of the adult, and the creation and growth of new life. It must be recognized that there is a limitation to the inner growth and development of the bachelor and spinster. The experience of sharing a common life doubles the dimensions of living. And in this respect each child also adds a new dimension to the life of its parents. This is the natural order of life.

I do not mean to say that the coming together of two people to form a family is the only way people can grow. There are other forms of association in which personal growth is possible because love unites the members for their mutual benefit. Among many primitive peoples the tribe was a larger grouping of individuals bound by ties of kinship but unified by the affection and love which each member felt for the others. In our own culture it has often been the love of country that brought individuals together in a common enterprise and made possible the personal growth of each citizen. More recently, love for humanity has become a force that relates people to one another and motivates meaningful activities that enable the individual to grow.

In all situations, love provides the security that makes growth possible. Two other elements, however, determine the process of growth. The feeling of love must lead to a joint activity or common enterprise the result of which is the experience of pleasure and the feeling of satisfaction and fulfillment. In the man-woman relationship, the fundamental activity is sex and the pleasure-satisfaction feeling is orgasm. Sex is not the only meaningful activity that expresses the love a man and woman feel for each other. Building a home is another such activity, one which humans share with other animals, and that is productive of pleasure and satisfaction. There are many more, including the basic activity of gathering and preparing food and consuming it together.

The progression from love to sex to pleasure is incomplete. One must ask: What force nourishes and promotes love? The answer to this question is that love has its roots in pleasure (love is related to the anticipation or expectation of pleasure). It emerges in consciousness through the awareness of shared pleasures. The progression has now become complete, being transformed into a spiral—which I call the spiral of growth.

If the quantities involved in these relationships were fixed, we would have a circle rather than a spiral and growth would be limited. Because each experience of pleasure enhances the feeling of love, growth becomes a continuing development. Stronger love feelings increase the tension of the relationship, resulting in a deeper and broader pleasure reward. Growth is a spiral that becomes progressively bigger with each cycle of the progression: love . . . sex . . . pleasure . . . love, etc. Growth is also an upward movement such as is seen in the tree, which grows taller as it grows bigger.

The motive force behind the spiraling progression of growth is our biologically rooted striving for pleasure. This pleasure drive motivates all the constructive activities of life: eating, sleeping, playing, sex, building a nest or home, the rearing of offspring, etc. The emotion of love develops from the feelings of pleasure recalled from the past or projected into the future. It appeared on the evolutionary scene when the process of growth demanded the protection and care of the helpless young. Whether one can say that a mother bird loves her fledglings is a matter of semantics. She acts as if she does. The same is true of a mother bear and her cubs. We know definitely that on the human level this pattern of maternal protection and care is consciously experienced as mother love. However, the motivation for this behavior, experienced as mother love, is the pleasure which the female derives from the fulfillment of her instinctual nature.

Nature has endowed the organism with the necessary instincts to start the process of growth. If the pleasure is not forthcoming, however, the progression collapses and the spiral of growth ceases. It should be pointed out that the aim of an instinct is always the pleasure to be derived from its satisfaction. Imperative as instincts are, they may fail to operate when their aim appears impossible of fulfillment. No instinct is more powerful than that which seeks to preserve life, yet persons will take their own lives when they lose all hope of pleasure or joy in living.

Animal mothers, for example, have been known to abandon or destroy their young. A female animal in captivity may reject her offspring, presumably because of her situation. But such behavior is also seen occasionally in pet animals and may even occur among animals in the wild. I would assume this happens when the mother animal loses or has no anticipation of the pleasure that nursing and caring can yield. Human mothers are not exempt from actions that are destructive to their children. One has only to read Joseph C. Rheingold's book *The Fear of Being a Woman* to realize the possible degree of maternal hostility. On the basis of my experience as a psychiatrist I would state without qualification that maternal hostility is directly proportional to loss of pleasure in being a woman and a mother.

In a woman the loss of pleasure in the feminine and maternal functions of life can often be directly traced back to experiences of deprivation and frustration that she experienced at the hands of her own mother, generally a woman who found little pleasure in her own feminine and maternal functions. The individual who was not fully accepted or loved by his parents cannot accept or love himself. Such a person poses a psychiatric problem, namely, how to separate his present attitudes from their origin in his past. In a sense, such an individual has become fixated in the past, that is, his spiral of personality growth slowed down or stopped when the motive force of pleasure diminished or ceased to flow.

The spiral of growth starts deep in the biological processes of the cell and body. These processes are largely unconscious. They reach consciousness in our perception of pleasure and pain. In one respect pleasure may be defined as the feeling of expansion and growth of an organism while pain is felt when an organism is in a state of contraction or arrest of growth. On a higher level of consciousness, love is the attraction that draws the organism into those relationships with persons and things that promote his function and his pleasure, while hate is the reaction to persons or situations that threaten to inflict pain.

Biologically, the progression that creates the spiral of growth starts with the body's function. If this produces pleasure, it will lead to love. Sex is, of course, one of the bodily functions. It operates even in those animals whose consciousness is still largely undeveloped. We can assume that it is associated with some feeling of pleasure and we know that it is a creative act in that it produces new life. In the more highly evolved animals such as man, the emotion of love is indispensable to growth. This is because man is a psychological organism as well as a biological one. His biology, however, determines his psychology.

In treating disturbances of growth or, to put it more positively, in developing the human potential, we cannot be one-sided. We cannot set the spiral of growth in motion by overemphasizing the importance of love. If we do so, we tend to become involved in a psychology that leads to metaphysical speculations or ends in the oft-repeated cliché that "love is all." We cannot ignore the importance of love if we are to retain the dignity of being human, that is, creatures who are conscious of their past and aware of their future possibilities. We cannot, on the other hand, deny the role of the body and its functions. From our basic animal nature we inherit the qualities of beauty and grace as physical attributes of our being. We can be psychologically sophisticated in the meaning of love, yet we will be mechanical and unfeeling in our bodily movements if we are dissociated from the body.

Uniting body and mind, biology and psychology, sex and love is the concept of pleasure. Its roots are in the somatic functions and its aspirations are in the psychic realms. Without pleasure, a body moves like a machine; without pleasure, love is an empty word. These relationships between body-pleasure-mind, sex-pleasure-love, biology-pleasure-psychology are the axioms which determine how we, in the Institute for Bio-Energetic Analysis, approach the problems of growth and human potential. These problems are the direct result of disturbances in the pleasurable functions of the body on the one hand and the pleasure aspirations of the mind on the other. The disturbed individual cannot experience pleasure in the present nor anticipate it in the future. Or to put it another way, his pleasure potential (growth) is limited by the nature and extent of his disturbance.

If we ask what is disturbed, the answer is the motility of the body. By motility I mean the natural, free, and spontaneous movements of the body. Because it is a closed system containing an inner charge or excitation, the living body has an inherent motility. It is in constant motion, awake or asleep. The heart beats, the blood flows, the lungs expand and contract, and the digestive apparatus functions continuously via peristaltic waves. In addition there are the larger movements of the head and neck, the arms and legs, and the whole body as it moves about. In man, some of these movements are conscious and willed but many more are involuntary and spontaneous. In a healthy individual these movements flow easily and are characterized by their coordination and rhythmicity. The disturbed person is hyperactive or hypoactive. In the first case, his movements are rapid, jerky, and uncoordinated. In the second, they are reduced, constricted, and slow.

The quality of motility has a direct bearing on the experience of pleasure or pain. Pleasure can be defined as the perception or sensation of a flowing, graceful, coordinated, and rhythmic body motion. The four adjectives are words that describe how such motion impresses the observer. The subjective experience is one of ease and pleasure. Movements that appear mechanical, forced, constrained, or spasmodic are experienced subjectively as painful. The person feels ill-at-ease or in a state of dis-ease. Dancing is a good example. The person who dances with grace and rhythm feels the pleasure of dancing. For the person whose movements are awkward and unrhythmical, dancing is almost painful. He does not and cannot enjoy dancing.

What is true of dancing is equally true of every other activity. Sex is pleasurable when the sexual movements are easy, spontaneous, and rhythmical. When sex is enjoyable, undulatory waves pass over the body synchronous with the breathing. If the breath is held, these waves are blocked and one feels a sense of constriction and pain. There are pulsatory movements in the vagina and penis which also contribute to the pleasure of sex. But even mundane activities can be pleasurable when the movements are rhythmical and graceful. Of course, the moment coercion enters the scene, the movements become forced and pleasure is impossible.

The natural motility of the body is disturbed by the chronic muscular tensions that result from the inhibitions and frustrations of infancy and childhood. These tensions not only block the expression of feeling but, if severe, prevent feeling from arising. The word emotion, composed of the prefix *e* and the root *motion*, denotes a movement outward. The constriction of movement creates a restriction of feeling. Unfortunately, by the time a person reaches adulthood these chronic tensions have become largely unconscious. His movements have become limited and his pattern of behavior has become structured. He is aware of an inability to express himself freely and fully, but he is generally ignorant of the fact that this inability stems from the rigidities and tensions in his body.

Each chronic muscular tension shackles the spiral of growth. When the body is beset with such tension, growth is reduced and limited, and we have the typical picture of an immature personality. In such cases love, alone, is not enough. Unless the physical tension can be released and the body restored to its natural motility, the pleasure of life is missing and love remains an ideal not a reality.

The feeling when the tensions are released is one of joy—the joy of freedom to live and to love. The person whose body is free from tension knows the joy of being alive. Most of his activities are pleasurable and most of his relationships are loving. The person who suffers from bodily tension, whether he is aware of them or not, sees life as a struggle. Burdened by tension, his every move is a painful effort. Imprisoned by his own rigidities, he dreams of a utopia governed by love.

I am no believer in utopias. If we talk of love, we must not separate it from the pleasure in which it has its origin. We love that which gives us pleasure. If we wish to understand pleasure, we must know that it is a quality of bodily response, the ability to become excited by and react spontaneously to the varied aspects of life. The child literally claps its hands in pleasure and jumps for joy. When we restrain our impulses and inhibit our movements, we become mechanisms devoid of life, joy or love.

3

The Hidden Taboo on Love

Joe K. Adams

History poses a challenging problem to anyone who believes that man is basically a decent, rational, and lovable animal, for no other species has behaved in a manner that is so mean and crazy as has man. If we were to observe a colony of apes, for example, solemnly feeding their infants into a blazing furnace, and forcing the mothers to watch, without attempting to save their young or even uttering a cry, we would draw the conclusion that the whole colony was mad in a way both hideous and bizarre. In ancient Carthage such a ritual actually existed; according to some accounts, as many as three hundred living children in a single day were sacrificed in this manner to the great god Baal-Haman.[1] Over a thousand years later considerable progress had been made; throughout most of Western Europe mothers were being burned alive and their children were being beaten at the scene of the burning; occasionally the children were forced to watch.[2] Still later, in our own century and in one of the most highly "civilized," industrious, "clean," and personally "moral" (a reputation the Germanic tribes have held since the time of ancient Rome) nations, millions of men, women, and children were exterminated by being locked inside huge chambers and gassed, hundreds at a time, while observers watched through one-way mirrors.[3]

For some theorists there is no great problem, because their theories, including all those dominant at the present time, present men as basically a kind of oafish robot. These theories, although thought by those who hold them to be products of the twentieth century, are actually continuations of the very old doctrines that man is basically deprived (as held

27

by the Catholic theologians of the Middle Ages) or depraved (as held by Calvin). Erich Fromm was possibly the first to point out that psychoanalysis, at least in the hands of some practitioners, is an especially vicious and destructive form of Calvinism.[4] Solomon Asch demonstrated the basic similarities of behaviorism and Freudian analytic theory in their shabby and unwarranted assumptions about human nature.[5]

Cynical doctrines such as these, however, are dominant not only among experts but also among the general public. The average person, although not readily classifiable as Calvinist, behaviorist, etc., does not hold to a very elevated view of basic human nature. The views of learned authorities, in fact, are almost always little more than an elaborate, codified, and more or less esoteric formulation of doctrines already dominant in the society. In the societies of Western civilization, the unworthiness of man in one form or another has been hammered into the general population for thousands of years, the only possible exception being portions of ancient Greece during relatively short periods of time. These cynical doctrines result in a deceptive appearance of validation—if man is convinced that he is unworthy, then he may indeed cooperate in acting out the role to which he has been assigned. As there has never been a sane society, however (at least within recorded history), the existence of sane, decent, and noble individuals, however rare they may be, casts doubt on all the calumny that has been heaped upon basic human nature.

The solution to the problem of why, if man is basically decent, rational, and lovable, he has behaved in such a mean and crazy manner can be seen if we examine the methods whereby man has been governed. We are ordinarily not conscious of the fact that the average man or woman is potentially an extremely dangerous animal; this fact, however, becomes obvious when an individual goes into a rage, when it may take three strong men to hold the human animal down, and when a demonic cleverness may enable the individual to act out destructive impulses without being stopped until after a great amount of damage has been done.[6] The problem of governing man, or of social organization, therefore, should never be taken as lightly as it is by many Americans.

Granted that almost any man is potentially dangerous, there are still many different approaches which might be followed in devising a means of social control. One would be to trust man as we might trust a pet Saint Bernard on which we shower food, affection, and sufficient freedom to be as healthy and happy as possible, so that although there would be numerous occasions on which our huge pet could easily dispose of us, we would be confident that no such urge would seize him. Another approach would be to avoid placing ourselves in any situation in which man could harm us, even if he wanted to do so. Another would be to trick him in some way, so that although he could harm us he sees no way in which to do it.

If we hold to a cynical doctrine of basic human nature, then we will naturally govern the human animal with a view to keeping him under control as the major objective, the welfare or happiness of the animal being secondary. We might, therefore, attempt to accomplish the following:

1. Keep men as weak as possible, except when in the service of fighting our enemies.

2. Keep men as ignorant and deluded as possible, so that they can be easily deceived.

3. Keep men as frightened as possible.

4. Keep men as alienated from each other as possible, so that they cannot band together for some purpose of which we might not approve.

It would be possible to accomplish these objectives by somehow preventing people from loving each other. By "love" I mean a sentiment, i.e., a feeling for another person, which, though as indefinable as any other feeling, is accompanied by desires and impulses to be intimate in some way (physically, emotionally, intellectually) with the loved person and to bring about pleasure, joy, relief from pain or fear, for the latter, and includes the ability to experience pleasure and joy when such impulses and desires are consummated.

The need for love is more basic than the need for sex. Without love, physically expressed, infants will quite literally shrivel up and die. The need for love persists throughout life, and love deprivation always leads to some kind of weakness, strong though the individual may become in some respects (he may, for example, become able to function much like an unfeeling machine). The strength and courage to act *as an individual* is dependent upon feeling loved by an individual. Any affection which one receives solely because of group membership is contingent upon conformity to the rules of the group; his strength and courage exist only as long as he acts as an acceptable member of the group.

Without love, communication becomes not a form of intimacy, or even relatedness, but a means for manipulation. Thus deception, intrigue, and withholding of information, all of which create ignorance and delusion, will be prevalent.

Deception, intrigue, and withholding of information will also create fear and alienation.[7]

It would be convenient, therefore, for tyrannical governments to taboo love; as this taboo, if effective, would help to keep men weak, ignorant, frightened, and alienated. A direct and straightforward taboo, however, would be no more effective than other direct taboos, such as those placed upon adultery, prostitution, homosexuality, or "sex perversions." To be fully effective a taboo must be hidden, i.e., indirect in the sense that the population is unaware of its existence. To understand what is effectively tabooed we should try to see what rarely occurs. The most strongly tabooed activity would be one which never occurs, and which we would presumably have difficulty in imagining, in the same way that Cook Islanders had difficulty in grasping the notion of suicide.

In order to taboo an activity effectively it is necessary to *prevent the conditions which lead to it*. If this is done, the tabooed activity itself may be directly encouraged without any danger that it will actually occur. This is particularly true in the realm of feelings and emotions, which can be neither forced nor summoned up voluntarily. Thus, people can be encouraged or even commanded to "love" each other without any danger of their doing so if the conditions which would lead to love are not permitted. Furthermore, it would hardly occur to the average person who is admonished to "love his fellow man" to make a serious inquiry into how this could be accomplished, as he has learned early in life that those activities which he is morally admonished to engage in are seldom if ever any fun.

The ways in which love is tabooed become clear if we first list some of the conditions which are necessary for love to flourish, and then consider how some evil genius might prevent those conditions from existing.

Three necessary conditions [8] for love which are of central importance to our argument are as follows:

1. Internal freedom, i.e., availability of impulse and feeling.
2. Self-respect, including a *sense* of self.[9]
3. Respect for others, including some *knowledge* of others, so that one can know whom he respects; in other words, respect for other people as they actually are and as we know them to be, not for people as we falsely imagine them to be.

In terms of availability and impulse and feeling the average middle-aged person is quite dead in comparison with a lively, healthy child, and this terrible result is accomplished by social processes; it is not simply a biological result of aging. If an impulse or feeling cannot be appropriately expressed, then the impulse or feeling itself will gradually disappear or be transformed into some other impulse or feeling. For example, if anger cannot be expressed in some fairly direct manner, such as striking, shouting, looking belligerent, cursing, or at least admitting that one is angry, then the anger, which is a "hot" emotion, may gradually freeze into hatred, a "cold" emotion which may not even be recognized as such. Hatred is expressed by "cold," "cutting" remarks or actions, which are intended to hurt but may be delivered with a "smile" instead of a belligerent or "blazing" expression as in the open expression of anger. A cold person, however admirably or effectively he may cope with certain kinds of difficult situations, is much further from being able to love than the "hothead"; many women know this, or intuitively sense it, in searching for a lover. The "cold-blooded killer" who can plan a murder and effectively carry it out is much more dangerous and farther from rehabilitation than the man who commits a "crime of passion." [10]

Another possible result of the much too stringent curbs on the expression of anger is apathy instead of hatred. The apathetic person has given up; he no longer fights back, except possibly by passive resistance. Apathy is sometimes the successor of hatred, and is even farther along the scale of deadness.

I have dwelt upon anger because it is one of the key emotions in keeping alive and thus in being able to love. Curbs upon the expression of other emotions, however, are perhaps of equal importance. The social taboo against crying, for example, has an effect upon emotion and impulsivity that can hardly be overestimated. Any one of several quite different emotions can accompany the impulse to cry; one of these is that rarest of jewels, joy (as in the expression "tears of joy"). The taboo on crying is, therefore, among other things a taboo against the expression of joy, and thus indirectly a taboo against joy itself.

Another emotion expressed by crying is a kind of intense poignancy, aroused in some people when they witness an act of kindness, sweetness, innocence, or generosity, character change for the better, or a "happy ending"—in other words, when they witness some kind of strong gratification or fulfillment, either in real life or in the theater. Sadness (not necessarily unpleasant), grief, self-pity, an intense feeling of loneliness or abandonment, and even fear or anger coupled with a feeling of helplessness or impotence are still other emotions which can accompany the impulse to cry. The taboo on crying, therefore, has very far-reaching and destructive effects, granted that being able to "bear up" or "not give in to one's feelings" does enable people to "carry on" in some situations.

There are, of course, taboos on the expression of love itself, such as a friendly hug or kiss, but I will discuss these later. The point to stress here is that the taboos on the expression of emotions play a vital role in the deadening or cooling of the person and thus in destroying his capacity to love. The removal of external restraints upon the expression of love itself, as in marriage, is not in itself sufficient to permit love to flourish, if the restraints upon the expression of other emotions remain too rigid. The release of emotions, on the other hand, as in revival meetings, can rejuvenate the capacity of love, despite strong taboos against some forms of expression of the latter emotion.[11]

As it is by means of our emotions that we sense ourselves—i.e., know "who we are"—the taboos on the expression of emotions, with the consequent loss or transformation of the emotions themselves, result also in a lack of sense of self. Even more directly, these taboos prevent knowledge of other people and result in a widespread feeling of alienation. Everyone becomes a stranger, even to himself. Under these conditions, extremely dependent relationships may form, and may be called "love," but such relationships do not include love as I have defined it.

The taboos on the expression of emotions form only one class of explicit taboos which indirectly destroy the conditions under which love can exist. The explicit taboos on sexual activities form another class. Unlike the taboos on emotional expression, the sex taboos have the remarkable property of effectively destroying the conditions for love *even when they are completely ineffective in their ostensible function, which is to prevent or minimize certain sexual activities*. There is good reason to believe that the sex taboos in Western civilization have never prevented or even minimized the forbidden sexual activities themselves. The "Kinsey Report" shocked many people, but it probably did not shock many of those familiar with the bizarre history of this subject.[12] Nevertheless, the sex taboos have been quite effective in driving the forbidden activities underground, in producing guilt, shame, fear and cynicism, and in forcing people to *pretend*.

Even those who do not violate a taboo (e.g., the taboo on adultery or homosexuality) may find that they must pretend to be in agreement with it, when in fact they may not be, or else be severely censured and perhaps suspect as well. Pretense invariably brings about a loss in self-respect and a loss in respect for others, when the latter are perceived to be pretending. To force someone to pretend is in fact an old shaming device, still practiced by bullies and pompous tyrants. Furthermore, pretense, when habitual, entails a loss in internal freedom—the individual can no longer differentiate himself from the roles he is forced to play. Finally, and even more obviously, pretense prevents people from knowing each other and produces feelings of alienation, which has been called the social disease of our time.

In order to maximize pretense, the activities chosen to be explicitly tabooed should be widely practiced and either harmless or at least clearly within the rightful prerogatives of the individual, so that many people will privately believe the taboo to be unjustified or even absurd. The ideal taboo to maximize the destruction of the conditions for love would be placed upon an activity which is universally practiced and well within the individual's rights, the only danger being that someone would succeed in pointing out the absurdity or injustice of the taboo to the entire population or to a very powerful segment of it, which might then rise up against the taboo or against the authorities who are perceived as responsible for it. The taboo on masturbation, which is by no means entirely dead, perhaps comes as close as any to meeting this criterion.

The advantages of absurd or unjust taboos are partly illustrated by adolescent groups, which usually develop conventions of dress, manner, attitudes, taste, and speech to which strict adherence is required, at the same time that they are freeing themselves from parental domination. By submitting to rules which are *arbitrary* the individual clearly submits to the authority of the group; *just or rational rules cannot possibly perform this function as there is always the possibility that just and rational rules will be obeyed simply because they are seen by the individual as just and rational.* The arbitrariness of adolescent group rules sets the stage for a repetition of the rearing of offspring in a way that is just as conventional and irrational as that in which the young rebels themselves have been reared. Their offspring will thus be prepared to accept arbitrary and irrational rules of their own adolescent groups, and thus an endless cycle is perpetuated.[13]

As stated before, the ideal taboo would be one which is clearly absurd or unjustified. The *pretense* which is forced upon the individual, however, should not be seen by him as absurd or unjustified. The *absurdity of pretense* is one of the forbidden perceptions; a person who has seen the absurdity of pretense has indeed eaten of the forbidden fruit of the tree of knowledge, and may have great difficulty in living within any existing society.[14] Many people who violate a sex taboo are quite aware of the injustice of the taboo which they happen to be violating, and many are aware of some the harmful effects of the pretense which is forced upon them; but very few are aware of the destructiveness, confusion, and unnecessary suffering entailed by pretense, which, when seen clearly, exposes pretense as an absurd condition of society. Many middle- and upper-class people will, in fact, take private "misbehavior" more or less for granted as long as it is sufficiently "discreet." An open admission of such misbehavior, however, horrifies them. It is this blind spot concerning the absurdity of pretense which has led to generation after generation of "messy" private lives among these classes, coupled with great fear of scandal, which has broken out repeatedly. The acceptance of pretense as right and necessary has resulted in great profit to those whose professions involve knowing the "secrets" of prominent members of the community.

To destroy love, along with suitable explicit taboos, an ideology (i.e., a doctrine of "human nature") should be constructed which makes it extremely difficult to attack the taboos effectively, no matter how absurd or unjust they may be. Ideology is usually unnecessary among adolescent groups, as the members are satisfied on an intuitive basis; they simply "see" and "feel" that their group is right, and quickly expel anyone who bores them with rational arguments. Most adolescent groups, as well as many groups of adults, are in this respect protototalitarian.[15] Among adults, however, there are sometimes some who will attempt to attack the taboos on a rational basis. To counter such attacks an ideology should be constructed of sufficient complexity to deceive the ideologists themselves into believing that they can construct adequately rational answers. Ideology should also include methodological principles which make it impossible to provide acceptable proofs of anything very important about human beings, so that it can be shown that the burden of proof, which is always on the heretic, has not been met.

In order to destroy love an ideology should, in addition to supporting the taboos, destroy self-respect and respect for others by presenting man in as unfavorable a light as possible. In other words, an ideology should encourage perceptions of oneself and others, and of human relationships, in such a way that love cannot develop.

A dominant ideology is embodied not only in the abstract formulations of learned authorities but also in the everyday life of the members of the society; as stated previously, the former tends to grow out of the latter. For example, a learned and dignified treatise reducing all of man's impulses or thoughts to the basic drives of hunger, sex, dominance, etc., is congruent with much cruder expressions of the same belief in everyday life, such as a sneering laugh or, in a heartier vein, a loud guffaw when someone expresses a noble thought or feeling, as though there is some self-centered objective for which the thought or feeling is merely a mask. Cynicism is expressed differently depending upon ethnic group, social class, etc.; a mere lifting of the eyebrows, a sharp, cold rebuke, or a condescending smile may express the same basic assumptions about human nature as our previous crude examples. Furthermore, many communications within the society which at first glance seem antagonistic to the dominant ideology are actually entirely congruent with it. For example, books and motion picture films which present tabooed sexual activities in a morbid manner may superficially seem at odds with our Calvinistic heritage, but in reality they are reiterating the message of Romans vi, 23, "The wages of sin is death." [16]

Although Christian ideology originally emphasized love much more than "sex morality," emphasis shifted more and more to the latter until by the tenth century many theologians were writing about little else. It is not surprising that some members of the clergy became obsessed with this subject, in view of the long struggle to force celibacy upon the priesthood.[17] The extent to which "sex morality" eventually overshadowed all other kinds of morality is indicated by the following quotation from the historian H. C. Lea:

How the estimate placed on purity increased as virtue diminished is fairly illustrated in a characteristic legend which was very popular with ecclesiastical teachers in the thirteenth and fourteenth centuries. It relates how a pagan entering a heathen temple saw Satan seated in state on a throne. One of the princes of Hell entered, worshipped his master, and proceeded to give an account of his work. For thirty days he had been engaged in provoking a war, wherein many battles had been fought with heavy slaughter. Satan sharply reproached him with accomplishing so little in the time, and ordered him to be severely punished. Another then approached the throne and reported that he had devoted twenty days to raising tempests at sea, whereby navies had been wrecked and multitudes drowned. He was likewise reproved and punished for wasting his time. A third had for ten days been engaged in troubling the wedding festivity of a city, causing strife and murder, and he was similarly treated. A fourth then entered and recounted how for forty years he had been occupied in tempting a hermit to yield to fleshly desire, and how he had that night succeeded. Then Satan rose and placed his crown on the head of the newcomer, seating him on the throne as one who had worthily achieved a signal triumph. The spectator, thus seeing the high estimate placed by the Evil One on ascetic chastity, was immediately converted, and forthwith became a monk.[18]

It is extremely dangerous to emphasize any kind of morality which has nothing directly to do with honesty, fair play, or kindness, because such an emphasis can easily lead to self-righteous cruelty. Without the help of this principle it is, I believe, impossible to understand the injustice and cruelty of the Inquisitions, which dominated most of Western Europe for about 500 years. There is a great lesson to be learned from the fact that men who professed to "love" their fellow men could justify both torture and deceit (both of which, Lea assures us, "were resorted to freely and without scruple, and there was ample variety to suit the idiosyncrasies of all judges and prisoners"); could allow their victims to spend months or years chained in dungeons without even being brought to trial; and could finally "abandon" the condemned to the secular arm, with a hypocritical "plea for mercy," it being clearly understood that their "love" objects were to be burned alive.[19]

The overemphasis on "sex morality" was accompanied by denigration of the body and thus of the self, with inevitable loss of self-respect and respect for others. The extent of denigration of the body and of the sex act is illustrated by Lotario de' Conti, a young man in the late twelfth century, who later became the most powerful Pope in history, Innocent III:

> How filthy the father; how low the mother; how repulsive the sister . . . dead, human beings give birth to flies and worms; alive, they generate worms and lice . . . consider the plants, consider the trees. They bring forth flowers and leaves and fruits. But what do *you* bring forth? Nits, lice, vermin. Trees and plants exude oil, wine, balm—and *you,* spittle, snot, urine, ordure. *They* diffuse the sweetness of all fragrance—*you,*

the most abominable stink. . . . We who shrink from touching, even with the tips of our fingers, a gob of phlegm or a lump of dung, how is it that we crave for the embraces of this mere bag of night-soil? . . . [God has decreed that] the mother shall conceive in stink and nastiness.[20]

The denigration of the body and the attitude that sexual "sins" outweigh all others has continued right up to the present day. In our prisons, as well as among more respectable citizens, the attitude that sex crimes are worse than murder or torture is not unusual. The greatest murderer of all time apparently expressed not one word of remorse or guilt about his millions of innocent victims before committing suicide; he was, however, very conscientious in marrying his mistress.[21] Although pogroms of Jews and others could be openly proclaimed, Hitler was very careful never to allow the public to hear of his relationship with Eva Braun (very few Germans even knew of her existence). This kind of inverted morality was not confined to Hitler and a few other Nazi leaders—at least not in their opinion, which was probably correct.

Christianity is no longer a sex-centered ideology, especially among the younger and the leading theologians. Rising to take its place as a more influential ideology, however, is Freudian psychoanalytic theory and its many derivatives. Just as socially deviant behaviors were codified into "sins," and "sins" were codified into laws, so socially deviant behaviors, "sins," and crimes have now been codified into "mental illness." [22] Psychotherapists have now taken the bulk of the lucrative guilt-and-confessions business from the clergy, and are now the ones who know the "secrets" of prominent members of the community. Love and truth are the greatest enemies of "mental illness," and mental health experts are no more likely to encourage love and truth to flourish than the clergy were to eliminate "sin" by advocating a moral code that the population could actually live by, instead of one that insured an ample supply of "sin." It is not at all surprising, from an historical and sociological perspective, that the strongest pleas for tolerance of sexual misbehaviors have come not from mental health experts but from religious leaders and organizations.

The idea of loving a warm-blooded animal without expressing one's affection physically would probably strike most people as very strange. In choosing a pet, few people would select a dog which they knew would not allow himself to be petted, for there would be little pleasure in having such a pet, to most people's way of thinking. Yet men have repeatedly been forbidden to love each other physically, however much physical affection they have been allowed to bestow upon males of other species. This prohibition has been brought about by the simple device of labeling physical affection between men as "homosexuality," which was thought by many ancient peoples to be normal (if coupled with affection and desire for the opposite sex), then was discovered by Christian theologians to be a serious "sin," and more recently has been discovered to be a form or sign of "mental illness." [23]

The way in which this taboo, supported by the ideologists, has hampered physical affection between men is illustrated by a cartoon which appeared early in this century in *Simplizissimus*, a paper published in Munich. The cartoon depicts the Weimar Poets' Monument (in which Goethe and Schiller are holding hands) with Goethe cautiously withdrawing his hand and saying to Schiller, "Fritz, let go! Here comes Magnus Hirschfeld!" Dr. Hirschfeld was a sexologist who frequently appeared as an expert witness during a witch hunt for homosexuals which occurred during that period.[24] Although he said the laws were wrong, he had acquired a wide reputation as someone who helped to track down the "third sex," as he called them. Although the meaning of the cartoon was clear enough, it is doubtful that the readers realized its full implications, which are actually more sinister than humorous. Yet it can hardly be denied that the danger, real or imagined, of being categorized as "homosexual" has tended to make men fearful or cautious of any spontaneous expression of affection for each other.[25] It is not unusual, at the present time, for American fathers to be afraid of expressing any physical affection for their own sons, even when they are still quite young! This is a most dangerous and unsavory result of this taboo, as the lack of love from both sexes while young is even more damaging than it is later in life.[26]

Analogous statements can be made for the official taboo on adultery and, especially for women, even on simple fornication. These taboos have the actual, though unintended, result of placing millions of women, especially those who live in small communities and who cannot afford extensive travel, in the position of never being loved physically by a man. It is absurd to expect a population to be healthy, mentally or physically, under such conditions.

One cannot help speculating what might have happened if the leading ideologists of Germany, instead of supporting a witch hunt for homosexuals, had told the people of Germany that it was all right to love each other, even their own sex! Until the leading ideologists of some country in Western civilization take this radical step, we cannot know the answer to this question.

Although I have stressed the role of the taboos on emotional expression and the sexual taboos, any kind of taboo which places an unreasonable restriction upon the individual and which is widely violated can do much to destroy the conditions under which love flourishes. The 18th Amendment ("Prohibition") is generally acknowledged to have created an enormous amount of crime, hypocrisy, cynicism, and disrespect for the law (as well as for one's parents). These conditions are incomptaible with those necessary for love to flourish.

Love is the greatest source of pleasure and joy, and to the extent that it is effectively prevented, the more men will turn to the accumulation of power, status, and material possessions (the latter frequently being enjoyed primarily for the status they bring), and the more savage, unethical, and ruthless the competition for these goals becomes. Competition of this kind in turn breeds hatred and alienation, making love still more difficult; thus, a vicious cycle is created.

In summary, I have tried to make the following points:

1. To a far greater extent than any other species, man has behaved for many centuries in a mean and crazy manner. Those who believe the world has only recently "gone mad" are unfamiliar with history.

2. Love has been tabooed, though in a hidden and unintentional manner, as a result of the rules which have automatically developed within society and which have tended to destroy the conditions necessary for love. Among the most important of these rules have been:

a. Taboos on the expression of emotions, which lead to the loss or transformation of the emotions themselves.

b. Taboos on sexual activities, which destroy the conditions necessary for love even when they fail in their ostensive function of preventing or minimizing the sexual activities themselves.

3. Ideologies have been constructed which, though unproved, have made it very difficult to attack the taboos, no matter how absurd the latter may be.

Despite the pessimistic tone of this essay, I should like to conclude in a more hopeful vein. Despite the fact that many people, perhaps most, are love-starved, even more than sex-starved, there is a vast potential for love and joy. As McLuhan has emphasized, we are living in an "electric age" in instantaneous communication, and our leaders have not yet realized that we are in a position to alter opinions and attitudes with a speed not conceivable fifty years ago.[27] If my thesis is correct that unreasonable taboos constitute a hidden taboo on love, then it may be possible, with courageous leadership in attacking these taboos directly, to create a society in which love and joy can flourish within a much shorter time than has been thought possible by the mature and responsible segments of our population.

NOTES

1. Will Durant, *Caesar and Christ,* Vol. III of *The Story of Civilization* (New York: Simon & Schuster, 1944), p. 42.
2. H. C. Lea, *Materials Toward a History of Witchcraft* (Philadelphia: Univ. of Pa. Press, 1939; New York & London: Thomas Yoseloff, 1957).
3. W. L. Shirer, *The Rise and Fall of the Third Reich* (New York: Simon & Schuster, 1960, and Fawcett World Library, 1962).
4. Erich Fromm, *Escape from Freedom* (New York: Farrar & Rinehart, 1941).
5. Solomon Asch, *Social Psychology* (New York: Prentice-Hall, 1952).
6. Carl Jung emphasized the cleverness accompanying the rage during the experience of the "magician" archetype.
7. J. K. Adams, "Deception and Intrigue in So-called 'Mental Illness,' " *J. Humanistic Psychol.,* 1964, 4, No. 1, 27–38.
8. This is not intended as a *complete* list of conditions necessary for love.
9. Erich Fromm maintains that self-love, which he carefully distinguishes from selfishness, is essential to loving others. Besides using the word "love" in a somewhat different way, his stronger assertion, while it may be true, is not necessary to the present argument. See his *Escape from Freedom* (ftnt. 4) and *The Art of Loving* (New York: Harper, 1956).
10. Our laws recognize premeditated murder as more culpable than impulsive murder.
11. It is for this very reason that revivals, both in the U.S.A. and in England (especially during the days of John Wesley), have often been considered somewhat scandalous. See W. Sargant, *Battle for the Mind* (New York: Doubleday, 1957).
12. G. R. Taylor, *Sex in History* (New York: Vanguard, 1954). J. K. Adams, "The Overemphasis on Sex in Western Civilization," *J. Humanistic Psychol.,* 1963, 3, No. 1, 54–75.
13. The arbitrariness of rules performs another extremely valuable function, that of allowing group members to consider themselves superior to all outsiders. This function is most clearly illustrated by the fact that language, especially the way in which words are pronounced and the use of a specialized or esoteric vocabulary, is one of the oldest, most important, and most frequently used bases of perceived status.
14. According to Alan Watts, the solution for the enlightened person is to become a "joker," one who plays social games but with the difference that he now sees their arbitrariness. As Watts would presumably agree, however, the life of a "joker" can become unbearably lonely. See his *Psychotherapy East and West* (New York: Pantheon Books, 1961). See also J. K. Adams, "Psychosis: Experimental and Real," *Psychedelic Rev.,* 1963, 1, 121–144.
15. Fascist philosophy, with its constant reiteration of the command to "respond to the Leader" rather than to engage in the insipid activity of thinking, had a strong appeal to the young people of Italy and Germany in the 1920's and 30's. Many of the young people today are in a very similar state of mind.

16. A page of motion picture advertisements from a recent issue of the San Francisco *Chronicle* (Dec. 7, 1967) illustrates this point quite adequately:

"The Fear. It offers a chance to talk about pornography . . . a voyeur's delight . . . a most graphic display of aberrant, sexual impulses."

"The Obscene House. Goes farther than underground. Nothing like it ever shown before."

"Carmen, Baby. The total female animal."

"Exposed. The vice capital of the world. It out Frenches the French."

"A program of erotica. These films were never intended to be shown in theatres."

"Her Bikini Never Got Wet."

"Strange Lovers. Love among the gay set."

Prudishness and pornography often present sex in the same light; differing only in that one advocates avoidance of "filth" whereas the other invites one to wallow in it.

17. H. C. Lea, *History of Sacerdotal Celibacy in the Christian Church,* third edition, revised (London: Williams & Norgate, 1907).

18. *Idem,* Vol. I, pp. 433–434.

19. H. C. Lea, *The Inquisition of the Middle Ages* (New York: Macmillan, 1961). (Abridged version of a much longer work first published in 1887–1888.) See also G. G. Coulton, *Inquisition and Liberty* (London: Heinemann, 1938).

20. This quotation is taken from Aldous Huxley's essay "Hyperion to a Satyr," in his collection *Tomorrow and Tomorrow and Tomorrow* (New York: Harper, 1956), pp. 151–153.

21. Shirer, *op. cit.*

22. T. S. Szasz, *The Myth of Mental Illness* (New York: Hoeber-Harper), 1961; *Law, Liberty, and Psychiatry* (Macmillan, 1963).

23. See, e.g., P. H. Heersema, "Homosexuality and the Physician," *J. Amer. Med. Assn.,* 1965, 193, 815–817.

24. R. Lewinsohn, *A History of Sexual Customs* (New York: Harper, 1958), p. 345. The term "witch hunt" is more than a metaphor. During the inquisitions homosexuality was considered a sign of heresy or witchcraft, and thus led to many burnings.

25. The way in which this category can override all others is spectacularly illustrated by the fact that Hitler was able to use a trumped-up charge against General von Fritsch, Commander in Chief of the German Army, not only to get rid of Fritsch but to relieve sixteen other generals of their commands and to transfer forty-four others, thus greatly weakening the power of the Prussian military aristocracy, the last obstacle in his path to complete power in Germany (Shirer, *op. cit.*). The fact that homosexuality usually leads to the categorization of the individual as "homosexual" instead of "bisexual," even in instances when the latter is clearly more accurate, tends to force many individuals into exclusive homosexuality. An anthropologist found that the members of a Melanesian society had never heard of exclusive homosexuality and were incredulous; in their society all the males are bisexual!

26. The homosexual taboo sometimes results not in an inability to love the same sex so much as a splitting of love and sex (a process already begun within the family, fostered by the incest taboo), so that men are loved while women are simply sex objects, housekeepers, and mother surrogates. Many women have complained that men do not love them, or do not know what love is.

27. Marshall McLuhan, *Understanding Media* (New York: McGraw-Hill, 1964).

4

Some Dimensions of Loving Experience

Sidney M. Jourard

❢

Ol' mas' loves wine, and miss loves silk, the piggies they love buttermilk,
The kiddies love molasses, and the ladies love a ladies man.
       I love to shake a toe with the ladies,
       I love to be a beau to the ladies,
       Long as ever I know sweet sugar from sand,
       I'm bound to be a ladies man.
                  —FOLK SONG, southeastern USA

Love is a many-splendored thing . . .
                  —POPULAR SONG, USA, 1950's

What is this thing called love?
                  —POPULAR SONG, USA, 1930's

Love, O love, O careless love. . . . You see what careless love has done.
                  —FOLK SONG, USA, nineteenth century

Plaisirs d'amour, ne durent qu'un moment. Chagrins d'amour durent toute la vie.
                  —FOLK SONG, French, very old

I sowed the seeds of love, and I sowed them in the springtime. I gathered them up in the morning too soon, while the songbirds so sweetly sing.
                  —FOLK SONG, British, c. sixteenth century

Amor patriae (motto).
For the love of God . . . (sometimes a prayer, sometimes not).

I

Eros and *agape*. *Gemeinschaftsgefühl*. Love as an art. Love as behavior. The beloved as a reinforcement magazine. As a sex object. As an object of worship and reverence. What does it mean to love? I will discuss love from the perspective of existential phenomenology. From this vantage point, love is a stage of being, it is an experience, it is a commitment and a relation.

Who is the lover, and who or what is the beloved? I will focus on love of persons by persons.

What is a person?

To a biologist, a person is a mammalian organism, a system of organs. To a general, a person is cannon fodder, a warm body to carry a rifle, a means to storm a position. To an existential phenomenologist, a person is that which makes a specific view of the world, time and space come into being. And a person is an origin for action which changes the world for himself and for others, for weal or woe. Further, a person is a situated being who embodies *projects*—plans, inventions, creations—that in time will be disclosed to the world. Projects can be seen as vows or commitments to transform the self and the world in some way that first exists in the mode of imagination, like a work of art. When consummated, they become perceptible to others and to the person who first invented them.

I experience another person in diverse modes. The other person can be likened to a source of disclosure about its being. A tree redundantly discloses its treeness, 24 hours a day, 365 days a year, to all who would receive these "messages." A person discloses his personality to all who come within his range, so long as he lives. To receive these transmissions is another way of saying "perception of the person." I can see, hear, feel, smell and taste the other, as I can the tree.

But I don't spend all my time perceiving the other. I form a concept of the other, close off my perception, and perceive the disclosures of other beings that exist. Even if I stand before the other, I may not pay attention to his incessant disclosure, because I know enough to contend with him. My questions about him, for the time, are answered.

The other person exists for me perceptually and conceptually. If the other dies, or simply passes from my field of perceptual experience, I can "re-call" him, in the recollective mode. And I can imagine him in all possible ways, so that he exists for me in the imaginative mode. I can dream about him. And I can experience him in the fantasy mode, as one who "sucks me dry," or who "fills me." In any or all of these modes for experiencing the other, I can know an affective *quality*—of joy or sorrow, fear or anger, excitement or depression, eroticism or indifference.

The other is my experience of him in diverse modes. But if I touch him, especially if I touch him or if he touches me, he takes on a dimension of *reality* that is more than if I just see or hear him. And he is more real if I smell and taste him. But perhaps he is most real if I touch him. "Touching is believing."

All I experience of the other is his appearance before my several perceptual systems. But I infer that behind and beyond appearances there is a center, a source that is free. I may try to control and direct his behavior, his appearances, but his center always eludes me. If it does not, he ceases to be a person and becomes a machine or robot.

So to be a person, the other must have a source, a center that he is privy to and I am not.

I can will his freedom, or I can set up the project of trying to destroy this freedom. He will know which of these options is mine by his experience of me. I may be able to conceal or misrepresent my intent for a time, but in more time, it will become known to him.

II

I love her. What does this mean?

I want her to exist for me, and to exist for herself. I want her alive. I want her to be, and moreover, to be in the way that she chooses to be. I want her free. As she discloses her being to me, or before my gaze, my existence is enriched. I am more alive. I experience myself in dimensions that she evokes, such that my life is more meaningful and livable.

My beloved is a mystery that I want to make transparent. But the paradox is that I cannot make my beloved do anything. I can only invite and earn the disclosure that makes her transparent. I want to know my beloved. But for me to know, she must show. And for her to show her mysteries to me, she must be assured I will respect them, take delight in them. Whether the mysteries are the feel of her flesh against mine—something I cannot know until it happens—or what she is thinking, imagining, planning or feeling. Why should she disclose herself to me if I am indifferent, or if I plan to use her for purposes of my choosing that are concealed from her? She would know me, the one who claims to love her.

If she would know me, then I must wish to be known. I must disclose my being to her, in dialogue, so that we know one another apace.

So soon as she discloses herself to me, I form a concept of her that is instantly out of date, for she has changed. As I reenter dialogue with her, my concept is shattered, and I must form it anew, again and again, unless she has made the commitment to appear before me in some constant way, a way that I may find reassuring or boring. If she is free and growing, then she will surprise me, upend my expectancies, "blow" my mind. Hopefully, in ways I like.

If I love her, I love her projects, since she is their source and origin. I may help her with them if she asks and wants my help; or let her struggle with them unaided, if this is meaningful to her. I respect her wishes in the matter.

If I love myself, I love my projects, since they are my life. If she loves me, she confirms me in my projects, helps me with them, even if the help consists of leaving me alone. If she tries to control me, she doesn't love me. If I try to control her, I don't love her. I experience her as free and treasure her freedom. I experience myself as free and treasure my freedom.

I am a body. I am embodied. So is she. I like to be embodied, and I like her way of being embodied. If I do not like the way she appears, I tell her, for our love is truth.

I am a sexual being. So is she. Together, we can produce an experience that is exquisite for us both. She invites me to know her sexually, and I invite her to know me sexually. We share our erotic possibilities in delight and ecstasy. If she wants me and I don't want her, I cannot lie. My body speaks only truth in this way. And I cannot take her without her giving. Her body cannot lie.

If I see and hear my beloved, I know her more than if I just see her. But if I touch, smell and taste her, I know her still more. But she will not allow me to come that close if she doesn't trust me, or want me to know her.

III

I love my friend, and he loves me. He loves a woman, and so do I. He loves his children, I love mine, and I love his. He loves my children, though neither he nor I know the other's so well as we know our own. But I love my friend. I want to know him. We make life richer, more meaningful, more fun for each other. My life is diminished without my friend being in it. I respect his projects, and he does mine. I help him when he wants it, and stand by when he does not. I wish him well in his projects. I know he reciprocates, because he has shown that he does. When he and I talk, there is no semblance between us. He discloses his experience to me in truth—he wants me to know him. And I do likewise. When he wishes to close off conversation he does so. I respect his privacy. He respects mine. I like the way he "refracts" the world. When he discloses his experience of his world to me, my experience is enriched, because he sees and does things I cannot do directly. Imaginatively, I live more through his experience.

IV

I love my children. They need me. They love me in their way, which is not my way. I am essential to their existence, and they know it. I want to help them become less dependent, to be able to cope with problems and challenges without my protection and guidance. And so I watch them and watch over them. I make guesses about how ready they are to be set more free. But I welcome them back when they are hurt or afraid —unless I judge that for them to endure the hurt will help them grow. I want to help, not hinder, the growth of their possibilities. I am often wrong in my judgments, but I mean well. I set them too free too soon sometimes. And I deny them freedom sometimes when they are quite ready to handle it. But I try to get better at my judgments. And they know I intend their freedom and growth.

V

The people I love give me a meaning to my existence beyond simply filling my gut, feeding my vanity, or giving me pleasure. I treasure them. And when they need help, I abandon the projects in which I was then engaged, and use my time and resources to help them live more fully, joyously and meaningfully. They give to me, and just as important, they accept from me. Their acceptance of my giving validates me, enhances my feeling of having worth. I know that I am a worthy being, but I feel more worthy when my existence enhances that of another.

There are billions of people in the world, but I don't love them in the concrete way I love my loved ones. I don't have the time. Everybody in the world needs someone to love and to be loved by someone, and I hope it happens. But I am more sensitive to the needs and the disclosures of need uttered by my loved ones. I respond to their cries for help sooner, and in preference to the cries I hear coming from others. This is too bad, but I have to choose. There isn't enough time. I respond to others when I can, with what I can spare from what I have pledged to myself and my more immediate circle of loved ones. If I neglect them in favor of others whom they do not know, I do so because it is meaningful to me. If they love me, and they do—then I expect and receive their patience and confirmation. I have to do what is meaningful to me, and I am entitled to confirmation by my loved ones.

I "tune in" on my loved ones regularly, to find out how it is with them. Since last we were in dialogue, a lot has happened to them. My concept of them and their condition is out of date, and I must renew it with fresh disclosures from them, fresh perception. I look, feel and listen.

VI

When I love someone—myself, family, friends—I see them in a special way. Not as the product of what they have been, of their heredity and schooling, though I notice that. I see them as the embodiment of incredible possibilities. I see, imaginatively, what they might become if they choose. In fact, in loving them, I may invite them to activate possibilities that they may not have envisioned. I lend them my creative imagination, as it were. If they are weak, I invite them to invent themselves as stronger, and to take the steps necessary to actualize their latent strength. If they have been shy or self-concealing, I invite them to try on boldness and self-disclosure for size, to be more creative artists-of-themselves. Just as I can be the artist-of-myself, if I love myself. And I do. In fact I am the artist of myself to the extent I am aware of my freedom and my responsibility. My situation includes my "facticity" *and* my freedom. The givens—my past upbringing and present habits; my body; my place; the people I am involved with and the relationships I now have with them and that they want to have with me—all these "givens" can be viewed as exact analogues of paint, canvas and brushes. They are what made me as I now am. As an artist in paint, I can produce pictures that I first imagine, limited only by my skill, my imagination, and the plasticity of the medium. As the artist of myself and my world, I can reinvent myself again and again. That is what I usually do, day by day, but my inventions each day are well-nigh a carbon copy of yesterday's. I can invent a new me, and strive to bring this into being. If my loved ones love me, they'll help me fulfill this new possibility, or tell me truly that they don't like it. In fact, they can serve as artistic consultants, to help me bring the image into fruition.

I can serve in the same capacities for my loved ones. Inventing and reinventing ourselves, playing with our possibilities, and picking those that please.

VII

My relationship with each of those whom I love becomes stale and habit-ridden. Predictable. When it comes to pass that I have no more pleasant surprises, and the predictability begins to bore and strangle me, I begin to reflect. What is happening? If the other is my peer, I let him or her know. She reveals that I am neglecting her, spending too much time at work, or at play with others. I reveal that our ways of sharing time, satisfying up to last year or last week, are now boring. But she still likes these games. And I like my new ways of spending time, apart from her. We are at an impasse. What will we do? If she does not wish to come along with me, or if I do not want her along, one of us is going to feel hurt, and the other guilty. If we love, we have to disclose this. We may have to start to reinvent our relationship. We may, for a time, spend less time with each other, more time with others, feeling somewhat sad and nostalgic for former good times that have passed and are no more.

We may have to reexamine our projects, to see which have least meaning—our joint projects, or our singular projects. It may happen that we cannot invent or discover joint projects that infuse our life together with zest and meaning, that we have to go separate ways. This becomes poignant if we are married, because we may decide—one, the other, or both—to become divorced. Or we may discover some new way to be married that looks like a "marriage of convenience"—no passion, not much delight, but some affection, trust, and goodwill. She might take a lover, I might take a mistress. That might be hurtful to all concerned, or perhaps not. If we have loved each other, and still do, the most loving thing to do might be to part, to dissolve the legal connection, and live separate lives with the hope of finding someone new to love. It happens.

There is no end to this chapter, or to loving. Unless, afraid of possible hurt, we decide not to love, but to control and use.

5

Love as an Adventure in Mutual Freedom

Colin Wilson

I write this as a phenomenologist. But since there are apparently as many kinds of phenomenology as there are phenomenologists, I had better begin by explaining what I understand by the word. I must also explain the way in which my phenomenology is a radical departure from that of Sartre, Heidegger, and Merleau Ponty—even, to some extent, from that of Husserl.

Most European psychology in the nineteenth century sprang from David Hume, who noted that when he looked inside himself to find the essential "me," he only stumbled upon thoughts and impressions. For Hume, free will is an illusion, and our apparent freedom to think what we like, a misunderstanding. Man's mind, he maintains, gives an impression of free, purposive movement, just as the leaves on a windy autumn day seem to be in a hurry to get somewhere. But the leaves move because hot air rises, and our thoughts move because physical stimuli blow them around.

But Husserl objected that there is one important respect in which the mind differs from a windy day. When I think or feel or see, I think *about* something, I look *at* something; I fire my attention at its object like an arrow. A leaf doesn't care where it goes, but when I think, the thought cannot get started unless it knows its objective in advance. When I look at something, I must know what I am looking at before I can really grasp it. If I wake from a drunken sleep underneath a cane chair,

I cannot grasp my situation until I have answered the question: "What is this curious, angular-looking object over my face?" Until my mind has, so to speak, pinned it down by making an act of "chair-ness," it hovers nervously over the chair, staring blankly. What is more, that act of chair-ness is exactly the same act you make if you close your eyes and imagine a chair. In other words, in order to see anything, we must imagine it. To look at a thing without this act of imagining would be not to see it, rather like reading these words with your mind on something else, and not taking them in. If your attention is an arrow fired at an object, this presupposes an archer. So Husserl denied Hume's assertion that there is no "essential me." He called this essential "me" the transcendental ego.

Although Sartre claimed to be a disciple of Husserl, he reverted to the old Humeian position. He agreed that consciousness is intentional, but not because it is *fired* at its object by the essential me. It is, in fact, *sucked* toward its object, as air is sucked into a vacuum if you remove the cork, or as the tides are sucked by the moon. There cannot be an essential me behind consciousness, according to Sartre, because consciousness has no "behind," any more than there is really a room behind the mirror.

It is hard to see how man can be free if Sartre is correct; however, according to Sartre, he is free, in some Pickwickian sense. The contradiction here should be easy to see. If consciousness has no "inside," it has no "works." A parallel situation would be this: Someone hears about the earth moving around the sun, and says, "Ah, it must have clockwork inside it." Someone else replies, "No, it is quite solid inside. Its movement is due entirely to the sun." The same goes for Sartrian consciousness—there is no clockwork, or anything else, inside.

My disagreement with Sartre is easily expressed. For Sartre, consciousness is a simple unity, like a plane mirror. But this leaves out of account one of the mind's most important parts: the robot. When I learn some new skill—a foreign language, typing, driving a car—I quickly pass it from my conscious mind to a subconscious robot, who does it far more efficiently than I can do it by conscious effort. So the mind is neither a unity nor a mirror. Its most important level is hidden in darkness. The full significance of this observation will appear in a moment.

There is an even more important matter that both Sartre and Husserl leave out of account. This is a quality of consciousness which I call "relationality."

This first came to my attention some years ago, and in order to make it clear, it would perhaps be simplest to explain the circumstances. I was driving through the Lake District, in a state of great mental clarity and intensity. I know the area well, and I observed that I was very clearly aware of what lay on the other side of the hills around me. I could say "Over there lies Derwentwater, and over there Helvellyn," and experience these places *as realities*, almost as if I could see them. Chesterton pointed out that we say thank you when someone passes us the salt, but we don't *mean* it. In the same way, I could now close my eyes and conjure up a picture of Derwentwater; but I wouldn't mean it. Yet, if some smell blown on the wind suddenly reminded me of Derwentwater, my mental image would take on reality; I would mean it.

In trying to define this state of mind, I found myself calling it "web-like consciousness." I had in mind the image of a spider in the middle of its web. It cannot see certain parts of its web which are hidden behind leaves. Yet it knows what is going on in every part of its web, since it can feel the vibration of every breeze, every slight movement of a leaf brushing a strand of web. In moments of intensity, consciousness seems to put out filaments of web to other times and other places.

Two years or so later, it suddenly struck me that *all* consciousness is weblike, by its very nature. If, for example, I am reading a book late at night when my brain is tired, I can understand each individual word or sentence, but it means nothing to me. Reading is a two-handed activity. One hand picks up the meanings of individual words or phrases, and passes these to the other hand, which holds all the meanings accumulated so far—rather in the manner of someone who picks up scattered sticks, picking up each stick with the right hand and passing them to the left hand, or tucking them in the crook of the left arm. A one-handed man could not pick up scattered sticks; and when consciousness is one-handed, it cannot pick up *meaning*, only individual meanings. The act of grasping meaning is an act of relating the new meanings to the totality of old meanings.

Sartre has said that consciousness *is* intentionality; i.e., that a consciousness that was not intentional would not be consciousness. I am inclined to doubt this; but it would seem to me more to the point to say that consciousness *is* relationality. I find it hard to conceive of a consciousness that is not consciousness of a pattern. Or, to put this more clearly, I find it hard to conceive of a perceived object that is not perceived essentially as a part of a pattern.

To take a crude example, I read *War and Peace*, and when I have finished it, consider that my knowledge of this period of European history is now reasonably adequate. Some time later, I become absorbed in the relations of the French and Russian courts in the eighteenth century, and read every book I can find that sheds any light on this. This, then, leads me to study the history of France and Russia since the fall of Napoleon. Then one day I reread *War and Peace*, and discover, to my astonishment, that it seems to be a different novel, full of meanings that I had failed to recognize before. My perception of *War and Peace* as a part of a vast historical landscape has deepened the meaning of the novel itself.

An obvious kind of assertion, perhaps, but consider its central point. If your older self could say to your younger self, "There are things about *War and Peace* that you have simply failed to grasp," your younger self could read *War and Peace* with a microscope and still fail to grasp the deeper meanings. For these are not to be grasped within the novel itself, but through its relation to a larger canvas. The total meaning of the novel does not lie *in* the novel.

But then, surely there is such a thing as a meaning in isolation? Can I, for example, stare at my left index finger, and see in it isolation from the rest of my hand?

A moment's thought shows me that this is impossible. I know it as a finger; I know what fingers are for; and I know they are part of a hand. The reason I appear to see my finger in isolation is that the robot does the work of relating for me.

Or again, I glance at my watch while thinking of something else. A moment later, I have to look at it again to check on the time. I did not see the time, although I certainly saw the watch and the position of its hands. But "seeing the time" involves a lot more than saying "Half past two." It involves a more complex thought: "Half past two in the afternoon—an hour since lunch, two hours before tea time." To see the time is to place it in relation to the rest of the day.

But now, here, for me, is the decisive leap in the argument. I am reading Eliot's *The Wasteland*, and I read the quotation from the beginning of *Tristan and Isolde*, *"Frisch weht der wind. . . ."* I experience the tingling sensation that A. E. Housman declares to be the test of poetry. Why? What has happened?

Only this: I have been reminded of a work with which I am familiar, and which has often moved me deeply. It is rather like a place in which

I have been happy; it has established its own separate reality in my mind. Now this whole reality has been evoked by a single quotation. It is like the biscuit dipped in tea that reminds Proust of his childhood, in *Swann's Way*. The sensation of poetry is, in fact, merely an expansion of the ordinary relationality of consciousness. (It might further be remarked that the whole of *The Wasteland* is a series of such juxtapositions and evocations.)

One might, then, summarize this phase of the argument by saying that to see a thing truly is to see it in the widest possible field of relations. The "nausea" that Sartre describes in the novel of that name is the sensation of seeing objects almost completely divested of meaning—i.e., of relations. Yet this is not to say *completely* divested of relations. An object completely divested of relations would not be seen at all, for consciousness would need to be totally passive to "see" a thing in this way. (Even within the framework of Sartre's philosophy, there is a contradiction in his idea of nausea, for he implies that this nausea is pure perception, without prejudice or preconception—i.e., without *intentionality*; then, in the next breath, Sartre asserts that consciousness *is* intentionality.)

But we might symbolize an object perceived in nausea as a kind of tic-tac-toe square, like this:

where the *X* represents the object. There is a minimum of relationality around it. In normal everyday consciousness, the object is surrounded by far more relations:

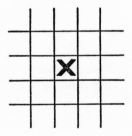

But the larger the graph, the more alive and meaningful the consciousness. My "weblike consciousness" must be thought of as a very large sheet of graph paper.

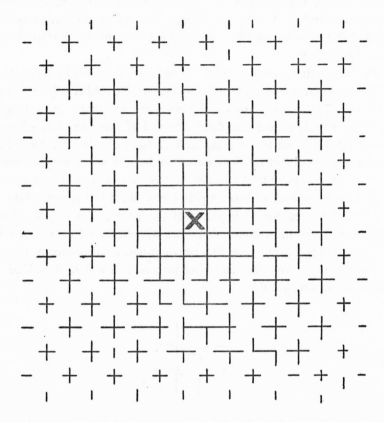

There is one more complication here that must be clarified. Even in limited, everyday consciousness, the graph is actually immense—but most of it is invisible. One must, as it were, imagine the lines of the graph continued with dotted lines to symbolize relations vanishing into shadowy realms beyond our "immediacy consciousness."

In experiences of weblike consciousness—poetic intensity—the dotted lines suddenly become solid.

This explains one of the basic problems of mysticism and poetry: the "ineffability" of their insights. Anyone who has experienced weblike consciousness can grasp the reason for this. What is seen in these intenser states of consciousness is, in fact, what is *already known* to ordinary consciousness, but only known conceptually. William James has spoken of the sudden vision of "horizons of distant fact" in states of mystical intensity, and this is very much to the point. The reason that the meaning content of weblike consciousness baffles expression is that it is already known to the limited everyday consciousness—but known conceptually, not perceptually. There is as much difference as between knowing a country from having studied a map, and knowing it from having lived there.

Now it can be seen why this notion of the relationality of consciousness throws a completely new light on phenomenology—in fact, virtually opens up new countries in phenomenology and existentialism. The existentialism of Sartre, Heidegger, and Merleau Ponty has a rather arid and sober nature; it seems to be largely an exhortation to man to face the unpleasant facts about himself. And all this arises from its theory of consciousness as a kind of helpless jellyfish, doing its best to deal with the world. The change of emphasis from intentionality to relationality suddenly reveals consciousness as possessing enormous and mysterious potentialities. In Sartre, states of poetic or mystical intensity are of merely "chemical" interest; they do not affect his basic view of the nature of consciousness. For Sartre, consciousness is a jellyfish with blunt pseudopodia that appear to reach out, but which are really dragged out of it by the gravity of objects. There would be no point in examining the jellyfish through a microscope; it has no inside and no cause. The only interesting thing about consciousness lies in the nature of the intention that connects the jellyfish with the objective world.

I have tried to show that this view oversimplifies. The intentional act is, admittedly, interesting in itself; but far more interesting is what takes place within consciousness in any intentional act. As the intention reaches out to the object, inner intentions stretch out into the realm of the robot, striving to send spurts of power into the invisible areas of the web. Sometimes, for no understandable reason, the resistance of these inner circuits drops; the power flows into the hidden areas and we have a sensation that can only be described as being like the exclamation "Of course!" These are the states in which all great poetry is written, and they are obviously a *perfectly ordinary potentiality* of human consciousness.

One further point. Hume divided sensations into two types: physical impressions and feelings, which are clear and definite, and mental impressions (memories, imaginings, thoughts), which are merely a *dim carbon copy* of physical sensations. On the whole, psychology has accepted this distinction.

Weblike consciousness denies it. What happens here is that our mental world, which normally seems so dim and feeble in comparison to physical actuality—a mere candle compared to the sun—suddenly takes on a glowing intensity. A kind of chain reaction starts, as in nuclear fission, and the result is a state of mind that is anything but a carbon copy of physical sensation. It exists in its own right, and may burn with such intensity that it is the physical world which becomes the candle against the sun.

It should be clear why it was necessary to say all this before entering upon the main subject of this chapter—the question of love and freedom. As is well known, Sartre's *Being and Nothingness* devotes a great deal of space to both subjects, and produces singularly discouraging conclusions. Love, according to Sartre, is a hopeless attempt by consciousness to escape its own loneliness; it could be summarized in Rupert Brooke's lines about lovers taking "Their own poor dreams within their arms and lying/ Each in his lonely night, each with a ghost."

Sadism and masochism are also vain attempts to escape this "lonely night," according to Sartre.

This view is a natural outcome of the Sartre view of consciousness as a passive emptiness, longing to feel itself filled. This can be seen with singular clarity in the following quotation from Simone de Beauvoir's *Pyrrhus and Cinéas*:

> I look at myself in vain in a mirror, tell myself my own story, I can never grasp myself as an entire object. I experience in myself the emptiness that is myself, I feel that I am not.

This is what one would expect from Sartre's psychology. Behind her eyes sits consciousness, like a shallow pool. It is basically a reflection of her environment—and at the moment, the main item in her environment is her own face in the mirror, with which she is completely, boringly familiar. Naturally, she feels nothing, and it seems to her that this state is an honest perception of what consciousness is really like. Feelings would only stir up the mud in consciousness and prevent her from seeing how shallow it is.

One might contrast this with the passage in Hesse's *Steppenwolf* in which the hero experiences a moment of weblike consciousness, about which he writes:

For moments together my heart stood still between delight and sorrow
to find how rich was the gallery of my life, and how thronged the soul of
the wretched Steppenwolf with high eternal stars and constellations. . . .

This, in fact, is the experience whose possibility Simone de Beauvoir is
denying. If Steppenwolf were to look into a mirror at this moment, he
would not feel that "I can never grasp myself as an entire object," for
that is precisely what he is doing—or, at least, he is well on the way to it.

When the relational nature of consciousness is grasped, we see that
Simone de Beauvoir was merely describing an extreme of low-pressure
consciousness, close to nausea, and assuming it to be an accurate picture
of all consciousness.

It is hard to see how one could convince Mlle. de Beauvoir of her
error. One might try saying to her, "You are starting to itch—first your
left knee, then your right ear . . ." And then, as she reaches out to scratch
herself, asking "Where did it come from? Not your 'consciousness'—you
were watching it closely. Yet you undoubtedly made yourself itch. It follows that there is a part of your mind, not open to your observation,
which produces the itch." Or, even more simply, one might ask her to try
to recall a tune, or the name of a character in a certain famous novel.
After a moment's hesitation, she recalls the tune or the name. You then
ask: "But where did the tune come from? It walked into your consciousness, drawn forth by an act of intentionality. From where?"

I have tried to establish—and, I think, have established successfully—
that the subject of love and freedom can be dealt with by phenomenological psychology, and, what is more, dealt with positively and creatively,
not negatively and destructively, as does Sartre. Let us now undertake a
more detailed analysis of love, attempting to remain within the phenomenological framework.

The aim of phenomenology is to brush aside preconceptions or assumptions that are not recognized as such. It once seemed self-evident
that the sun revolved around the earth; it was necessary for Copernicus
to perform a Husserlian epoché, a suspension of belief, before he could
examine the truth of this assumption.

What, then, are the human assumptions about love that need to be
suspended? They are so taken for granted that it is difficult even to state
them clearly. In the romantic fiction of the nineteenth century, as well as
in today's women's magazines, love is some immense, irresistible force
that picks up human beings by the scruff of the neck and involves them
in emotions that are the deepest they will ever experience—*Wuthering*

Heights and so on. People "fall in love"; they establish what Goethe called "elective affinities," which somehow dissolve their separateness, creating a sort of unity.

I apologize for this vagueness; it lies in the matter under discussion.

Consider the alternative view. According to Blake, "What men in women do require" (and vice versa) is "the lineaments of satisfied desire." That is to say, male-female relations are a transaction, like buying a cabbage from the grocer. What lovers are after is personal satisfaction, exactly as in a commercial transaction. They may be so mutually satisfactory that they are finally willing to give one another unlimited credit, offering satisfaction without the demand for immediate return. But it is "established credit," just as in business; not pure generosity.

There is also the matter of "falling in love." But this will hardly bear scrutiny. Young people are very prone to fall in love—but then, they are emotionally hungry, and liable to fix on the most unsuitable objects, which would seem to suggest that they are projecting their desires rather than trying to enter into a two-sided relationship. We are inclined to label this emotion "puppy love" or "infatuation," indicating that we recognize its highly subjective nature.

Unfortunately, this recognition usually leads to a landslide of skepticism about the whole subject. The poet W. J. Turner writes:

> Can the lover share his soul
> Or the mistress show her mind?
> Can the body beauty share
> Or lust satisfaction find?
>
> Marriage is but keeping house
> Sharing food and company,
> What has this to do with love
> Or with the body's beauty?
>
> If love means affection, I
> Love old trees, hats, coats and things,
> Anything that's been with me
> In my daily sufferings.*

And it is only one step from this to Rupert Brooke's "each in his lonely night, each with a ghost," and Sartre's total nihilism on the subject.

Here is the analysis of love that I would propose as conforming to a fairly stringent reduction. Let me first of all state it flatly, without elaboration.

I would suggest that the normal use of the word love is inaccurate,

* The Author wishes to thank the estate of W. J. Turner and Messrs. Chatto and Windus for permission to quote from Mr. Turner's poetry.

that it contains several false assumptions. I have never heard of a case of falling in love that could not be analyzed along the lines of the grocer and the cabbage. When the statue in *Man and Superman* protests that he has often been sincerely in love, Don Juan retorts: "Sincerity . . . ! To be so greedy for a woman that you deceive yourself in your eagerness to deceive her!" This kind of "love"—greed for a desirable person—is surely a matter of possessiveness combined with self-deception.

On the other hand, the kind of love I feel for my children—particularly when they are babies—is an instinctive protectiveness. I have included them within my personal radius, so that the protectiveness I normally feel for myself extends to them too. Protectiveness, in some respects, goes deeper than love. Is it self-love that makes me fling up my hands when I stumble? Obviously not; it is something much more primitive. My feeling toward my children is an equally primitive protectiveness.

I can think of no example, either known to me personally or through literature, of any case of love that could not be broken down into the two elements of sexual desire (lust) and protectiveness. There may or may not also be involved an element of intellectual or personal sympathy of the kind that exists between ordinary friends. (I can think of a great many marriages in which it is lacking.)

I have to admit that, so far, I have said nothing with which Sartre would not agree. But it is at this point that I would part company with his analysis.

The last stanza of Turner's poem *Epithalamium* runs:

> I have stared upon a dawn
> And trembled like a man in love,
> A man in love I was, and I
> Could not speak and could not move.

In the same way, Shaw's argument in the third act of *Man and Superman* is that love is given its peculiarly obsessive quality by the fact that the lovers are in the grip of an evolutionary force that transcends their personal involvements.

This, of course, is an argument that Sartre would condemn as completely unphenomenological. Phenomenology is an extension of Humeian skepticism. It deals in observables. To speak of an evolutionary force is not only bad psychology; it is bad biology and bad philosophy. The "evolutionary force" is wishful thinking. Julian Huxley commented that to attribute evolution to an *élan vital* is like attributing the motion of a train to an *élan locomotif*.

But it is always easier to demolish an argument by swinging a sledge-hammer of skepticism than to demonstrate it by detailed and careful analysis. In this case, there are a number of reasons why I cannot accept the sledgehammer approach. To begin with, Merleau Ponty has used phenomenological analysis to show that pure behaviorism cannot account for all mental activities. Arthur Koestler's attack on behaviorism in his important trilogy *The Sleepwalkers, The Act of Creation,* and *The Ghost in the Machine* follows similar lines, although for some reason, Mr. Koestler shows no awareness of what Merleau Ponty has already done. There is also a powerful movement, led by Sir Karl Popper and Michael Polanyi, to try to place the philosophy of science on a less positivistic basis. Some of Popper's arguments in *The Logic of Scientific Discovery,* particularly in the appendices added to the latest edition, strike me as quite conclusive.

Most important, for my purposes, is Maslow's contribution to psychology. Let me try to summarize this as I understand it.

Men differ from animals chiefly in that they may be driven by "values" that cannot be reduced to such lower terms as the Freudian libido, the need for territory, food, security, etc. "Man has a higher nature that is just as 'instinctoid' as his lower nature. . . . This higher nature includes the needs for meaningful work, for responsibility, for being fair and just, for doing what is worthwhile," he writes in the preface to *Eupsychian Management* (1965). Aldous Huxley once made a similar suggestion when he remarked that if man possesses a subconscious basement containing all his darker desires and instincts, why should he not possess an attic, equally inaccessible to conscious reflection?

It may be a relatively small proportion of human beings who urgently experience this need to live in terms of higher values, but it is also the most important section of the human race.

Man is an evolutionary animal. Of all animals, he is the one who most hates inactivity. A bored man will tap his foot or tap his finger against a chair arm. A bored animal will merely go to sleep. Man wants to move, to go. He is a big engine that needs to be geared to worthwhile labor if he is to operate at maximum efficiency. Or he could be compared to a river that must flow forward. If the river gets dammed up for some reason, it tends to run back up the valley and form a lake, which now becomes an amplifier of every minor frustration or neurosis.

Maslow's basic assertion is obviously that man's impulses toward higher values exist in their own right; they are not a sublimation of some lower impulse, a *faute de mieux*. In fact, Maslow's experiments with monkeys in the early nineteen-thirties seemed to demonstrate that monkeys will solve intellectual problems for the fun of it, and that therefore even a monkey cannot be wholly summarized in terms of its lower impulses.

What happens when the river gets dammed up is also the central theme of Frankl's psychology. There is Frankl's story of the schoolboy who stuttered badly—until asked to play the part of a stutterer in the school play, after which he was unable to stutter. Man was not intended for static self-contemplation and lack of purpose. He is only at his best when driven by purpose—the higher the better. This is the theme of Shaw's *Man and Superman*, and, more recently, of the Spanish existential philosopher Zubiri, for whom man is only truly himself in action.

I am here summarizing a large body of evidence in a hasty and unsatisfactory manner; lack of space demands this. This evidence has not in any way contributed to my own conviction that the evolutionary drive cannot be dismissed as wishful thinking; this was already the central theme of my book *The Outsider* (1956), written before I was aware of any of this evidence. I refer interested readers to the six volumes of my "outsider cycle" (1956–65), and to my *Introduction to the New Existentialism* (1966).

All this should make it clear why, although I accept Blake's "lineaments of gratified desire" view of love, I have no sympathy with the Sartre vacuum.

Maslow, then, has answered Nietzsche's question "Freedom for what?" with an evolutionary affirmation. "Freedom for the expression and development of man's higher instinctoid nature." Love in itself is not necessarily a part of this higher nature; it may be a fairly low-level expression of lust, protectiveness, and the need for emotional security. But it may become a vital part of this higher instinctoid expression, blending it with it so as to become an indistinguishable part. The love story of the Curies offers a convincing example of this. But this higher expression need not necessarily be connected with love. There is no evidence that Bernard Shaw's marriage made the slightest difference to him as a creative thinker, except to provide him with three meals a day. H. G. Wells' sexual relations were frankly promiscuous and physical, but there is no evidence (in his work) that his "higher nature" was in any way starved. Clearly, he was in some ways an immature person, which explains the obsessive need for seduction; to judge by his later work, however, his creativity was unaffected.

But the really interesting problem is the question of the nature of freedom for modern man. And here I must admit that I do not see how this word can be defined except in evolutionary terms. Man is probably about two million years old. For about three quarters of that time, he showed no advance at all. Then the rate of evolution slowly accelerated. One of his greatest advances was his collaboration with the dog, and his realization that certain animals would obey him instead of fleeing from him, if he treated them right. Then came husbandry, with the discovery that he could survive by growing things instead of hunting, as the next greatest advance in human history. And it was probably this slower, more contemplative pace of life that caused the development of religion and then of art.

Art, as Julian Huxley never tires of pointing out, is perhaps the greatest advance of all. For it is basically the discovery that man is not permanently "stuck in the present," like a needle tracing its inevitable course over a gramophone record. He possesses a mental being, "those thoughts that wander through eternity," as Milton says. According to Robert Ardrey, this was the beginning of his downfall, for he now had to see himself as something more than a part of nature; he had to believe that he was somehow the center of the universe. Whether one agrees with Ardrey or not (and I don't), it has to be admitted that all real evolution —truly human evolution—has sprung from this belief in his central significance. It endowed him with a new, altogether more aggressive attitude toward nature. One has only to read any popular book on Stonehenge to grasp clearly what this means; read of the enormous effort entailed in quarrying stones in Wales, then dragging them overland on rollers, then floating them on rafts up the Bristol Channel, then more rafts, then more rollers—until they are finally dragged to the middle of Salisbury Plain, to take their place in a monument that probably took a hundred years to build.* To imagine that state of mind of the priests when they looked at the finally completed temple is to realize that the human will to achieve is a force that makes glaciers and volcanoes and earthquakes seem modest and feeble. It is this force that has continued to operate, from Archimedes' pulleys to the discoveries of Pasteur and Fleming, and that has

* Recent evidence suggests that these stones could have been brought to Salisbury Plain by glaciers. However, considering the sheer engineering skill and patience required to erect Stonehenge, I feel my example remains valid.

made man the most incredible phenomenon that this planet has ever seen.

But the changes of the past two hundred years have been too abrupt. We cannot adjust to them. And as a result of this feeling of confusion and bewilderment, we have Samuel Beckett's tramps looking blankly at the universe and muttering "Nothing to be done," and Sartre's assertion that "man is a useless passion." We are at our best when responding to challenges; and compared to human life five hundred years ago, our civilization is a huge feather bed.

The problem of freedom now arises. We have plenty of freedom in the physical sense; we are surrounded by it. And now the Frankl syndrome begins to operate. Left to itself, with no purpose, consciousness begins to feed upon itself. Frankl's story of the stutterer makes this clear enough. When told to use his conscious control to go ahead and stutter, the will goes into gear; energies flow into their proper circuits; the being is unified by purpose. And the neurotic symptoms vanish. Man becomes what he *should* be—what evolution intends him to be. (It is worth commenting here that the sexual orgasm offers man one of the clearest insights into what consciousness *could* be like if he could learn to unify his being through purpose with the same intensity that his sexual instinct can unify it.)

Man is not himself without purpose. And it has been the great achievement of humanistic psychology to recognize this from purely experimental premises, without wishful thinking or idealizing.

It may seem that this paper has failed to come to grips with its subject: love as an expression of mutual freedom. But, in fact, it has been necessary to argue in this somewhat roundabout way in order to reach this subject.

The kind of unity of being provided by a strong sexual stimulus is largely nonreflective; it rises from the realm of the robot. But most of our purposive activities are less powerfully instinctive, so that they require a conscious self-image to hold them together.

Here is an anecdote that illustrates my point. When the BBC built the first soundproof studios for broadcasting music, they discovered that orchestras played badly in the "dead" studio. An orchestra likes to *hear itself*, to hear its sounds bounced back off the walls of the concert hall. A friend of mine was given the amusing job of connecting up a circuit that would pick up the sound of the orchestra, and relay it back to them a fraction of a second later through loudspeakers situated around the studio, thus producing an artificial echo. As soon as they could hear themselves, the orchestra played twice as well.

We all need "mirrors" to reflect our activity if we are to function at our best. And this is surely the deep significance of the male-female relation. There is, of course, the simple fact that in merely stimulating one another sexually, they are providing one another with an experience of deep instinctive unity. But the sexual side of marriage is bound to be affected by habit, so this aspect is hardly important over a long period. But the way in which each of the partners operates as a mirror for the other remains of permanent importance. Freedom cannot operate on a long-term basis without a clear self-image, and the purpose of the marriage partner is to provide this self-image.

There are, of course, many other ways of providing a self-image. To mention only one: a writer produces his book because it is his mirror, which confirms the direction of his evolution. While Alexander's slave was told to whisper "Remember you are mortal," a writer's book is there to whisper "Remember you may be immortal."

Ideally, a love relationship serves the same purpose. Each of the partners is provided with a new self-image, one that differs radically from the reflection thrown back by parents and schoolteachers and work colleagues. Each serves as a magic mirror in which the other sees himself reflected *in terms of potentiality*. (It also follows, of course, that sexual relations can be the most destructive thing in the world if either of the partners lacks belief in the other's potentiality.)

Let me finish on a warning note. It is true that a love relation is, ideally, an illumination of one another's freedom: that is to say, potentialities for evolving. But real evolution—of the kind we see in the case of great artists, musicians, philosophers, scientists—is not dependent upon this kind of encouragement. Would Beethoven have been a greater composer with an admiring wife? Would Goethe have been a greater poet if he had married an intellectual equal instead of the stolid and peasant-like Christine Vulpius? Almost certainly not. On the other hand, a downright unsuitable marriage—such as H. G. Wells's first marriage, or Einstein's—may actively hinder creativity.

While love undoubtedly presents the possibility of an immensely important adventure in mutual freedom, I have to admit frankly that I cannot call to mind a single case of a great man—or woman—whose evolution has been heavily dependent upon the freedom mirrored by the love relation. And the reason may be the one given by Socrates in the

Symposium: that in highly evolved human beings, the love of another person tends to serve as the stepping-off point for more universal enthusiasms. And at this point in the discussion, it may be that psychology gets uncomfortably close to theology.

6

Communication in Love

Herbert A. Otto

Communication in love has been a challenge throughout the ages. Catullus, in ancient Rome, said, "Let no woman believe a man's oath, let none believe that a man's speeches can be trustworthy." [1] This thought was echoed by Sir Walter Scott, when he noted:

> False man hath sworn, and woman hath believed—
> Repented and reproached, and then believed once more. [2]

Shakespeare also expressed the same sentiment. He, however, ascribed this point of view to the feminine sex:

> When my love swears that she is made of truth,
> I do believe her, though I know she lies. [3]

Similar ideas are found in contemporary poetry and literature.

Nonverbal communication in love also occupies a prominent place in poetry and literature. John Donne concluded that verbal communication can be an actual impediment to love: "For God's sake hold your tongue, and let me love." [4] In this lyrical poem he was more explicit about nonverbal communication in love:

> Our eye-beams twisted, and did thread
> Our eyes, upon one double string;
> So to, engraft our hands, as yet
> Was all the means to make us one. [5]

The literature abounds with similar observations. Dryden, working with the same metaphor, said, "When eyes meet far off, our sense is such,/ That . . . we feel the tenderest touch." [6] More briefly, Ovid noted that "There are often voice and words in a silent look." [7]

The literature of past ages and cultures and contemporary literature both contain explicit references and even verbatim accounts of the types of communication which occur between persons in love. When we analyze this material, we find that, paradoxically, communication in love seems to be characterized by two main features: (1) confusion and lack of clarity; and (2) increased clarity and comprehension. Many of the great lovers, both male and female, complain of difficulties encountered in expressing their feelings and difficulty in understanding what the beloved person intended to communicate to them. Often, we find references to the stammering and stuttering of persons not ordinarily afflicted with speech impairments, while some lovers describe themselves as "being struck dumb."

Lovers often display a tendency to read too much into each other's utterances, to look for hidden meanings, symbolism and depth in communication which may or may not be there. At times, lovers characterize the other person as "speaking in riddles" and talk about "the mystery of her (his) words."

Conversely, we find that many lovers throughout the ages and in many cultures characterize communication in love as having exceptional clarity. They understand the communication of the beloved as they have understood no previous person's communication; they are then inspired to compose poems, letters, and essays which both lovers cherish for their qualities of clarity and understanding. In some instances, lovers have been observed to communicate verbally with a free-flowing quality and fervor which almost amounts to a distinct poetic speech form.

Contemporary premarital counseling literature, on the other hand, is heavily laden with accounts of people in love who do not communicate adequately and who do not verbally explore many areas which need to be explored in relation to continued togetherness and marriage. The writer's own research bears this out and lead to the development of a set of premarital counseling aids * designed to foster communication between couples. With the contemporary emphasis on the importance of communication has come the recognition that *self-disclosure in love is espe-*

* *The Otto Pre-Marital Schedules,* Palo Alto, Calif. (Consulting Psychologists Press, 1961).

cially desirable and necessary, as this helps to establish a relationship characterized by optimal personality growth for both lovers.

The premises of this point of view are that personality growth can be a lifelong adventure and that two persons in love can grow with and through each other by the continuous development of a communication system which is characterized by maximum openness, freedom, and self-disclosure. An opposing point of view holds that both the man and the woman should maintain a "mystique"; that they should not expose themselves too much to the other person, or say too much, or communicate too much. Implicit in this point of view are the folk sayings that "mystery attracts" and that "familiarity breeds contempt."

These points of view are not necessarily bipolar. The human being is essentially a mystery; the phenomenon of love is a mystery. Although we believe we understand love better than we ever did before, it is necessary for us to acknowledge that this was a conclusion reached by preceding generations. What we are faced with, then, is man, the mystery, entering into a mysterious state of being (love) and attempting to communicate out of the depth of this mystique. Can man, engaged in that state of being we call love and loving, really communicate a great deal about what is going on within himself? Conversely, how much of what he communicates is really understood by his beloved? It seems that even with the most persistent thrust and desire to communicate and understand fully, there will always be elements of the mystique present in the man, the woman, and the relationship.

An interesting aspect of nonverbal communication is symbolic communication. Women seem more responsive to symbolic love communication and symbolic love offerings than are men. A woman's responses to a single red rose or a surprise gift of perfume are likely to differ qualitatively, on a feelings level, from a man's response. The woman seems more sensitive to the symbolic implications of communication and tends to ascribe more meaning to a symbolic gift. She also seems to value such symbolic communication more. Despite the eagerness with which such symbolic communication is received by the woman, only rarely will a man consistently and freely use the varied symbolic possibilities which are available to two people in love. This despite the fact that maximal use of such symbolic communication between lovers seems to greatly strengthen and foster the relationship.

Until recently, comparatively little attention has been paid to the nonverbal aspects of communication. The literature on love has long recognized the importance of nonverbal elements and as previously noted, many a line and verse stresses the importance of, for example, eye play and other nonverbal communication in love.

Nonverbal communication has always been part of man's communication stream—only the marked interest and scientific study of the subject are of comparative recent origin. For thousands of years human beings have been reading each other's smiles, shrugs, winks, voice tone, posture, position, movements, and mannerisms. The new insights being gained today also enrich our understanding of the ways such communication may be offered and accepted.

For generations, some people have been considered "sensitive" while others have been seen as "dull" or "insensitive." Even as some people have an impairment of their sight or hearing, others have an impaired sensitivity to nonverbal communication which in turn has crippled their relationship to people. However, this type of impairment is correctable. Today, it is widely recognized that sensory awareness, including awareness of nonverbal communication, can be developed and tremendously sharpened by training. There is also increased realization by scientists that verbal skills represent only a fraction of man's communications spectrum. For example, the psychologist Albert Mehrabian concludes that when communicating, total impact breaks down as follows: 7 per cent is verbal, 38 per cent is vocal, and 55 per cent is facial.[8] If we acknowledge the importance of nonverbal communication in love and, in particular, its role in the preliminary phases of the sexual relationship and during intercourse, this raises the intriguing question of whether training in nonverbal communication should not be an integral part of preparation for love and marriage.

Certainly, acquaintance with the concept of nonverbal communication should be an integral part of every course and curriculum which attempts preparation for marriage and family living. Group experiences, intensive experience seminars, and group marathons on nonverbal communication can add new dimensions of quality to life and love and improve and extend the total spectrum of communication.

Few of us are very aware of principles that apply to nonverbal communication. A few of the more important principles and findings are as follows:

1. Spontaneity is the key word in nonverbal communication. Perhaps 85 to 90 per cent of nonverbal communication is spontaneous, free-flowing response. Spontaneous self-expression through dance and some

forms of acting seem to foster and encourage the development of richer, more varied, and more expressive nonverbal communications.

2. The studied and conscious use of nonverbal communication segments as an integral and controlled part of the verbal communication stream can have a very far-reaching and profound impact on those participating in this event. The emotional thrust of the nonverbal message seems to be greatly amplified by controlled use and timing.

3. One of the major values of increased sensitivity to nonverbal communication is the clarification of feeling states. "From the way you are slumping, I get the impression you feel a little blue . . ." "The way you move, I know something good has happened."

4. Awareness of one's own nonverbal communications can lead to enlarged self-understanding, change, and growth.

5. The better we get to know a person, the more accurate should be our perception and understanding of his nonverbal communication. These are multiple signs and signals—the signals he sends by body movements, eye movements and posture, the timbre, quality and tone (not necessarily content) of his verbalizations. Feeling states, attitudes, and emotions are conveyed by a turn of the head, the lifting of an eyebrow, inclination of the body, or twitching of a foot. Unfortunately, most of us prefer to close ourselves to the nonverbal communications even of those close to us, as it is often more convenient, and our own pressures and needs are of more paramount importance.

6. As Mehrabian points out,[9] nonverbal communication is influenced by the status of the participants and their feelings about each other. For example, the more we like a person, the more time we will spend looking into his eyes as we are talking to him.

7. The "after the event" recall of nonverbal communication can add to our understanding of what happened. Since we are often too involved in the here and now of the communications stream, it may be desirable to view high points of the nonverbal aspects of the communication with another person some time *after the event*. Significant insights and increased awareness of the other person's communication stream can be obtained through this process. For example, in reviewing our interaction with a person, we may recall his getting up and pacing up and down at a certain point in the conversation. This nonverbal clue, to which we may not have paid much attention at the time, may greatly increase our understanding of what had transpired.

The foremost investigator of communicative body motion or kinesics (nonverbal communication) is Dr. R. L. Birdwhistell. He has concluded that ". . . body motion is a learned form of communication, which is patterned within a culture and which can be broken down into an ordered system of isolable elements." [10]

The importance of nonverbal communication received new impetus as a result of a comparatively recent research report. Dr. W. S. Condon of the Western Psychiatric Institute and Clinic of the University of Pittsburgh School of Medicine used high-speed cinema photography for his study of "Communication-Dancing" which he reported in 1968.

> When a person talks, his or her body "dances." The listener's body also "dances." A leader in this research, Dr. Condon said that the behavior of doctors and patients and of others in mutual communications was recorded by a special sound film device in which controlled time flow was registered in fractions of seconds. Complex "dance" patterns were brought to light in frames of time pictures.
>
> In one record, a doctor and a woman patient, both young and handsome, appear engaged in a "courting dance." Obtaining diagnostic information from the patient, the doctor sits down, plucks his trousers, then both the doctor and the woman begin to lean toward each other at the same time frame.
>
> The physician and the woman continue to come forward until their heads are about two feet apart. They move their heads upward and then they begin to move back. Both carry out such body changes at the same time frames, one frame being 1/24th of one second.
>
> Men particularly seem to be "dancing" all the time. . . .[11]

What is perhaps most surprising when we survey communication in love is the almost complete absence of research in this field. What *are* the communications of people in love? Is voice frequency, timbre, and tone affected by the love experience? Are posture and body motion patterns so affected? If we are in love, does our nonverbal communication increase in frequency or intensity, or change in its nature? Are there particular body communications patterns peculiar to the male and female in love? Are we perhaps here dealing with a *human love dance* on the body communication level alluded to in the Pittsburgh Research Report on communication dancing? Perhaps with the new photographic techniques it would be possible to identify people who are strongly attracted to each other and who may even be in love without knowing it.

In view of the importance of love as a regenerative force in our personal lives and in our relationships to society as a whole, it is my hope that there will be more research in the very neglected field of communication in love. All of us are the product of love, for without love, we would have died in infancy—just as today many people are dying for no other reason than lack of love. *For most of us the prospect, reality and communication of love remain the most dynamic and hopeful events in our lives.*

NOTES

1. Catullus, *Odes,* Ode IXIV.
2. Sir Walter Scott, *The Fortunes of Nigel,* Chap. 20.
3. William Shakespeare, *Sonnets,* Sonnet CXXXVIII.
4. John Donne, "The Canonization."
5. John Donne, "The Ecstasy."
6. John Dryden, *Marriage à la Mode.*
7. Ovid, *Ars Amatoria.*
8. A. Mehrabian, "Communication Without Words," *Psychology Today,* Vol. 2, No. 4, p. 53.
9. *Ibid.,* p. 54.
10. R. L. Birdwhistell, Kinesics and Context (Philadelphia: University of Pennsylvania Press, 1970), p. iv.
11. Los Angeles *Herald Tribune,* July 1, 1968, "Body Dance, Part of Talk," p. 8.

7

Love and Women's Liberation

Rosalind Loring

THERE'S A ME [1]

Tell me not about your love
I know it well
I've felt it in your glance
Felt it from the lash of the whip
And worse
From out your tongue
Tell me not of your love
It is so fluid
It has drowned me
And mine
In its burning intensity
I have but few places left unscarred
The heat of your love has all but consumed my brain
The security of your love has rendered me fatherless
The gift of your love branded me bastard
The testimony of your love has imprisoned me
Your song of love has made me voiceless
I shall sing no more
I am no more
You have loved me into oblivion.

Filled with anger, hostility, pain, hurt, grief, the poem expresses well the radical feminist movement's view of love. Anti-male, it rejects "his" love because the women in this movement believe that inevitably love has and will continue to cause their downfall. Second class status, loss of identity, lack of autonomy . . . all are due to love. Love has been used as a tool both by men and institutions of society to keep women in their place, and historically that place has been defined by men. The result has kept women from achieving their potential, from gaining ego strength, from being fully functioning human beings.

Because the consequences of love have caused women to feel and to be powerless, where they see men as being powerful, those in the movement frequently express their views in economic and political terms. Clearly stated by Kate Millett, author of *Sexual Politics*,[2] through her book's substantial 363 pages, a constant theme is reiterated. . . . The relationship between men and women throughout all societies has been a political relationship, one which has reached into every arena of life. In the language of today's interpretation of politics, love is an institution where power expressions are found. Dominant/submissive . . . win/lose . . . decision maker/decision receiver . . . leader/follower . . . all are role relationships in which women are the receivers. Today's radical feminist no longer agrees that this must be. Thus she will reject love, regretfully but firmly, occasionally raucously. Even the poet, in her dramatic intensity, speaks of "the lash of the whip," "imprisonment" and finally of the love that "has made me voiceless."

Radical feminist women, searching for the causes of their depressed and denigrated state, have decided that the achievement of love has meant the loss of self. The trade-off has been detrimental to a woman's best interests. The anguish heard throughout all the rhetoric of the movement is the feeling of betrayal. *"You have loved me into oblivion."*

That sense of oblivion is less tolerable for almost all of today's women. As well educated as men, as healthy, as aware, they, too, strive for recognition and for equality. It has not been found in our past. The pages of history books, especially in the Western world, are almost bare in reporting the contributions of women in the development of culture and society. (Old Mother Hubbard's cupboard?)

On the other hand, throughout recorded history, relationships of men and women have been reported and commented on. The writings of radical feminists are replete with quotations from the Judeo-Christian Bible, both the Old and the New Testaments. Even the Eastern religions and the polytheistic religions of the Greeks and Romans expressed strong reservations about the abilities of women and delight in being male, rather than female. So that love by men has been substituted for equal valuing and acceptance of a whole person.

It is particularly interesting to note that concepts popularly held today, past the middle of the twentieth century, still contain strong elements of romantic love as defined in the twelfth century. "It is generally accepted that western patriarchy has been much softened by the concepts of courtly and romantic love. . . . In comparison with the candor of machismo or oriental behavior, one realizes how much of a concession traditional chivalrous behavior represents." [3] Yet historians of courtly love rarely mention that the raptures of the poets and practitioners had no effect upon the legal or economic conditions of women. It appears that the 'courtlier' the love, the less it was exposed to the rigors of marriage. "Cinderella" was a fairy tale, not an historical document.

Kate Millett and others point out that chivalry has been used as a way of saving face while subordinating women's roles and hiding the injustices of women's social position. Much has been made of the gimmickry, the falseness of the pedestal position. As one comic strip female capsulated, "Man places woman on a pedestal because we 'bug' them at eye level." Statues are static, not living, breathing, feeling humans. The traditional words 'respect,' 'honor,' 'protect' and 'admire' have a hollow sound to those contemporary women who are also congruent with their situation.

The idealization of romantic love became ironic when Marx and Engels presented the premise that the family unit was not based upon love, but on economic considerations. The influence of the Industrial Revolution in shaping the family merely confirmed the notion that love and marriage were separate entities, sometimes joined. Further, Engels and others argued that marriage is a form of prostitution; that is, sex and household services are made available in return for money or financial security. Because of the dependency of women, Engels believed that only when men and women were equal would sexual love cease to be used as a form of coercion. But the priority of economic stability necessitated the cohesion of a patriarchal family and the authority of its head as well as the economic dependence of its members. At least, that condition existed until the recent movement into the Post Industrial society.

Thus the anger, the frustration, and indeed the ambivalence that can be heard throughout the radical feminist literature, are based upon an inability to separate the effects of economic condition and political subordination from those due to romantic love. Love is experienced not only as a weapon, but also as a ruse, a technique, a method for concealing the true meaning of men's intentions regarding women. Their distress is so frequently expressed in terms of trickery. Queries one young woman of twenty-four, a recent college graduate, in a quiet little feminist bookstore in Venice, California, "Do you believe love is the psychosocial malfunctioning of a human being?" Says Ti-Grace Atkinson, one of the major leaders and codifiers of the movement, "Marriage means rape and life-long slavery. Love has to be destroyed. Friendship is reciprocal, love isn't." [4] Germaine Greer in *The Female Eunuch* [5] charges, "Men have reduced heterosexual contact to sado-masochistic patterns by exploiting love and fantasies of romance."

Again the language of power politics, the symbols of revolution. But this is not strange when one realizes that the current radical women's movement began in response to the experiences of young women, bright, intelligent, and capable who thought that their involvement in radical social movements (race, youth, anti-war) would include their participation in activities on an equal basis with young men, white and minority. Much to their dismay, distress and disillusionment, they found that the men in those movements, their peers, expected from them the typical services and roles. There was no difference from being part of a labor union or a business establishment. They became increasingly uncomfortable with the same sexual behavior, the same put-downs, the same group definition via sex role. It is not surprising, then, that the movement is nation-wide. Numerous organizations have sprouted throughout the country, from Boston to Florida, from New York through Iowa to California. Although there are variations in the language and feelings, the intent of these groups is to deny the value of love as long as love denies them other values of their society.

The radical feminist movement and its views on love are frequently accused of being primarily a function of the white, educated, middle-class. Apparently this is not true. Puerto Rican women have stated, "Machismo is fascism," and the diatribes of the Black Women's Alliance against love and men are as firm and as hardy as any of their sisters.

Hatred of men is not a function of any single period. According to mythologist Richard M. Dorson,[6] "Little Red Riding Hood, erstwhile a dawn maiden, has become a virgin ready for seduction. Her red cap is a menstrual symbol and her wandering in the woods is her straying from the path of virtue. . . . The wolf eating the girl is the sex act. . . . The wolf is properly punished when Little Red Riding Hood stows stones, a symbol of sterility, in his insides. This copulation drama turns out to be a tale of women who hate men and sex." Again, in *Meanings of Myth*[7] Harry Levin quotes folktales in which the most persistent motif is regarding heroines, "the unappreciated woman."

What is new is the openness, the confronting, the willingness to encounter. Today this resistance to the after-effects of love culminates in the question posed by Shulamith Firestone, one of the founders of the radical feminist movement in New York,[8] "Do we want to get rid of love?" Obviously there are many prices to be paid for getting rid of love (if indeed this is possible). She offers a variety of alternatives, none of them very palatable to most women. In the process of doing so she quotes Theodor Reik as he describes the ambivalence of women as they recognize their dependence on men at the same time they reject what this dependence means. Reik quoted a patient, "All men are selfish, brutal and inconsiderate, and I wish I could find one."

The dilemma has been faced by many women active in this movement. If love for men is antithetical to one's own best interests, if it produces more pain and anguish than pleasure, then there must be substitutes. For some women the question is answered in terms of homosexual love, or homosexual relationships. Not just as a substitute for physical or psychological purposes, but with recognition that love for another woman can replicate the experience of the love relationship without inequality, without superiority. Lesbian literature contains a depth of awareness of values and attempts to be rational. Nonetheless, this type of love appears to be one of the greatest threats to American, even European, males and females in the twentieth century. Although from centuries past there are reports and tales of homosexuality and lesbianism, this has been among the most taboo of all love relationships. It is still almost impossible for most men to accept the concept and fact of this kind of love.

Another option has been sought in the communes which have opened other new and loving relationship possibilities to women. Again, love for men is denied, as exemplified in an article in *Everywoman* magazine,[9] which described the benefits to be derived from starting a collective. The author stated, "That women by starting their own collective are saying two things at the same time, 'f--- men' and 'up with the new revolution.'" Economic equality and nonpedestal positioning makes it possible for women to depend upon each other for psychological and social approval. "Once we trust, rely upon and love each other, it will give us faith and strength to convince other women because they really are worth our time and effort." Here friendship seems to be the cohesive element.

Still it would be a serious mistake to view even the organized radical feminist movement as unilateral in belief system regarding love or in the practice of individual members regarding their own love relationships. Some are married; some have children; some are bisexuals; and some few live their lives in full expression of the views described above.

Liberation II

As with other social movements, women's liberation is not a single strand. Variations are located along the continuum as the *Everywoman* editor commented further, "While the feminist community in Los Angeles could well benefit from such a collective, the women's liberation must go beyond hatred of males to find new ways of living and working together." [10] Other variations are apparent in some of the most recent public statements which recognize the after-effects of love and lovemaking, and contain an acceptance that heterosexual sex and love still are a vital part of most women's lives. For example, students while decrying the nature of the nuclear family and its impact upon work, still make demands for *free* child care centers, *paid* pregnancy leaves, *free* abortion, *free* birth control and *free* access to self-defense classes. These hardly seem to be eliminating men. But the power relationships may indeed change. As yet, the number of raised voices (to go with the raised clenched fists) are minuscule indeed. But both represent, I believe, the growing resentment of large numbers of women who are beginning to recognize the dichotomy present in visions of love and the realities of every day (and night) life.

"In our society, men are unsexed by failure, women by success," says Margaret Mead. Women, having become conscious of their own need for self-fulfillment and their potential for growth, are attempting to prove that assessment inaccurate. They are re-directing their energies toward self-love in order to avoid failure. Joined together in groups through educational programs and therapeutic experiences, they intend to give voice to their resentment of their status and to find new ways for self-determination. In the company of other women they contribute to "consciousness raising," the creation of a sense of self, the discovery of the universality of their being. The small group, focused on the exchange of opinions, ideas and experiences, has helped them to increase their self-esteem, their *self-love*. Lucy Komisar in her article, "The New Feminism," [11] describes this as "an exhilarating experience" and declares that "self-hatred is endemic." Reports of the value of experiences are repeated again and again from groups throughout the country: from the Hawaiian Women's Liberation to groups in Baltimore and Birmingham.

Based upon Edmund Bergler's conviction that "All love originates in self-love," the psychoanalytic view has stimulated women to acknowledge their concern (love) for themselves and to seek self-development. A major goal is the cessation of the playing of games, the separation of true inner self from the presentation of outer self. In "The Right to be Plain," [12] Varda One expresses rather strongly her view that it is time for women to stop meeting the traditional PRETTY view of what women should be and instead accept the fact that regardless of appearance women can contribute, can be a valuable part of human society on their own terms. She asks the question, "Why is it wrong to put down a person racially, but not to reject a woman because she is homely? Aren't they both cases of discrimination?" Again, this is a question of acceptance and love—by others or by self. This style of life may not be pleasing to men, but the problem of priorities has been posed. This new approach of self-love is a response, a reaction to the constant charge that women are their own worst enemies and have a lower opinion of their own sex than do men. If this is true, then some women seek to change the prejudice.

Interestingly enough, it is women who are making group experience possible for other women; it is women who are most distressed by the alienation of women. For example, William Ryan in his challenging book, *Blaming the Victim*,[13] has developed a realistic and hard-hitting theory that when we, the American public, are uncomfortable with the results of society's patterning, we search for reasons. We blame the victim rather than blaming the real villain. Throughout Ryan's book he has exposed the consequences of this behavior upon the minorities, the downtrodden groups. But never once does he mention that education, business, industry, government, organizations and public and private individuals blame not men for what happens to women and their lack of quality, but rather blame women themselves. As with other intellectuals, he does not refer to discrimination of women and its affects. Perhaps unintentionally, he sex casts using sex roles, when he talks about the principal *he*, the teacher *she*. In response to this type of role definition which re-affirms the second class status of women, women interested in development toward self-love have turned to those devices helpful in disavowing the traditional view of who women are and what they can be. It seems that if women are to accept themselves, they must be capable of equality. They must be able to accept success, they must believe they could be fully functioning, that they can continue to grow and contribute both to themselves and to their society. For these women self-love is primary.

A special kind of hatred is reserved by the women liberationists for psychoanalysts and psychiatrists who in their treatment of women have encouraged them to adjust, to accept their status and who inscribe books to "my loving wife without whose help this book would not have been possible." Post-Freudians, in an effort to validate their belief-systems, have made global statements which were eagerly accepted by most men and even most women. Theodor Reik, in *Of Love and Lust*,[14] says, "Women need to be loved more than men." And again, "Women want to be proud of their men." It is as though the very resource intended to free the human spirit and to make human development most possible has been the device used to prevent self-love by women. Professional women are particularly bitter about growth psychologists who have espoused and aroused the aware community with a concern for self-love and self-determination and who conceptualized that experiences of participation and involvement were crucial in the documentation of self. Yet pitifully few have found places by their sides for women as professionals, as their peers in training, teaching and lecturing. *The Radical Therapist*,[15] a news and opinion collection of articles ranging from "Brainwashing and Women," to "Consciousness-raising and Intuition," to "An Open Letter to Psychiatrists," is full of commentary about the damage to self-love wrought by therapists. In an open letter from Red Stockings (a radical women's liberation organization) there is a list of suggestions for action by truly concerned women. Number one on their list is to begin compiling a list of therapists in every city against whom malpractice suits may be filed. Another suggestion is "Mother is not public enemy No. 1. Start looking for the real enemy." (Shades of William Ryan!) The letter concludes with a challenge, "Off the couch, Off our backs."

Thus it seems that many women have established a priority for self-love and are quite willing to deny love of others if need be. They are making choices; and upon facing the restrictions which love for others has forced upon them, in many cases are selecting love of self first. This means that today's options for expressions of love: physical; the purely romantic expression ("till death do us part"); the intellectual religious (the cult of Mary); or the Cinderella love of illusion (fleeting, unobtainable) no longer offer a real choice for many women. In their search for new directions, their first option may be self-love. If this is achieved, then hopefully they will be available for other forms.

Liberation III

Where Is It Written? *

Where is it written
That husbands get twenty-five-dollar lunches and invita-
tions to South America for think conferences while
Wives get Campbell's black bean soup and a trip to the
firehouse with the first grade and
Where is it written
That husbands get to meet beautiful lady lawyers and
beautiful lady professors of Ancient History and
beautiful sculptresses and heiresses and poetesses
while
Wives get to meet the checker with the acne at the
Safeway and
Where is it written
That husbands get a nap and the Super Bowl on Sundays
while
Wives get to help color in the coloring book and
Where is it written
That husbands get ego gratification, emotional support,
and hot tea in bed for ten days when they have the
sniffles while
Wives get to give it to them?

And if a wife should finally decide
Let *him* take the shoes to the shoemaker and the children
to the pediatrician and the dog to the vet while she
takes up something like brain surgery or transcen-
dental meditation,
Where is it written
That she always has to feel
Guilty?

With pain and anguish and bitterness, a growing number of women who chose the normal, traditional path of love and marriage are seeking new emphases in their love relationships. Rejecting oblivion or guilt as

* From *It's Hard to Be Hip Over Thirty* by Judith Viorst. Copyright © 1968 by Judith Viorst. Reprinted by arrangement with The New American Library, Inc., New York, N.Y.

alternatives, their search is for a new amalgam, a new weighing of the usual elements. Committed to husband, home and children, nonetheless they will not relinquish self. And love with its multiple definitions and demands plays a major part in the determination of degree of change. Their education and society's technology have produced awareness, and awareness has heightened their self-concept. This strengthened self-concept has induced new priorities leading to self-actualization through love. Increasingly self-actualization is not found by living *through* one's husband, one's children, even by the full and free expression of one's love for one's family. Women who are "liberated" are less available for the "trap" which the romantic versions of love has long held for them.

Other women who have had satisfying love relationships within their homes are nonetheless responding to the expansiveness of the era. Freed by their families they, too, seek for continuous growth and experience. They are part of the restlessness and have joined the searchers of the society in an effort to find additional satisfactions in their lives.

So many factors coexist—affluence, longevity, economic and political autonomy, the relentless decrease in the valuing of women's traditional activities and attributes, "Portnoy" and "Jewish Mothers," youth groups and commuting husbands. Certainly the demise of the Puritan ethic with its emphasis upon delayed recognition and benefits is a major factor. Each has liberated women from what was; the process now is to identify what else can be.

Thus it is not only in the radical movement that literature throughout the land is full of strong statements and new demands. Liberated women, almost all of whom do not belong to any feminist organization, are living radically different life styles. They have contributed to the skyrocketing divorce rates and to the numbers of women now working. It can be expected that when a woman works for a full third to half of her life outside the home, her commitment to her love relationships at least will be different; perhaps even less. Therefore we are experiencing a major change in society, not through the radical women's open declaration of anti-male love, but through the liberated woman's withdrawal of the typical historical commitment to love as the basis for all her life's activities. "Love is a thing apart for man, for woman her whole existence."

Change in this direction has been incredibly fast. As recently as 1960, Morton Hunt in *The Natural History of Love* [16] referred to the fact that while women all over the world want emancipation which will enable them to love and be loved in the modern way, nonetheless over two-thirds of America's emancipated women stay at home after they are married. That figure is no longer true. In fact we are fast approaching exactly the opposite since well over 60 per cent of all women are working and it is estimated that 9 out of every 10 women will work at some point during their lives. Obviously this has an impact on family relationships and love patterning for women of all ages, educational and economic status. College students and middle-aged careerists, women heads of households and married women, demand institutions for such "freeing" activities as child care centers, cooperative nursery schools, all women communes, half-way houses for women changing their marital status, and abortion counseling. Thus freed to develop relationships outside the home, women are exorcizing the institutions of family and religion which have confined them through the centuries. In *Sisterhood Is Powerful*,[17] Robin Morgan says, "One thing does seem clearer as time goes on; the nuclear family unit is oppressive to women (and children and men)."

We are now seeing the broad band of the middle-class utilize the love patterns of the very rich and the very poor with other forms of the love/ sex relationship. While much has been written of quality rather than quantity, the end result has been that for both men and women there is less time to concentrate on love, its implications, its ramifications and its extensions. As women move away from their perceived traditional stress on love, and emotional concentration on children and husbands, those same energies are utilized in other types of activities. *The Church and the Second Sex* [18] by Mary Daly raises the now-often repeated view of the role of woman as mother. She recalls that in pagan religions the mother goddess was worshipped and that Judaism and Christianity represent a reaction against this. Women as mothers then and now are threatening in their role as life and love-giver. The difference today is that women who have been more and more restricted to the mothering role are reviled as their pent-up energy explodes over the family.

Mary Daly quoting psychoanalyst Andre Lussier states that, "Therapy often reveals a woman who has an impression of non-existence resulting from the annihilation of her personality identity by her duties as wife and mother. Therapy also reveals that there are men, and they are legion, for whom the person in the wife is non-existent. These men know the wife as a possession and mother of their children."

As women have gained psychic freedom for themselves, they have also freed their families. Much is made of male liberation! For many the freedom has created new dimensions in the male/female relationships including romantic love and in the ways of expressing love. For some this freedom is stated and acted out on a purely sexual basis. Certainly the media and mass magazines have created the climate and placed great emphasis upon sex. Others have experienced a new era of expressions of love. It is interesting that Dr. David Reuben writing in *McCall's* [19] magazine about the "Sexual Problems of Women Alone," mentions only sex but not love until his last paragraph. Then he remarks, "The tenderness, love and devotion that characterize the male/female relationship at its best is the right of every woman." It is this new reversal of "right" that carries the greatest potential for dramatic impact, of change in love relationships. In the achievement, the acting out of that right, by women as well as men, liberated women even more than women liberationists will change our notions and ways of love.

We have seen and felt the tremors as various sub-groups in society have demanded and achieved new status for themselves. With women as the largest "sub-group" it appears that the total society will quake as women *with* men identify the path from hatred through love of self to the meshing, growthful expressions of love which we believe to be possible. But no movement occurs without causing waves. In this case the tentativeness of creating new ways of relating have produced multiple signals of distress. From the words of rock music and country and Western music ("When things don't go right, think about things as they used to be." [20]) to the research of Drs. Anne Steinmann and David Fox and others [21] to the Swinging Clubs of middle-aged professionals earnestly changing sex partners in an effort to maintain their marriages, there is a wistfulness for "things as they used to be." It appears that the issue is not whether love ever was the dominant factor as described in poems, novels and myths. Rather, liberated women seem to be acting out the variety of ways and degrees in which love can be expressed and enjoyed. As that happens love has become only one of a number of valued feelings. The priority lists vary with each woman; love rates high on most of them. It is the certainty of priorities which indicates the impact of social revolution on love.

NOTES

1. Althea Scott, "There's a Me," *Everywoman,* Los Angeles, October 1970.
2. Kate Millett, *Sexual Politics,* Garden City, New York: Doubleday & Company, Inc., 1970.
3. *Ibid.,* p. 36.

4. Ti-Grace Atkinson, "The Oppressed Majority Demands Its Rights," *Life* magazine, December 12, 1969.
5. Germaine Greer, *The Female Eunuch*, New York: McGraw-Hill Book Company, 1971.
6. Richard M. Dorson, "Theories of Myth and the Folklorist," *Myth and Mythmaking* (edited by Henry A. Murray), New York, George Braziller, 1960.
7. Harry Levin, "Some Meanings of Myth," *Myth and Mythmaking* (edited by Henry A. Murray), New York, George Braziller, 1960.
8. Shulamith Firestone, *Dialectics of Sex: The Case for Feminist Revolution,* New York: William Morrow & Company, Inc., 1970.
9. "Women's Collective," *Everywoman*, July 31, 1970.
10. *Ibid.*
11. Lucy Komisar, "The New Feminism," *Saturday Review*, February 21, 1970.
12. Varda One, "The Right to be Plain," *Everywoman*, July 31, 1970.
13. William Ryan, *Blaming the Victim*, New York: Pantheon Books, 1971.
14. Theodor Reik, *Of Love and Lust*, New York: Farrar, Straus and Cudahy, 1941.
15. *The Radical Therapist*, Vol. 1, No. 3, August–September 1970.
16. Morton M. Hunt, *The Natural History of Love*, London: Hutchinson & Co. Ltd., 1960.
17. Robin Morgan, *Sisterhood Is Powerful*, New York: Random House, 1970.
18. Mary Daly, *The Church and the Second Sex*, New York: Harper & Row, 1968.
19. David Reuben, M.D., "Sexual Problems of Women Alone," *McCall's*, February, 1971.
20. Simon and Garfunkel, "Bridge Over Troubled Waters," Capitol Records.
21. Anne Steinmann, Joseph Levi, David J. Fox, "Self-Concept of College Women Compared with Their Concept of Ideal Woman and Men's Ideal Woman," *Journal of Counseling Psychology*, Vol. 2, no. 4, 1964, and numerous other articles.

8

The Behavior of Love

Clifford H. Swensen

Although love has been discussed from time beyond memory, very little research has been done on the topic. There are many reasons for this, but perhaps one of the most important reasons is that love is elusive, and difficult to define. As the popular song of some years back says it, "Who can explain it, wise men don't even try." But where wise men shy away, there are always fools who are willing to make the attempt. This chapter is the description of one attempt to describe love, as a first step toward understanding love better.

The first problem to be faced in studying love is defining what it is that is to be studied. *Webster's New World Dictionary* defines love as "strong affection or liking for someone or something." This definition is not very specific—certainly not specific enough to serve as a beginning for a research program. C. S. Lewis (1960) describes what he calls four loves: affection, friendship, eros, and charity, all of which are directed toward people. He adds a fifth love that he calls liking, which is directed toward nonanimate objects or situations (e.g. "I love golf"). In his descriptions Lewis defines love in the ways people usually use the word. But he, like us, is primarily concerned with love as it applies to the relationship between two people, and so devotes most of his small book to what he sees as the four different kinds of love that exist between two human beings. In a sense, he describes what might be termed four different patterns of interaction between people.

The approach to love to be described here is similar to Lewis's in that it assumes that the kind of love in which we, as human beings, are most interested is that which occurs between two people. So, when we talk about love we are really talking about a special subclass, called "love," of the general class of phenomena called "interpersonal relationships." We interact with other people every day in many different ways. Some of these interactions are instrumental. That is, they are designed to accomplish some purpose that has nothing to do with interpersonal relationships. An example of this would be our interaction with a clerk in a drugstore when we buy a tube of toothpaste. Our primary goal is to obtain some toothpaste, with little concern about whether or not the interaction is pleasant or unpleasant, although the interaction might be quite memorable if the clerk is particularly enchanting and solicitous. During the course of an ordinary day we have many similar kinds of ordinary "interpersonal interactions." Over the period of our lifetimes we collect a sizable sample of interpersonal interactions, ranging from the very negative and stressful to the very positive, constructive, and enjoyable. If we tallied the universe of our interactions with other people, the resulting graph would probably look something like the normal distribution curve. At the negative end of this curve would be the especially unpleasant personal relationships that we call "hate" while at the positive end of this curve would be the especially positive and constructive relationships that we call "love." The accompanying figure illustrates this conceptualization of love. Love is conceived here as a positive, enjoyable, constructive interpersonal relationship.

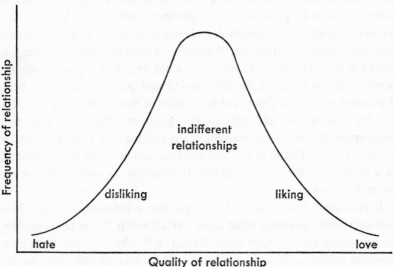

Positive, constructive interpersonal relationships come in many different patterns. These patterns vary, depending upon whether or not the person with whom we have the relationship is a mother, brother, friend, husband or wife. All of the relationships are called "love" although they differ from one another in the ways in which they are expressed. Therefore, any attempt to study love must either choose to study the varying patterns of love, or it must specify which particular pattern it chooses to study, and confine itself to that particular pattern.

The studies described in this chapter derived from thinking about love in the manner described above. That is, there are many different kinds of interpersonal relationships. These relationships may be rated along a continuum ranging from negative, unpleasant relationships at one end to positive, constructive, enjoyable relationships at the other end of the continuum. Love is composed of those relationships located at the extreme positive end of the continuum. But love is not an object or a concrete "thing" in the sense that a horse or a house is a concrete object. Love is conceived as a process or, more specifically, a relationship between two people. As a relationship, love is dynamic. That is, it is not static, or fixed at a certain position, or confined to certain kinds of feelings or behaviors. Rather, love between two people is a relationship between two people, and as a relationship it is constantly changing. This process of change is sometimes a function of changes in the people themselves, and sometimes a function of changes in the environment within which those involved in the love relationship are living. The kinds of changes that take place could be illustrated within any kind of love relationship, since all relationships change over time. A father-son relationship changes as a function of changes in both the father and the son, from the son's childhood to the father's old age, with the boy being dependent on his father in the first period and perhaps the father being dependent on the son during the last period of the relationship. The relationship of a husband and wife also changes over a lifetime. The intimate relationship that occurs during courtship and the first years of marriage tends to become less so as the husband becomes involved in the demands of a career and the wife's attention is absorbed by small children and caring for a home.

Even though love is defined as a positive relationship, we still have nothing specific to study. What is this "relationship"? It is not something we can touch, see, hear, or smell. Rather, it is what we infer from more concrete evidence. That is, we cannot study love directly, but we can study the effects of love. The studies described in this paper are not directly aimed at studying love itself. Rather, they are designed to describe the consequences of love. If we cannot measure love itself, we can study the things people who love each other do for each other, or say to each other, or say they feel about each other. The studies summarized in this paper were designed to discover how people expressed their love to each other, and the different kinds of patterns of this expression of love that occur in various relationships.

The Development of the Scale of Feelings and Behavior of Love

The simplest way to find out how people behave or feel toward those they love is to ask them. This is not the most precise procedure, since people neither observe nor remember accurately their own behavior or the behavior of those with whom they are emotionally involved. However, it is a first step which has some advantages. The first advantage is that a far larger sample of different kinds of behavior can be obtained than could be obtained by observing people. It also makes accessible behavior that could not be observed. A person's feelings toward another, for example, must be obtained from the person who is doing the feeling. An observer can merely infer what another is feeling, and the inference may be incorrect. The final advantage is that it is much less time-consuming to ask people how they behave toward others than it is to follow them, observing how they behave in certain situations.

Three hundred people were asked to describe their relationship with those whom they loved. They were asked to list the ways they behaved, the things they said, and the feelings they had that differentiated the relationship with the person they loved from another person who was just an acquaintance. Some of these lists of behavior were obtained in interviews, but most were written. The subjects who provided the lists ranged in age from eighteen to thirty-eight. The various kinds of behavior or feelings that were listed, when duplications were eliminated, provided 383 different items that were inspected and classified into eight different categories (Swensen, 1961). These eight categories were: (1) Material evidence of love. This included any sort of material demonstration of love, such as giving gifts or providing financial support. It also included performing specific tasks such as washing dirty clothes or running errands. (2) Nonmaterial evidence. This included items that indicated concern, providing encouragement and moral support, giving advice, and showing interest in the activities of the person loved. (3) Shared activities. This included any activities that were performed jointly, such as attending church, taking trips, or golfing. (4) Similarity of values and goals. This included items indicating similar religious, ethical, moral, or political beliefs shared with the loved person. (5) Self-disclosure of intimate personal facts. These items are similar to those described by Jourard (1958), and include intimate personal facts that the subject had disclosed to the loved person. (6) Verbal expression of affection. This included statements of affection made to the person loved. (7) Feelings. These were descriptions of feelings the subject had for the loved person, but which had not been verbally expressed to the loved person. (8) Physical expression of love. This included hugging, kissing, and other physical ways of expressing affection. In addition to these eight categories, there was a ninth category composed of a few miscellaneous items that did not appear to properly belong in any of the eight listed categories.

At this point in the research two questions arose. The first question had to do with whether or not the eight categories of verbal description of love behavior listed above were enough, too few, or too many. The second question was whether or not different kinds of love relationships would produce different patterns of scores on the different categories of items. The first question could be answered through a statistical technique called factor analysis. The second question could be answered by having subjects answer the items in the categories for several different love relationships.

To answer those two questions, the scale, with the 383 items divided into the eight categories described above, was answered by 592 subjects. These subjects ranged in age from seventeen to forty-two, and included 286 men and 306 women. The subjects completed the scale for their love relationships with five different persons: father, mother, closest brother or sister, closest friend of the same sex as the subject, and closest friend of the opposite sex (who was defined as their spouse if the subject was married). The subjects were instructed not to answer the scale if they did not feel they loved the person in a particular relationship.

The answers given by the subjects to the items in the scale were factor-analyzed (Swensen and Gilner, 1964). In factor analysis the answers given to each item are correlated with the answers given to every other item in the inventory. Those items that correlate highly with each other are assumed to be measuring approximately the same dimension or factor. This procedure was performed for each relationship for which the subjects completed the scale. The results obtained in these factor analyses were similar, with seven factors consistently being identified. Six of these factors corresponded to six of the eight categories described earlier, but one of the factors had not been apparent in the rational classification of the items. The six categories of items that were confirmed by the factor analytic procedure were: (1) verbal expression of feelings; (2) self-disclosure; (3) nonmaterial evidence of love; (4) feelings that had not been verbally expressed; (5) material evidence of love; and (6) physical expression of love. The new factor revealed by the factor analytic procedure was (7) willingness to tolerate the less pleasant aspects of the loved person. This seventh factor was composed of items from each of the eight categories of the original classification scheme, and consisted of items that appeared to be negative. It included such things as attending events you do not enjoy in order to be with the loved person, and having the loved person tell you the event in their past of which they were most ashamed.

The factor analytic procedure had confirmed six of the original categories and revealed a new category that had not previously been apparent. However, this procedure had been performed on data obtained from subjects who were mostly young adults. Would the same factors continue to appear in the verbal descriptions of the love relationships of older people? This question was answered by an additional study (Gilner, 1967) which obtained data from 553 subjects classified into three age groups: young (aged eighteen to twenty-six); middle-aged (aged twenty-seven to fifty); and older (aged over fifty). This study confirmed four of the factors revealed in the earlier studies, provided some less consistent evidence for three of the factors, and revealed no new factors. The four confirmed factors were: (1) verbal expression of affection; (2) self-disclosure; (3) nonmaterial evidence of love; and (4) feelings not verbally expressed. The three factors that were less consistently supported were: (5) physical expression of love; (6) material evidence of love; and (7) toleration of the less pleasant aspects of the loved one.

In addition to the general factors that have been listed above, each of the factor analytic procedures revealed small factors that appeared to be specific to specific relationships. For example, both the first factor analysis and the last one produced a factor that looked like a "parent" factor.

This factor included items describing such behavior as providing financial support, giving advice, and administering discipline.

The results of these studies suggest that there are about seven consistent factors, or dimensions, in the expression of love. The data were obtained from over 1,500 persons, aged seventeen to eighty, for five different kinds of relationships, and classified into categories by both rational and statistical methods. Repetition of this procedure thirty times, by relationship described, by age of the subjects, and by the sex of the subjects, consistently support the conclusion that there are about seven factors in the expression of love, as it is verbally described.

At this point in the discussion let us recapitulate what was done and what was found. The original scale was obtained by asking people to list the ways they talked to, behaved toward, or felt about people they loved that distinguished their relationships with those they loved from relationships with ordinary acquaintances. The items obtained were then rationally classified into categories. The items obtained from this procedure appeared to belong to about eight categories of behavior. To determine whether or not these apparent categories would be empirically confirmed, this scale was given to over 1,000 subjects to complete for five different relationships, and the data obtained was factor-analyzed. The factor analytic procedures fairly consistently revealed six factors contained in the original rational classification of items, and revealed an additional factor that had not been apparent in the original inspection of the items. These results suggest that there are approximately seven basic dimensions to the verbal descriptions people give to the ways they behave, talk, or feel in love relationships. These basic dimensions are: (1) verbal expression of affection; (2) verbally revealing intimate facts about themselves to the loved person; (3) giving emotional and moral support to the loved person and being interested in the affairs of the loved person; (4) giving gifts and money, and performing physical chores for the loved person; (5) having feelings for the loved person that are not verbally expressed, such as feeling happier when the loved person is near and feeling completely secure and relaxed in the loved person's presence; (6) expressing affection physically by hugging, kissing, or other overt behavior; and (7) tolerating the demands or other negative aspects of the loved person in order to maintain the relationship.

The most surprising thing about the factors listed above is not in the factors that were obtained so much as it is in the factors that were omitted, or that were not confirmed. It is not surprising that those who love express it verbally and physically, have special feelings for one another, or are willing to tolerate unpleasantness for the sake of the relationship. Man has been aware of this for centuries. What is surprising is that the categories named "shared values and goals" and "shared activities" disappeared when the empirical method of factor analysis was applied. But the items classified under those categories did not emerge in an empirical analysis of the data. The implied conclusion is that shared opinions, goals, values, interests, and activities are not a part of the expression of love.

The failure of shared values and interests to survive as a factor in the expression of love suggests that love goes beyond mere "liking" or "friendship." Many studies (e.g. Newcomb, 1961; Byrne and Nelson, 1965) suggest that individuals are first attracted toward those who hold similar opinions and interests, thus supporting the conclusion that this is a factor of importance in more casual relationships. The data reported here, however, suggests that similarity in outlook ceases to be of major importance when a relationship becomes love. This aspect of love has been described repeatedly in literature. Romeo and Juliet fell in love despite the fact that they belonged to feuding families. The author once knew a couple that had been happily married for years, although she was a Catholic and politically conservative while the husband was a politically liberal Protestant. Love is not togetherness but, rather, transcends togetherness.

Patterns of Expression of Love

Love is expressed in different ways in different relationships. In the course of obtaining the data used to determine the basic factors or dimensions in the expression of love, much information was obtained from the subjects that described how they expressed love in various relationships. The relationships were with the mother, the father, the closest friend of the same sex, and the closest friend of the opposite sex or the fiancé or the spouse.

The patterns of expression of love can be viewed from two points of view. One is to analyze the expression of love by the kind of relationship —that is, from the point of view of the relationship. The other approach is by the manner of expression—that is, from the point of view of the factor or dimension of love expression. In this section we will discuss the expression of love from both points of view.

The data upon which this section is based was obtained primarily in three studies (Swensen, 1961; Fiore, 1966; Shapiro and Swensen, in press). The first study included 50 men and 50 women, the second included 151 men and 99 women, and the third study involved 30 married couples.

Before entering a discussion of the factors that typify various kinds of love relationships, it should be pointed out that two factors appear to be general factors since they appear in all of the relationships. These two are toleration and nonmaterial evidence of love, which includes moral support, interest and encouragement.

Parents. Love for parents is expressed largely through material means, through toleration and through advice, encouragement, and moral support. The relationship with the mother is usually expressed materially through performing chores. For college students the chief expression of love with the father was money, with the direction of flow being from the father to the student. One item in the original long form of the scale was "I have prayed for them" and, interestingly, the only love relationship for which this item was checked with any consistency was for the relationship with the father.

Brothers and Sisters. The relationship with brothers and sisters was expressed through the same factors as the relationship with parents, but the rate of expression was much lower. Of all the relationships investigated, the relationship with siblings appeared to be the weakest.

Closest friend of the same sex. Love in these close friendships was expressed largely through verbal means; that is, through disclosures of intimate facts about the self, or through encouragement, advice giving and other nonmaterial methods. Material methods of expressing love were absent in these relationships.

Closest friend of the opposite sex, fiancé, and spouse. The relationship with the opposite sex is the strongest of any of the relationships in that it is expressed through all of the factors, and is expressed more intensively in all of the factors than any other relationship. This strength was particularly apparent in the relationship between husbands and wives, which was expressed the most strongly of all relationships in all factors. Opposite sex relationships for those who were not married were also expressed strongly in all factors except the material factor. Material evidence of love for the unmarried was more strongly expressed to members of the immediate family, such as parents and siblings, than to members of the opposite sex to whom they were not married.

Spouse. Some rather interesting patterns of love expression within the marriage relationship were observed, in addition to those noted above. A comparison of the patterns before and after marriage reveals changes in the other love relationships, with men increasing the expression of love to their fathers and women increasing their expression of love to both parents. Advice giving and encouragement are the areas in which the increase is most noted. However, for men the relationship with the mother decreases, particularly in material evidence of love, but also in advice giving and encouragement. Apparently much of the mother's function in a young man's life is taken over by his wife when he marries. This empirical result suggests a basis for wife–mother-in-law conflict, particularly if the mother-in-law declines to relinquish her role gracefully. Probably the increased expression of love between a man and his father and a woman and her mother is produced by the increased similarity in their roles, with the man becoming a husband as well as being a son, and the woman adding the wife's role to that of daughter.

A comparison of the items marked by husband-wife couples as characterizing the expression of love within the marriage relationship found husbands and wives agreeing with each other on all of the factors except verbal expression of affection and self-disclosure. Further investigation disclosed that husbands and wives agree on the affection they have verbally expressed to each other, but disagree on the frequency with which the affection is expressed. Both husband and wife agree that the husband has told his wife "I love you," but the husband is inclined to believe that he says it more frequently than his wife thinks he does. Apparently husbands and wives have different standards by which they judge the frequency of verbal statements of love.

With self-disclosure of intimate facts about themselves the disparity was reversed, with husbands stating that the level of self-disclosure was lower than the wives thought it was. More detailed investigation revealed that both husbands and wives overestimated the amount of accurate self-disclosure, with the wives' overestimate being larger than that of the husbands. Husbands and wives disclose much about their feelings, attitudes, beliefs, and sexual lives to their spouses. However, they disclose relatively little about finances and their feelings about their work. Apparently one spouse takes primary responsibility for finances, and the other spouse ignores that aspect of the marriage most of the time. In the case of work concerns, apparently after marriage a division of labor occurs, so that communication about work-related subjects declines. One interesting finding was that although husbands and wives are quite knowledgeable about each other's personalities, this knowledge was not obtained through verbal disclosure. Apparently they learn about their spouses' personality through observation rather than discussion.

Now let us briefly consider the expression of love from the standpoint of the factors involved.

Material evidence of love. Expressing love through material means is largely confined to the family. Relationships with friends, even close friends of the opposite sex, are not typically expressed through material means. When the relationship to a member of the opposite sex changes from that of fiancé to that of husband or wife the expression of love through material means becomes typical. Most of these relationships are symmetrical. That is, it is expressed materially equally by both members of the relationship. The exception to this is the father who does a lot of expressing materially, but receives relatively little material evidence of love in return. This disparity is especially pronounced if one of the partners in the relationship is a college student.

Verbal expressions of love. The expression of love by verbal means, including both the verbal expression of affection and self-disclosure of intimate facts, is largely confined to relationships with peers, such as brothers and sisters, friends, and husbands and wives. The level of expression is lowest for brothers and sisters and highest for husbands and wives. Verbal expression of affection tends to be confined to members of the opposite sex.

Nonmaterial evidence of love. Support and encouragement (including such items as giving advice, showing an interest in the loved person's activities, and showing respect for the loved person's attitudes and opinions) is the most general factor in the expression of love. This factor occurs in all of the relationships, with its highest level occurring in the relationships with parents and the opposite sex and the lowest level with brothers and sisters. A man will accept an attitude from his fiancée that he would not tolerate for two seconds in his sister. What happens when his fiancée becomes his wife has not yet been investigated.

Physical expression of affection. The physical expression of affection is largely confined to relationships with the opposite sex, with the expression of love through this factor reaching its highest level in marriage.

Unexpressed feelings. This has been a difficult factor to deal with, probably because it is difficult to define. It has been retained in the studies because it keeps reappearing among the factors obtained from the factor analytic procedures. Basically, it consists of a feeling a person has for one he loves, but which he has never verbally revealed to the loved person. It appears to be highest in the relationship to the mother and to the closest person of the opposite sex, and lowest in the relationships with the father and the closest friend of the same sex.

Toleration of the less pleasant aspects of the loved person. This factor also is a general one, in that it characterizes all love relationships to a fairly high degree. It is highest in the relationship with the opposite sex, particularly with the spouse, which would seem to be obvious, in view of the interminable battle of the sexes, but why it should be lowest in one's relationship with his mother is not quite so apparent. The most probable reason is that the mother, being the first person loved in a man's life, sets a kind of standard. What mother does seems natural and is expected. The behaviors that have to be tolerated are those that are not expected.

Factors, Patterns and Theories of Love

Discussing the results presented earlier in this chapter within the context of prevailing theories of love is both easy and difficult. It is easy to discuss within the context of more specific approaches, such as that of Lewis, since his four loves correspond, to a degree, to the relationships investigated. The results are difficult to discuss within the context of more general theories, because these theories are general, and therefore difficult to relate to specific behavior.

Isidor Schneider (1964), in his summarization of theories of love, concludes that most theories view love as "a principle in which forces are exerted for unification and growth. . . ." Perhaps the best modern statement of this view is that of Erich Fromm (1956) who defined mature love as "union under the condition of preserving one's integrity. . . . In love the paradox occurs that two beings become one and yet remain two." How shall we relate love expression in seven factors (or three, or thirteen for that matter) to a union? There are aspects of the data presented that can be fitted to such a conceptualization. Each of the eight categories in the original scale was divided into two parts. One part listed items describing behavior the subject had expressed toward the person he loved, while the second part listed behaviors the loved person had expressed toward the subject. Inspection of the completed scales revealed a high degree of reciprocity between the subject and the person he loved. Further, the matrix of correlations among all of the items confirmed this reciprocity. That is, we tend to express love toward other persons in the same way they express it toward us. If they encourage us, we encourage them. If they are open and frank about themselves in talking with us, we tend to be open and frank with them. The only relationship in which this almost exact reciprocity does not exist is between parents and children for the material expression of love. Even here, the only substantial imbalance is in financial support, which flows chiefly from the father to the child, and this imbalance is redressed somewhat by the child performing chores or other useful tasks for the parent. Thus the data can be viewed in a way that fits the fusion conception of love.

Relating the results to Lewis's concepts appears a little more obvious. Lewis divides love into two kinds, need-love and gift-love. His two kinds of love are similar to A. H. Maslow's (1962) "deficiency-love" and "being-love." The basic idea is that one kind of love derives from a person's deep need for another, while gift-love or being-love flows, or overflows, from one mature person to another. The data presented here does not appear, in a general way, to support such a categorization of love. Needs and gifts do seem to be an element in the relationship between a parent, particularly the father, and a child in the material realm, but outside of this particular factor and this particular relationship, the most striking observation is the reciprocity in the relationships. Even in the child-parent relationship there appears to be an attempt on the part of the child to provide some sort of balance between what he receives and what he gives. After considering this division of love, Lewis himself seemed, in his book, to lose interest in it as he pursued his classification of love into four kinds.

Maslow's classification, however, bears further investigation. In an earlier book (1954) Maslow discussed the love of self-actualizing people, and listed some of the characteristics of these people. He concluded that it was characterized by much openness and spontaneity, by a fusion of the hierarchy of needs of the pair so that the needs of one were the needs of both, and a respect of each for the individuality of the other. I decided to follow up Maslow's lead, and did a small study (1960) in which I compared some matched subjects from my own large pool with some "self-actualized" people. The data for the self-actualized people were obtained from biographies of these people. The love scale items were completed for the relationship of the members of each group with their closest friend of the same sex. The two groups were then compared by items. The differences between the two groups did indicate some element of difference between the love of the self-actualized and the love of the ordinary person. The items that particularly characterized the close friendship relationships of the subjects taken from my pool of subjects could be characterized as indicating considerable interest in the other person and openness in disclosing personal facts about one's self to the other. Nine items differentiated the self-actualized persons' relationships from the relationships of the subjects from the pool, and these items might be described as attempts to help the other person develop to the fullest. These items included such behaviors as giving good or useful advice, teaching values and ideals, and inducing in the other a desire to live up to his own ideals. These items might be termed a "helping the other to self-actualize" factor. These items all correlate highly with, and are included in, other factors on the scale, so it would appear that this is a factor that only emerges clearly in certain mature, self-actualized love relationships. This sketchy data suggests that what Maslow termed "being-love" is not so much a giving love, in the sense that it is given by one person to another, as it is a love in which one person provides the kind of relationship that induces the other to develop toward the best that is within him.

Lewis's four loves appear rather easy to fit to the data. His "affection" is described as a "warm comfortableness" that takes in all sorts of objects, animals, and eccentric people. Nothing in the love factors seems to fit, but Lewis's affection was undoubtedly defined out of consideration of the original instructions to the subjects. "Friendship" fits with the friend relationships for which the subjects answered the scales. Lewis viewed friendship as being somewhat out of fashion these days, and as the least natural of the loves since it has no biological basis. In Lewis's view, the basis of the formation of friendship is the discovery of a mutual insight. When we find another who has seen the same truth that we have seen, friendship is born. This phenomenon probably requires similar experiences, if similar insights are to be acquired. The data reported here do not support Lewis's view of friendship. The items describing shared activities, goals, values and attitudes did not emerge as a factor, even in the friend relationships. Rather, friendship seems to be expressed by mutual interest and support, mutual toleration, and a mutual personal openness about oneself. A friend appears to be one with whom we can be relaxed, comfortable, and open. Perhaps the discovery of a shared insight is a necessary precondition to the development of this comfortable relationship, but nothing in the data could be construed to indicate this.

Eros, or sexual love for the opposite sex, has its counterpart in the factor scores for the relationship with the opposite sex. Lewis makes much of the sexual aspects of this relationship, but the data presented here suggests that it should be viewed somewhat differently from the romantic view. Romantic love may, as de Rougement (1956) suggests, have death as its aim. If so, it does not fit in with love as defined here by the behaviors through which love is expressed. Probably romantic love is, as both the ancients and Theodor Reik (1958) have suggested, best viewed as an emotional aberration rather than a particular kind of love. The data obtained from the factors indicates that eros is different from the other kinds of love in two respects. First, it is a love that is expressed by all of the factors involved in the expression of love, including the physical expression of love at the most intimate level. Second, the expression of love for all factors is higher in this relationship than in any other. Or, to put it simply, eros is different from other kinds of love in the breadth and quantity of its expression, not in the introduction of some new quality that is missing from other love relationships.

Charity is a kind of love Lewis relates particularly to God, which he describes as "wholly disinterested and desires what is simply best for the beloved." This kind of love does not emerge from the factors of love, but does seem to be a case of the love for friends of self-actualizing people, which was differentiated from ordinary friendship by nine of the items on the scale.

REFERENCES

Byrne, D., and Nelson, D., "Attraction as a Linear Function of Proportion of Positive Reinforcements." *Journal of Personality and Social Psychology*, 1965, 1, 659–663.

de Rougement, D., *Love in the Western World*. Garden City, N. Y.: Doubleday and Co., 1957.

Fiore, A., "A Two-Dimensional Approach to the Measurement of Interpersonal Behavior." Unpublished M.S. thesis, Purdue University, 1967.

Fromm, E., *The Art of Loving*. New York: Harper and Bros., 1956.

Gilner, F., "Self-Report Analysis of Love Relationships in Three Age Groups." Unpublished Ph.D. dissertation, Purdue University, 1967.

Jourard, S. M., "Some Factors in Self-Disclosure." *Journal of Abnormal and Social Psychology*, 1958, 56, 91–98.

Lewis, C. S., *The Four Loves*, London: Geoffrey Bles, 1960.

Maslow, A. H., *Motivation and Personality*. New York: Harper and Bros., 1954.

———, *Toward a Psychology of Being*. Princeton, N. J.: D. Van Nostrand, 1962.

Newcomb, T., *The Acquaintance Process*, New York: Holt, Rinehart and Winston, 1961.

Reik, T., *Of Love and Lust*, New York: Grove Press, 1958.

Schneider, I., *The World of Love*, 2 vols. New York: George Braziller, 1964.

Shapiro, A., and Swensen, C. H., "Patterns of Self-Disclosure in Married Couples." *Journal of Counseling Psychology*, in press.

Swensen, C. H., "The Compleat Man and the Compleat Relationship." Paper read at Southeastern Psychological Association, Atlanta, 1960.

———, "Love: A Self-Report Analysis with College Students." *Journal of Individual Psychology*, 1961, 17, 167–171.

Swensen, C. H., and Gilner, F., "Factor Analysis of Self-Report Statements of Love Relationships." *Journal of Individual Psychology*, 1964, 20, 186–188.

Swensen, C. H., Shapiro, A., and Gilner, F., "Validity of the Self-Report Measure of Love and Self-Disclosure in Married Couples." Paper read at Southeastern Psychological Association Convention, New Orleans, 1966.

9

Love and Companionship

Henry Winthrop

1. Introduction

If an author starts out to discuss the nature of love and companionship
—the latter being understood in the sense of friendship—he had better
make clear to his readers exactly what is intended by the use of each of
these terms. It is obviously quite possible for different writers to mean
different things by each of these terms. It is certainly possible to have
some forms of love without any form of companionship. It is also possible to experience certain forms of companionship without these being
accompanied by any form of love—more so, of course, between members of the same sex than between those of opposite sex. To make matters more difficult, where some form of the psychological state we call
love is accompanied by, or blended with, one of the types of personal
relationship we usually designate as companionship, we then obtain a
configuration whose attributes are likewise different from those of either
of the two separate component states when experienced alone. The literature is replete with insightful classifications of human love and
human companionship. Curiosity about these two states which mean so
much to human beings is perennial. Agreement as to the number of different forms love and friendship may take or agreement as to the characteristics of each form in which these two states are said to be
expressed, has never been achieved. These states and the processes in
human experience to which they refer are definitely a proper concern for
a humanistic psychology and an existentialist outlook.

102

But why should we be concerned with the place of love and companionship in human life? Because in their quest for community, these are precisely the two intangibles which men and women seek. The quality of love and companionship men and women seek will depend upon many things. That quality will depend upon the grade and quality of consciousness which characterize the individuals involved, the degree to which they are egocentric or ego-extensive, and the level of maturity they exhibit. That quality of love and companionship will also depend upon the range of human interests and concerns displayed by the individuals involved, their sense of continuity with selected themes from man's past, and their identification with the world line of man's future which they choose to make uniquely their own. Nor are these all the intangibles which determine the mode of both love and companionship for which men and women may thirst.

Man's quest for community consists of two parts: the dyadic relationship he seeks in a mate, and the wider, nonsexual relationships he seeks either in personal friendship or group affiliation. In the history of advanced and civilized societies, the relationship of man to woman has been regarded by *most* people—or, if you prefer, the *average man*—as the major source of supply for both love and companionship. Seen, however, from the viewpoint of the religious impulse and from the various forms of social altruism which have emerged historically, it is the non-sexual dyadic relationships and group affiliations which have been seen as the real soil for the growing of more mature forms of love and companionship. But most members of humanity are not yet ready to strike so disinterested and transcendental a posture. Different forms of spiritual growth and holistic awareness, however, clearly can be facilitated by mature relationships of either a personal or an ego-transcendent type.

One thing is certain and inescapable. There can be no sense of an improving and evolving community, no sense of an authentic and fulfilling relationship between man and woman, and no authentic answer to the question "What is the good life?" unless mature blends of both love and companionship are made possible. The human condition is largely the result of the errors and misjudgments, shortsightedness and superficiality that derive both from human satisfaction with crude forms of love or companionship and the even cruder forms of relationship between them which are frequently sought. For all the preceding reasons, then— and many more which limitations of space make it impossible to mention here—we can clearly involve ourselves in a discussion of love and companionship and the many forms taken by their association. It is to this discussion, then, that we shall now turn.

2. Forms of Love

A preoccupation with the forms and the classification of human love has appeared throughout history. In our own time, however, the apparatus of modern scholarship and learning, combined with insights from psychiatry, psychology and the social sciences in general, have been brought to bear upon this subject in order to achieve systematic treatment. The result has been a series of distinguished efforts from the pen of such writers as de Rougement,[1] Lewis,[2] Nygren,[3] Berl,[4] D'Arcy,[5] Fromm,[6] Maslow,[7] and many others. One of the earliest distinctions, still widely and insightfully employed, has been to dichotomize human love into *eros* and *agape*. In the everyday treatment of these two forms of love, the first is superficially regarded as referring to erotic or carnal love and the second to transcendental forms of love. By the latter is meant those love relationships in which he who loves supports and nurtures the object of his love without recompense or any necessary return of love. In agape he who loves is unmotivated by any desire to allay anxieties about his current condition or his extramundane future. He loves and admires the object of love for its own sake and for the properties, real or imagined, with which it is invested. In this sense agape is a nonbookkeeping form of love, completely opposite in spirit to the motto so characteristic of Roman life *Do ut dat*—"I give in order that thou mayest give in return."

In a somewhat more sophisticated form of this distinction, eros is regarded as egocentric or self-centered love in all forms and agape is seen as theocentric, when its roots are religious in nature, or descularized, when the object of love is either the set of attributes of a generalized and idealized humanity or when the nature of Creation, itself, is the object of concern. In this more sophisticated form, agape is expressed through a persistent monistic assumption that all Being is one, and through an unswerving effort to blend with this all-pervasive attribute of Being. More accurate and more subtle interpretations of eros and agape abound and they are quite varied.

One such central and highly sophisticated interpretation defines eros in such a way as to constitute the very negation of the common but somewhat erroneous interpretation of this form of love as carnal and self-centered. In the sophisticated interpretation to which I am referring, the soul is regarded as aspiring to complete understanding. Because of this aspiration it rejects this finite world, eschews sexual activity and ever seeks to pass beyond desire (the achievement of Nirvana). All that is human is regarded as limited and the individual seeks some connectedness with the eternal through various regimes of meditation, self-denial, self-flagellation, withdrawal from society, self-mastery and similar taxing procedures. According to this same sophisticated interpretation—as it occurs in the Gospel—agape possesses four basic attributes. As a form of love it is (1) creative and spontaneous and not to be explained strictly on a biological basis, (2) it does not depend on how deserving of love is the human being who receives it, (3) it imputes worth, dignity and value to the loved one rather than *assuming* that such attributes are present before love is conferred, and (4) agape, in a very fundamental sense, freely declares the acceptability of the person who is loved, for the fellowship of man, and encourages that person to give expression to any moral principles which are imputed by the religious impulse to Creation itself.

There are numerous other distinctions which have been made between eros and agape and if they differ somewhat from each other, they have this much in common: they all recognize that there are both different kinds of love as well as different degrees of each kind.

In our own time Maslow [8] has seen fit to make a useful distinction between two forms of love which he has christened D-love and B-love. D-love refers to all forms of self-centered love in which A and B love one another only in the sense that the *deficiencies* or *needs* of each are met, in some way, by the behavior of the other. D-love of A for B is based upon the presence of some selfish objective in A which he or she expects to have satisfied through B. Thus the typical male in bourgeois society speaks of loving his wife primarily because (1) she is an outlet for his sexual needs; (2) she basks in the effulgence of whatever glories he achieves and she finds this derived status most satisfying; (3) she is happy to achieve the privileges and assume the responsibilities which stem from the respect the community tenders her husband, and she lets him know this frequently and in many subtle ways; (4) she is gay, decorative and charming socially and thereby increases his prestige; (5) she manages his ménage, feeds him, and assumes the total physical care of his children; (6) she accepts an inferior intellectual status, in relation to her husband, even if unwarranted; and (7) she sides with him when he meets opposition, whitewashes his errors and his sins, accepts many of his social and political convictions and adopts his biases and prejudices. All these are a small sample of some of her husband's deficiencies and needs to which a wife may cater in a middle-class marriage.

In turn the wife can count on her husband meeting some of her own deficiencies and needs. She speaks of loving him because her husband (1) is a good provider; (2) is a satisfying sexual partner; (3) is the guarantor of economic security and social stability both for herself and her family; (4) is a "real" man as defined by middle-class ideology —that is to say, he is "successful," takes responsibility and exercises good judgment in all the important decisions he makes on behalf of his family; (5) is "smart" or intelligent—and a lot more so than the husbands of other wives she knows; and (6) is a man who introduces novelty into her life, makes it exciting, and is understanding and forgiving whenever she proves to be trying. In short, she loves him for allowing her to be a "spoiled darling." Many more of the gratifications of D-love which the middle-class husband and wife bestow upon one another could be mentioned, but they are too many to be enumerated here. Although D-love is chiefly expressed in the relationship of man and woman, it should not be overlooked that it can also occur in the relationships between members of the same sex.

In contrast to D-love there is B-love—the love for the very being or presence of another person, that is, for the qualities, gifts, activities and aspirations of that person, taken in all their composite uniqueness. B-love is expressed chiefly through the relationship of the sexes but is quite capable of existing between members of the same sex. D-love is a sort of bookkeeping arrangement, no matter how deftly disguised. In B-love, in contrast, one gives of oneself without necessarily expecting any return. It is love unmotivated by any desire to fulfill some personal need or some selfish aim. B-love is not possessive, it nurtures the growth potentials of the person who is loved, and those who are capable of B-love enjoy the qualities of the loved one as these latter are given in the lover's experience. The person who is loved is not seen routinely day after day as a human being with a given, finite set of qualities. Instead, new qualities in the loved one are noticed from time to time, as the years go by, and familiar qualities are seen freshly every now and then.

In B-love between a man and a woman neither ever feels threatened by the other, a relationship of mutual trust develops easily, the lovers are comfortable in each other's presence and if their interests are different each enjoys hearing about the world, the work and the activities of the other. Magnanimity, generosity, and complementary autonomy are the attributes found in B-love. There is always depth of understanding and a genuine spiritual encounter between men and women who experience B-love. In D-love the fact that the focus of attention is upon the exaltation and aggrandizement of self and personal needs tends to constrict the focus of attention and narrow the horizons of consciousness. In B-love the spectrum of consciousness is enlarged, perception widened and a multiplicity of perspectives shared.

D-love is fragmented. A male may enjoy his wife as a sexual partner in a strictly biological sense but despise her or deride her for her values, anxieties and interests. In this respect, full genitality in the Freudian sense is never achieved and the primal sexual drive is separated from the activities of the rest of the psyche. In B-love this can never happen. The lovers respond holistically to one another as unique persons. The sexual impulse and sexual activity are anchored in the love for, and delight in, the unique constellation of qualities of the other. Sexual union is heightened by the deep respect for, and enjoyment of, the ego-transcendent impulses and the social altruism of the loved one.

One result of the preceding is that in B-love the blending of the sex drive with the drive for psychological depth and growth-producing propensities results in a love relationship whose quality has nothing at all in common with D-love. It resembles the latter neither sexually, psychodynamically nor socially. B-love may rightly be called "psychedelic love," in the sense that one takes a consciousness-expanding trip with it and finds oneself a fuller person following sexual congress than one was before participating in the psychophysical act itself. The common but erroneous belief expressed by the phrase *post coitum omne triste* (after cohabitation the whole world seems sad) may very nearly be true for the sexual act when consummated in D-love. After consummation in B-love the whole world seems glorious, offering new possibilities for the sharing of novel experiences which can bind the lovers to one another in new depths still to be explored.

There is an extremely important aspect of B-love which must be highlighted at this point. A man who is capable of B-love for a woman will succeed in escaping one of the worst features of the historically conditioned form of love between the sexes, which has prevailed in almost all cultures past and present. I am referring to the deeply ingrained masculine habit of looking upon woman strictly as a "female," that is to say, as the source of sexual pleasure, personal beauty, and mother to the race. In Western culture the tendency to invest women almost solely with their sexual value—although hypocritically pretending to value their nonsexual qualities—is so marked as to be reflected in the risqué story, ribald humor, and in the esoteric, intrasexual vocabulary of the immature male. This same tendency is reflected in the sexual obsessiveness of the culture, as displayed in the excessive preoccupation with sexual themes, in the "respectable" arts, and as displayed in the masculine "underground" culture of pinup girls, beauty contests, girlie magazines, pornographic films and similar marginal phenomena.

The existence of this anthropocentric attitude makes it almost impossible for the male to see a woman as a person. From the standpoint of this attitude, personhood in woman is either thought to be absent in the sex or, if recognized, is quickly repressed as an object of masculine attention. This is, of course, a species of intersexual tragedy, since women, too, are persons, and if it seems at times that they do not wish to so regard themselves, this attitude of self-debasement is simply one which has been uncritically introjected from the culture.

If women are not seen as persons and therefore, even in advanced societies like our own, not treated as capable of sharing the same interests as men, this is due to two separate sets of factors. One is the social constriction on the masculine role, which demands that woman be seen as intellectually and spiritually different because she is biologically and psychologically different. Various types of perceptual selection and perceptual distortion then come into play and make it impossible for the typical male to attribute personhood to woman. The other factor is the overeager adoption of role expectancies associated with being female, the uncritical and far too accepting attitude on the part of women toward the masculine denial of their personhood, the psychosexual mishaps which occur with males when a woman asserts her personhood in most cultures, and finally the tyranny exercised by other women toward a woman who really tries to be a person.

This potentiality for personhood, which is always latent in woman, is completely fostered and reawakened in a woman who exists in a B-love relationship with a man who is capable of that type of love. This is an extremely satisfying experience for a woman who seeks to express her own individuality and have it appreciated. It increases her depth of feeling for a man enormously. Far from costing her any measure of her femininity—which common masculine stereotypes assert must inevitably follow—it will actually increase enormously the stability and freedom of her psychosexual persona. The enrichment of the relationship of the sexes which recognition of woman's personhood generates makes B-love an intensely unique experience, without counterpart in the ordinary forms of D-love.

There is still another extremely important aspect of B-love which should be discussed here. It is an aspect of B-love which can best be seen and understood in terms of one of the central ideas which underlie the work of Eric Berne.[9] In describing the games which people in our culture play with one another, this author has pointed out that people operate essentially on three different levels or in three different ego states. Each person has within himself (1) an ego state which resembles those of parental figures; (2) adult ego states which are unique to each individual, patterned by himself or herself and autonomously exercised and in which the subject tries to deal objectively and realistically with his environment; and (3) ego states which carry with them the psychological debris of childhood. These latter are accompanied by behavioral repertoires which were fixated in childhood, and which—precisely because they do not take stock of the *real* characteristics of an interpersonal relation and a current situation—result in behavior which is irrelevant to that situation. This will be true even though such regressive, childlike behavior may produce certain gratifications sought by the individual who displays it. Berne refers to these three ego states, respectively, as Parental, Adult, and Child.

In most relationships, but particularly in marriage, one or both of the partners is apt to act dysfunctionally in relation to these three levels of the personality. This dysfunctionality may be expressed in one of two ways. One or both of the partners may misjudge the ego state of the other or, even if that ego state has been gauged correctly, one of the pair may respond to it improperly. The other inappropriate pattern occurs when one or both of the partners rigidly and almost continually preserves an ego state in relation to the changing ego states of the other partner, and does so regardless of the inappropriateness of the hardshell posture assumed. This second inappropriate pattern reflects a psychological inelasticity which proves to be frustrating and painful to the more flexible partner and it produces a growth-repressive and growth-deflecting situation for that partner. In such a relationship the frustrated partner—or both partners if the inelasticity is mutual—is continually miserable. It should be clear, of course, that the dysfunctionalities, incongruities, and inelasticities of mismatched ego states in marital partners, such as those we have just described, are frequent in marital forms of *D-love only*. They are the inescapable inadequacies of such self-centered forms of love.

In B-love, however, this type of reciprocal inelasticity rarely occurs. One of the most fruitful characteristics of the B-love partnership and marriage is that each partner is well aware of the presence of any one of the three different ego states at different times in the other. Each partner understands the life factors and situational characteristics which can produce any one of these states in the partner, and this understanding generates more than tolerance. It generates sympathy and concern. Above all—and this is the central emphasis I wish to make here—B-love generates what I shall call the "proper, functional, ego state match."

By this phrase I am referring to the following behavior in each partner. When the woman seeks to function as an adult—the role and ego state which is most often present in B-love because of the greater maturity of the individuals involved—the man almost always matches the woman's adult ego state with an adult ego state of his own. And, of course, the reverse holds true. A woman in a B-love relationship— because of the press of unforeseen circumstances or because of the occurrence of an unexpected tragedy or bereavement or because of any one of a dozen other severely stressful or frustration circumstances—may be unable to keep from slipping into the helpless, child ego state and role. When this occurs the man she loves thoughtfully matches this ego state with the needed and corresponding parent ego state and role, thus meeting his partner's temporary emotional needs. At the same time he provides the sympathy, understanding and help which his partner's needs of the moment require. As a result her husband's or lover's parent ego state will sustain her in her trials and tribulations. And again, of course, the reversal of these roles occurs, whenever necessary.

There are even more significant matches of ego states in B-love than the two I have mentioned. If there are children in a B-love partnership, one never sees the children used as pawns in conflicts between the partners. In fact, such conflicts are few and far between. However, conflicts between marital partners rage frequently in D-love, and the children are almost invariably used as helpless pawns in such situations. In the first place conflicts—"disagreements" would, perhaps, be the more appropriate word—occur, as I have already emphasized, very infrequently in B-love. If they do occur they are not very intense and they will be quickly dissolved. This is because the adult ego state will take over in both partners. And when they do occur, both partners would find it utterly out of the question to use their own children, whom they both love dearly, as counters and devices in moves made to achieve personal, selfish and immature ends. Such conduct would be simply unthinkable in B-love. With respect, then, to their handling of their children, and at nearly all times, a couple whose relationship is characterized by B-love will almost always assume a common parental ego state. One can count on the couple's tendency to keep that joint parental ego state intact in relation to the welfare of their children, even on those rare occasions when differences arise between them.

But perhaps the most unique ego state match which occurs in B-love, and one which is among the more important of the ego state correspondences so characteristic of this type of love relationship, is the total pattern of behavior which occurs in the sexual relationship. In the sexual activity which accompanies the B-love relationship, both partners display, and accommodate to, a variety of quickly changing ego states. In sexual foreplay and in sexual congress itself, a child-child ego state match will be largely present. Each partner freely lets himself or herself go, not only in the expression of erotic impulses and behavior, but also in the uninhibited expression of states and feeling which accompany sexual enjoyment. These states of feeling are likely to be both quite rapturous and highly individualized. They will be quite suffused with poetical and aesthetic content and unusual types of sensitivities. In the intense blend of psychological interpenetration which accompanies B-love, all these childlike (*not childish*) responses in the sexual relationship are common and highly desirable. They are not found to accompany D-love at all.

In the child-child ego state not only are the feelings of each partner during sexual congress uninhibitedly expressed but they are completely understood and constantly encouraged by the other partner. Following sexual climax B-love partners are likely to be highly articulate in discussing and reviewing their sexual and nonsexual feelings for one another and the meaning which these very feelings have for each of them. During these periods of articulation an adult-adult ego state correspondence frequently comes into play; and the maturity, intelligence and insight with which their shared love and sexual attraction for each other are explored and evaluated contributes quite meaningfully to the enrichment of the B-love relationship. In B-love the partners can make smooth, easy and desirable transitions from one of these two pairs of matched ego states to the other, a transition which they both enjoy and welcome. This ease of transition is far less frequent in the sexual relationship most typically found in D-love.

Although the matched ego states in B-love are chiefly of the child-child and adult-adult forms there also occurs frequently a parent-child correspondence. In this match male protectiveness toward the passive and cooperative feminine persona is displayed and enjoyed by both partners. Other ego state correspondences may occur in B-love but the points which I am trying to make in the present connection are the following: (1) The number and variety of such matched ego states and their accompanying nuances is greater in B-love than in D-love. (2) The transition from one such ego state to another is made more easily and is more readily welcomed in B-love than in D-love. (3) The matched ego states of the sexual relationship in B-love are much more growth-fulfilling and much more facilitative of the quest for personal identity than in D-love.

In fact, D-love is likely to be characterized by *parent-child* correspondence of ego states, the male rigidly assuming that the parent ego state and its roles is the proper one for him, while the female partner correspondingly assumes that the proper ego state and role for her is that of the child. These rigidities are, of course, fostered by tradition, social psychology, and role expectations. The child role invokes in the woman the role of helplessness, admiration for the strength of the male and for a wisdom he does not, in fact, usually possess. Unfortunately, it is also true that in D-love, nourished by the corny and childish, romantic themes of the mass media and cheap literature, the woman demonstrates a willingness to be used and admired strictly as a *sexual object*. The fact that in D-love the male is completely captivated by the woman's physical charms provides her with a tawdry sense of power—a sense of power which reinforces her willingness to bind the male to herself by complete *physical surrender*.

The parent-child ego state correspondence in D-love is, of course, socially conditioned by the cheap literature, cheap movies, and other sources of mass distractions to which I have already referred. These provide and reinforce the customary stereotypes regarding sexual attitudes and sexual behavior. This kind of sexual relationship, which is almost strictly biological in nature, is highly unimaginative and hopelessly inauthentic. It completely stunts the psychodynamics and growth potentials of either partner. It is rigid, comic and pathetic. It so narrows the focus of consciousness and so woodenly makes use of the erotic impulses that the sexual relationship with a given partner is almost bound to grow jejune and degenerate. It will become less and less satisfying, even on a strictly biological basis, with the passage of time. It is precisely this barren denouement of the sexual relationship in D-love which produces the crying need for a variety of sexual partners. What happens here is that each D-lover seeks to recapture the sense of the first flush of sexual novelty that was experienced in the early period of his or her marriage.

It is the freshness and expansion of consciousness in B-love and in the ability of both partners to share something new all the time and enrich the network of psychological investments they have with one another which makes sexual infidelity almost an absurdity. The sexual fidelity in B-love is not a function of moral restraint. Rather it is a function of the deep-lying, total psychological satisfactions and involvements which each partner pursues, and of the total set of values which each obtains in his or her marriage.

A great deal more has been said and can be said about the forms and characteristics of human love. The considerations stressed above are both synoptic and incomplete but they will have to do. But companionship or friendship has also played a major role in the quest for personal identity and community. It is to the forms of friendship and their characteristics to which we will now turn.

3. Forms of Companionship

The expression of friendship or companionship, like that of love, exists in several forms. The lowest grade of companionship will involve merely the desire to avoid *physical loneliness* and *isolation*. The highest grade of companionship will involve the desire to understand others and to be well understood by them. Thus one can see that one central need in companionship is for communication. Since communication, itself, runs the gamut from the desire merely to have a listener present to the point where one may explore any concern with another person and explore it to the full, both ideationally and/or psychologically, the conditions for satisfying the latter extreme are fairly uncommon. The latter expectation calls for several things. It demands (1) an interpenetration of consciousness and feeling; (2) the ability to keep the same object of attention in mind fully while sharing perspectives with regard to it. This last desideratum involves a shared expansion of consciousness in which two people genuinely wish to sustain each other's inner life. This, in turn, calls for a companionship of mutual dependency in a psychological sense—a dependency which carries no implications or overtones of psychiatric undesirability.

There is a second aspect to all those higher forms of companionship which contribute to the quest for personal identity and to the growth objectives of self-actualization. This is the aspect of "care." When care is present, each of the two companions is concerned with the personal fortunes, changing situations, life-style, happiness and needs of the other. The relation is a highly charged one of dyadic ego-extension, using this latter term with the meaning attached to it by Gordon Allport.[10] In companionship, as in love, there may be a locking of fates. In companionship, as in love, the motive for pairing may be to meet deficiencies and needs and to obtain certain forms of gratification. In this latter sense there is a D-companionship as there is a D-love. And in the highest form of companionship, namely, deep and abiding friendship, concern and care may involve willing sacrifice, if necessary, and a whole train of important activities. These activities will aim at contributing (1) to the other's pursuit of his own growth potentials and self-actualization; (2) to the free exercise of his talents; (3) to the untrammeled expression of his qualities; and (4) to the establishment and maintenance of the other's welfare. These objectives will be executed regardless of cost and expressed quite freely. This is because the individual enjoys and admires the qualities in the companion and deeply respects the latter's uniqueness. This then is B-companionship, the analogue of B-love, and B-companionship is, in essence, the most fruitful form of friendship.

If communication is the basic objective of the spiritually more valuable forms of companionship, and if the highest grades of companionship are inevitably transformed into the most deeply fulfilling forms of friendship, then a most conspicuous phenomenon arises in the relationship. This is the phenomenon of sharing. Each of two companions will almost unhesitatingly offer the other the temporary or permanent use of his possessions or, usually without being asked, he will allot portions of his time and the use of his talents to provide any services which the other may need. This type of sharing is "symbolic sharing." It is a token of esteem, goodwill, and a sign of care. It reassures the receiver of the continuation of the friendship that the companionship involves. But in the companionship of people with qualities beyond the ordinary, sharing becomes an entirely different phenomenon. The kinds of people to whom I am referring are those whose definition of the good life will involve what

Adler [11] has called social interest. In addition, these will be people who constantly work at perfecting themselves, morally, intellectually, and aesthetically.

People of this type become deeply and authentically involved with the spiritual struggles of their friends. A person of this type will explore with a friend nuances of the latter's inner questionings and doubts—even morbidly if necessary—in precisely the soul-searching and soul-searing fashion so frequently found in the great Russian novels. He makes himself a party to the companion's plans. He abandons all pretense and all role playing in order to engage himself psychologically in depth with that companion. He will share with a friend by offering him the fruits of his own experiences, his own past anguish, and his own agonies. He will spend sleepless nights looking for ways and means of extricating his friend from dilemmas. And if he cannot find a way out for his friend, he will insist on sharing that friend's suffering and dilemmas. In such trying periods we lay bare the perturbations that accompanied our own inner struggles. We draw aside the veil concealing our own self-doubts and inadequacies. We abandon our own projects for a period in order to make certain that our friend does not go under in his crisis. In every way we can, we offer our friend and companion all the empathetic sharing we can muster. We offer a free gift of ourselves.

Such sharing of depth in companionship faces certain pitfalls. In B-companionship one seeks to link one's fate with that of an authentic friend. Symbolically one declares for a spiritual partnership in the adventure men call life, and this partnership—if I may borrow a legal metaphor —is never a limited one. In B-companionship, as in B-love, the relationship sustains the personal autonomy of the other rather than demanding or expecting that the being of the other should serve the exigencies of one's own life. The pitfall to be avoided in such intense sharing is that of personally submerging one's identity in that of the other. Stewart [12] has reminded us of the distinction made in German between *Einsfühlung* and *Einfühlung*. He puts it this way.

... In Einsfühlung—being at one with another—we do not differentiate. We live in and with the feelings of the other. Practically speaking we completely agree on the meaning of certain experiences. . . . In Einfühlung —each implicitly confers on the other his identity by imagining the other to be what he is, after comparing some item of the other's behavior with behavior of one's own. In Einfühlung, therefore, the other gets his personal identity—insofar as he gets it, outside himself, from me. . . . (p. 36)

B-companionship demands *Einsfühlung* and is characterized by it. The pathological form of sharing, *Einfühlung*, will be found in D-companionship. It is, of course, not a form of sharing at all. It is a form of slavery and spiritual extinction and is to be avoided at all costs. Psychological masochism and sadism, wrapped in a mantle of *ersatz* companionship, is a travesty upon authentic friendship. Its motivational determinants and dynamics have nothing in common with those underlying authentic companionship.

In the *Nicomachean Ethics*, Aristotle [13] distinguishes three forms of friendship or companionship. There is first the friendship based on profit; second, the friendship which provides mutual pleasure; and third, the friendship which is based upon the *permanent* in us or—as we would say in the terminology made familiar by modern psychology—that which is based upon our true, inner self. This latter was understood by Aristotle to be a core persona which pursued the true, the good, and the beautiful. This core possessed a nascent and amorphous moral sense which the individual sharpened and gave content to, by the pursuit of virtue. This same permanent core sought wisdom through knowledge and reflection. It also sought beauty through the arts, both by contemplation and by active participation.

Aristotle recognized the *gradability* or *quality* of these three forms of friendship. The first is evanescent when one's companion no longer serves a useful purpose. It is striking to note that in our own culture, where the marketing orientation is so dominant, "success" is centrally dependent upon the ability to manipulate others in order to ensure that they shall serve our own purposes. These are usually obvious, although, of course, they may also often be hidden. What Americans call "friendship" is precisely that form of companionship in which other people are good "contacts" who may smooth the path toward our egocentric objectives. When this is no longer the case, perhaps because someone else has come into view who may be of even greater serviceability, they are then politely dropped. When this is done, a variety of excuses will be found for avoiding them.

American middle-class friendship or companionship, then, is an example of Aristotle's first form. Everyone knows that this is the way the game will be played. Is it any wonder that insecurity is so widespread in our country? In this form of "friendship for profit" everyone knows that he cannot depend upon his "contacts" to provide any form of authentic relationship. In this sense there is no one we can trust. One then needs another form of security to cushion oneself against the insecurity of profit-seeking companionship. And so one joins cliques, organizations, and political parties in order to retrench against the day when he, too, will be let down by those upon whom he depends. One perfects what Fromm [14] has called the "escape from freedom." And so, one makes an attempt to ward off the insecurity which began with an improper form of the relationship between man and man (the marketing orientation). One tries to ward off the day of reckoning by constructing other patterns of behavior with presumably built-in safety margins. One seeks to defend oneself against the eventual loss and failure which come to most of those who live by the marketing orientation. These associative patterns, to which I have just alluded, are meant to be a second line of defense. They are meant to be the various modes by which we seek to escape from freedom. They are therefore still aimed at shoring up "friendship for profit." For these reasons they are bound to fail—producing only a lonely crowd—since Aristotle's first form of companionship is not an authentic relationship at all. Our shenanigans are one illustration of the French adage *Plus ça change, plus c'est la même chose*.

The second form of friendship of which Aristotle speaks is likewise a radical departure from the authentic elements of friendship or companionship to which we have already brought attention. Companionship based on pleasure and distraction is fickle and superficial. When a more charming, more amusing, more charismatic, more widely experienced or more knowledgeable person comes along, we are very likely to adopt him as a friend—while simultaneously gradually or suddenly dropping our interest in another friend of long standing. Again, this form of companionship is common in American middle-class psychology. An attractive acquaintance adds to our stature, confers prestige, and reinforces those flattering self-images we have previously used for self-reinforcement. In this sense, American friendships are shallow. Those who seek this type of friendship also try to make themselves acceptable as a "friend" to many other people. The formula for doing this is either to be "a real nice guy," or to be "the life of the party," or to provide the best distractions at cocktail parties. This last is accomplished by keeping all conversation at the level of the light fantastic, by encouraging chitchat and avoiding the serious, and by being amusing, charming, and hospitable. In addition, one tries to have one's ears sensitively attuned to other people's psychic perturbations and not exacerbate them, by massaging other people's egos, by engaging in phratric communion, and by dozens of similar devices too numerous to mention here.

In all of this superficial activity, there is no common spiritual quest or joint intellectual adventure and no sharing of that type of understanding, interest, and curiosity which proceeds from an individual's authentic center of consciousness. The transiency of this second form of friendship is reinforced by the great mobility of contemporary American life. People know they are going to have to uproot themselves every few years, never again to see those they have left behind. This uprooting can most easily be done by establishing shallow forms of companionship which will create no real sense of spiritual emptiness and psychological deprivation if they ever have to be disrupted.

We have already stated what Aristotle meant by the third form of friendship and I think that a reading of the *Nicomachean Ethics* would warrant the statement that a good deal of what I have described as B-companionship could also be included in Aristotle's third form, or vice versa. We should note here, of course, that B-love, as we have described it in the previous section, *can* include B-companionship within its framework, *provided that the individuals involved are capable of B-companionship*. Unilateral B-love is possible between pairs of persons. This can occur, for instance, between mother and child. Thus B-love from mother to child may be wholly *unilateral* and occur at a time when the state of development reached by the child would hardly warrant the expectation that the child could return B-love. B-companionship behavior, however, both by definition and in terms of human experience, must be *reciprocal*. It is therefore, *a fortiori*, impossible between mother and child. In the typical mother-child relationship, the mother may extend B-love and the child usually extends D-love, but reciprocal B-companionship would be impossible.

But it is not the reciprocity of B-companionship which really distinguishes it from B-love. Rather it is the *quality of consciousness* and the personal level of spiritual development of the two companions involved which is the important thing. B-companionship demands a high level of awareness of self, a rich acquisition of knowledge, and a wide range of personal experience. This must be personal experience which has been well mulled over, and from which a great deal of knowledge concerning oneself and the motivational dynamics of men has been distilled. B-companionship also requires a social perceptiveness and a social altruism which render the participant highly and quickly insightful into human relations, human conflict, and, in general, the condition of man. The quality of consciousness, then, in B-companionship is philosophical, even if it does not result formally and explicitly in the construction of a philosophical system. Few people are suffused with the quality of consciousness I have just described. For this very reason few people are ready for B-companionship. The latter is very rare and, of course, most desirable.

The preceding material, then, reflects some of the *central features* which surround the nature of love and companionship. Quite obviously there is enough to be said concerning both of these to fill entire libraries. Nor will the last word ever be penned on these matters, considering the fact that love and companionship are subject to infinite variation as the human condition itself changes, and as men fashion new social psychologies to adapt to such change. It would be of real value, I think, to focus attention *on the relationships* between the forms of love and companionship, such as we find them among men. This is a matter which has been given insufficient attention. Unfortunately, however, the attack upon such a theme would be so far-reaching as to require considerable effort and substantial, separate treatment.

NOTES

1. Denis de Rougement, *Passion and Society* (London: Faber and Faber, 1956).
2. C. S. Lewis, *The Allegory of Love* (London: Oxford University Press, 1948).
3. Anders Nygren, *Agape and Eros* (Philadelphia: Westminster Press, 1953).
4. Emmanuel Berl, *Nature Of Love* (New York: Macmillan, 1924).
5. M. C. D'Arcy, *The Mind and Heart of Love: Lion and Unicorn. A Study in Eros and Agape* (New York: Meridian Books, 1956).
6. Erich Fromm, *The Art of Loving* (New York: Bantam Books, 1963).
7. Abraham H. Maslow, *Toward a Psychology of Being* (Princeton, New Jersey: Van Nostrand, 1962).
8. Abraham H. Maslow, op. cit.
9. Eric Berne, *Games People Play*. The Psychology of Human Relationships (New York: Grove Press, 1964).
10. Gordon Allport, *Becoming. Basic Considerations for a Psychology of Personality* (New Haven: Yale University Press, 1955).
11. Alfred Adler, *Superiority and Social Interest:* A Collection of Later Writings, Heinz L. and Rowena R. Ansbacher, editors (Evanston, Illinois: Northwestern University Press, 1964).
12. David A. Stewart, *Preface to Empathy* (New York: Philosophical Library, 1956).
13. Aristotle, *Nichomachean Ethics* (Cambridge: Harvard University Press, 1956).
14. Erich Fromm, *Escape From Freedom* (New York: Avon Books, 1965).

10

Homosexual Love—
Woman to Woman, Man to Man

Del Martin and Paul Mariah

Throughout history the homosexual has been defined primarily in terms of her or his sexuality. Very seldom was the lesbian or the male homosexual thought of as a whole person or as having the capacity to love. Yet the Bible, which is most often used by religious literalists to condemn homosexuals, vividly portrays in the most beautiful of love lyrics the union of love—woman to woman, man to man, Ruth and Naomi, Jonathan and David.

"So, Jonathan made a covenant with the house of David. . . . And Jonathan caused David to swear again, because he loved him as he loved his own soul. . . . And they kissed one another, and wept with one another, until David exceeded. And Jonathan said to David, Go in peace, forasmuch as we have sworn both of us in the name of the Lord saying, The Lord be between me and thee, and between my seed and thy seed for ever. . . ." [1]

And Ruth said to Naomi, "Entreat me not to leave thee, or to return from following after thee: for whither thou goest, I will go; and where thou lodgest, I will lodge; thy people shall be my people, and thy God my God; Where thou diest, will I die, and there will I be buried: the Lord do so to me, and more also, if aught but death part thee and me." [2]

The Book of Ruth is often referred to as a prose masterpiece, but most Biblical scholars are seemingly blind to its full significance. Considered in the light of Ruth's willingness to abandon not only her native

120

soil and her own family but even her God and her hope of burial with her ancestors, it is a compelling declaration of her compelling love for Naomi. H. M. and Nora K. Chadwick, in *The Growth of Literature,* point out that "it gives the impression of being written primarily for feminine circles." [3] Dr. Jeannette H. Foster, former librarian for the (Kinsey) Institute for Sex Research and author of *Sex Variant Women in Literature,* goes a step further. She contends, "By comparison with many treatments of the variant theme it might well have been written *by* a woman." [4]

When the psyche is engaged in any interchange between persons of the same sex, it is our contention that that interchange is homosexual—be it covert or overt, be it verbal or nonverbal. We who are involved in human liberation are always "at war" with the literalists, for they limit themselves to text and never context. When the flow of all energy opens new doors of perception, there are fingers of feelings, not found in all words, but behind the words, the veil, the last mask. Thus any relationship between two women evolves from/into a lesbian love. If it is filial, it may be restricted by family relationships; if it is social, it is restricted by church and society. Both the filial and the social involved the psyche—be that psyche expressed, repressed, oppressed, or impressed.

Michael Field, a "poet" of the late Victorian age, was the pseudonym for Katherine Bradley and Edith Cooper, aunt and niece respectively, who were much closer than the family relationship would indicate. Katherine wrote of the Brownings (Robert and Elizabeth Barrett): "These two poets, man and wife, wrote alone; each wrote, but did not bless and quicken one another at their work; *we are closer married"* (italics hers).[5] In Edith's account of her attack of scarlet fever while the two were traveling in Germany, she tells of Katherine's fighting an entire hospital staff in order to occupy the same room with her. "I have my love close to me. . . . Looking across at Sim's little bed I realize she is a goddess, hidden in her hair—Venus. Yet I cannot reach her. . . ." [6]

There are many historical references to "strong emotional friendships" between women. One example is the idyl of the "Ladies of Llangollen": Lady Eleanor Butler and Sarah Ponsonby, two seventeenth-century Irishwomen who eloped to the Vale of Llangollen in north Wales after Eleanor's mother tried to force her boyish daughter into marriage or a convent. While they were known as "The Platonists" among their literary friends, it is reported, however, that Lady Eleanor wore men's clothes, her journal spoke of "our bed," and the two were never separated, even for a single night, during the fifty years they lived together.

In Greek culture, as well as in most other cultures, past and contemporary, homosexuality is an integral part of man-to-man relationships. Plutarch wrote tenderly about a battalion composed only of lovers. Mentor-student, filial affairs are other patterns that have evolved. But pederasty is considered by society today as just above incest and bestiality. Society relegates no positive values—either emotional or intellectual—to a relationship between an elder man and a younger boy.

In a poem, "Two Loves" by Lord Alfred Douglas, a friend of Oscar Wilde, a reference to homosexuality is explicit as "The Love that dare not speak its name." During cross-examination in his infamous trial, Wilde was invited to explain. " 'The Love that dare not speak its name' in this century is such a great affection of an elder for a younger man as there was between David and Jonathan, such as Plato made the basis of his philosophy, and such as you find in the sonnets of Michelangelo and Shakespeare. It is that deep, spiritual affection that is as pure as it is perfect. . . . It is in this century misunderstood, so much misunderstood that it may be described as 'the Love that dare not speak its name,' and on account of it I am placed where I am now. It is beautiful, it is fine, it is the noblest form of affection. There is nothing unnatural about it, and it repeatedly exists between an elder and a younger man, when the elder has intellect, and the younger man has all the joy, hope and glamour of life before him. That it should be so, the world does not understand. The world mocks at it and sometimes puts one in the pillory for it." [7]

To be put in the pillory for the love of another human being is that part of dehumanization here with us as lesbians and homosexuals today through our laws and our social sanctions—even when the love is mutual and at the same peer level. In D. H. Lawrence's book ironically entitled *Women in Love,* we find the story is actually about the (social) love relationship between two men, Gerald and Birken, and Gerald's inability to accept it. After Gerald's death, Ursula asked Birken, "Aren't I enough for you?"

"No," he said. "You are enough for me, as far as a woman is concerned. You are all women to me. But I wanted a man friend, as eternal as you and I are eternal. . . . Having you, I can live all my life without anybody else, any other sheer intimacy. But to make it complete, really happy, I wanted eternal union with a man too: another kind of love." [8]

The term "homosexual" is applied to both sexes, although lesbians think of it generally as referring to the male because most discourses on homosexuality are written about males from a male point of view. Of course, there is always the implication that there are females too, and what is said applies to the women as well as to the men. This assumption on the part of sociologists, psychologists and psychiatrists is in gross error. We do not feel that the grid patterns of female and male homosexual relationships are parallel, lateral or linear. The common denominator is attraction/love for the same sex. It stops there. For this reason, we will speak of the female as lesbian and the male as homosexual. We are not the first to dissent in this matter. André Gide in *Corydon* spoke of it in separate terms; yet when Frank Beach, of Yale University, wrote the commentary for the American edition of the book, he could not agree from an academic standpoint with Gide about the distinctness of the two loves of homosexuality—man to man, woman to woman.

The term "lesbian" is derived from the isle of Lesbos where Sappho, the famed Greek poetess, loved and lived amid a following of young women during the early sixth century B.C. Described by Dr. Foster as "the most economical description of passion to be found in literature" is Sappho's celebrated "Ode": [9]

> It is to be a god, methinks, to sit before you and listen close by to the sweet accents and winning laughter which have made the heart in my breast beat fast, I warrant you. When I look on you, Brocheo, my speech comes short or fails me quite, I am tongue-tied; in a moment a delicate fire has overrun my flesh, my eyes grow dim and my ears ring, the sweat runs down me and a trembling takes me altogether, till I am as green and pale as grass, and death itself seems not very far away.[10]

There is no "known" lesbian literature, however, from the ancient times of Sappho until 1788, when Mary Wollstonecraft's novel, *Mary, A Fiction,* was published. In that long interim the women depicted by male authors as lesbians were always without a love relationship and limited to explicit sexual byplay—never to be taken seriously. The male ego could never admit that a woman existed who could love another woman deeply, or that she could experience sexual and emotional satisfaction without a man.

The absence of such literature can be related to this historical fact: Young Caesar, at the age of nineteen, went to Bithynia to borrow three ships from Nicomedes (with whom he slept) in order to conquer Mytilene, capital of Lesbos. Mytilene was the last city to hold out against western civilization, then known as the Roman Empire. After that fall there has been a conspicuous silence or silencing of women in their own civilization. The lesbian was twice silenced—first as a woman, secondly for the love of another woman. Women's Liberation today, because of mass media, is the first real vocalization of this 2,000 years' repression. Women's suffrage did not have the benefit of modern media.

Mary, A Fiction idealized an innocent variant relationship as the highest form of emotional experience. It was based on Mary's attachment for Fanny Blood, which began when she was fifteen and continued until Fanny's death twelve years later. Ms. Wollstonecraft is better known, however, for her *Vindication of the Rights of Women,* as a champion for her own sex and a biting critic of male dominance.

Women poets who followed generally concealed the sex of their beloved, and there has been much conjecture as to possible lesbian interpretation in the works of Emily Dickinson, Sara Teasdale, Edna St. Vincent Millay and Amy Lowell, among others. Renée Vivien, whose poetry has been pronounced the most perfect in form of any French verse in the first quarter of the twentieth century, received nothing approaching her due recognition because of the lesbian element in her work. In her adult years American-born Pauline Tarn acquired residences in Paris, Nice and Mytilene where, as Renée Vivien, she attempted to recapture the golden age of Sappho.

While Gertrude Stein's *Things As They Are* and André Gide's *Corydon* were first published as private editions in limited number, it was Radclyffe Hall who took the courageous step of coming out into the open. *The Well of Loneliness,* a novel which was to some extent autobiographical, was the first public plea for sympathy, understanding and acceptance for lesbian love. Though the book was censored in England, it was later translated into eleven languages and by 1938 (ten years after it was originally published) was enjoying an annual sale of 100,000 copies in the United States alone. It became the "lesbian bible," though as a work of art it can hardly be compared with the writings of Colette, Rosamond Lehman, Djuna Barnes, Gale Wilhelm and others who have also focused on the lesbian theme in their novels. Donald Webster Cory, author of both *The Homosexual in America* and *The Lesbian in America,* calls *The Well of Loneliness* "a social document, it is a cry for justice. It is the *Uncle Tom's Cabin* of homosexuality, male as well as female. It is the voice of those who had for years been voiceless, and literary merit or lack of it not withstanding, John (Radclyffe Hall) will ever be their hero, even as she is mine." [11]

Despite this opening wedge with the novel *The Well of Loneliness,* it was not really until the mid-1960's that there was a breakthrough in public media of any great significance. The barrage of lesbian novels found on the newsstands in the 1950's were written primarily by men for a male audience. Plot formula included titillating sex scenes for male enjoyment, a sordid and tragic depiction of lesbian life and the author's choice of one of two endings: the heroine either had to go "straight" or lose her life.

Through the media today we are only beginning "to speak its name"; for like the silencing of women and the distortion of the lesbian life-styles, love between men and the freedom to talk about that love has been deterred and therefore inferred, never spoken of directly, in plain honest terms. Homo*sex*uality by the nature of the word has been thought of almost solely in sexual terms, not in terms of love. The honesty of love overwhelms C. P. Cavafy, twentieth-century Greek poet, to bear witness to the truth, in the Kierkegaardian sense, as is the duty of all poets, as seen in "Before Time Changes Them":

> They were both deeply grieved   at their separation.
> They did not desire it;   it was circumstances.
> The needs of a living   obliged one of them
> to go to a distant place—   New York or Canada.
> Their love certainly   was not what it had been before;
> for the attraction   had gradually waned,
> for love's attraction   had considerably waned.
> But they did not desire   to be separated.
> It was circumstances.—   Or perhaps Destiny
> had appeared as an artist   separating them now
> before their feeling should fade,   before Time had changed them;
> so each for the other will   remain forever as he had been,
> a handsome young man   of twenty-four years.*

In the media and in public educational discussions on homosexuality, there seems to be an unwritten law that any positive stance (from the homophile community) must be balanced with the negative (religious and psychoanalytic doctrinaire). This is called "fair exchange." Ninety

---

* Translated and copyright 1961 by Rae Dalven. Reprinted from her volume *The Complete Poems of Cavafy* by permission of Harcourt Brace Jovanovich, Inc.

per cent of such ventures, in reality, while they may often open the avenues of communication to a much neglected and maligned subject, are misleading, confused, in bad taste, and certainly exploitive. The story of the homosexual is her or his own. It cannot be told or heard in debate. It must stand on its own, of its own merit, as a human testament.

Psychoanalysts, having largely adopted the theological doctrine of sex for procreation only, have made the value judgment that homosexuality is a "repetitive, compulsive sexual behavior." They have concentrated on the sexual activity thereof and have denied the possibility of any love relationship. From this perspective any individual, heretosexual or homosexual, who is incapable of love is bordering on neurosis or psychosis. To say that the homosexual *by definition* cannot love is the Big Lie, a gigantic hoax compounded for too many centuries.

Though many in the so-called "helping" professions agree with Frank Beach who claims that "homosexual behavior should be classified as natural from the evolutionary and physiological point of view," [12] they nonetheless profess, as he does, that this admission does not necessarily mean it is "socially desirable." [13] They recognize homosexuality as a preference, proclivity or propensity toward a same-sex "love object," a term with which we have serious objections because it, at once, dehumanizes the human beings involved. This use of terms, too, could very well be why these professionals, though they admit homosexuality is natural (or normal), are still unable to see homosexuality other than as a behavior. This use of terms is also a defense mechanism, for to accept homosexuals as persons is to condone homosexuality. And to condone homosexuality is to admit that homosexual love is equal to and on a par with heterosexual love. There lies the hang-up. But is it not true? Love is love. How can you put a limiting value judgment on orgasm, ecstasy, bliss, or the euphoric state, whether it is heterosexual or homosexual, if it culminates from the love of one human being for another human being? Is it the polarity, the joining of male-female and penis-vagina that makes a "marriage" whole and therefore "holy"? Isn't it rather the mutual respect and the mutual love for one another, each to and for the other as a human being, that makes the difference? And isn't love "socially desirable"?

Love is boundless. Throughout the history of humankind attempts by poets, writers, and lovers to capture its essence have filled thousands of volumes. Love is a subjective experience; it is abstract; it is feeling, and it cannot be confined, defined or measured. It does not lend itself to empirical science, to "detached objectivity." Yet in the guise of science, researchers are still trying to measure and confine homosexual "behavior" without taking into account that behavior as an expression of love. The results, because they address themselves merely to function and ignore this love factor, are useless. The researchers merely disclose the bias of their premises and their questions which, no matter how objective the intent, are based upon and compared with the heterosexual's subjective experience and white middle-class values. What do we know about black sexuality? There has been so little research done in that field. Yet if it, too, were pursued, how could science separate the black experience from sexual behavior to define their love? Can it be defined by white researchers in white terms? Can the homosexual be defined by heterosexual researchers in heterosexual terms? So far the only apparent interest by researchers is in sexual practices (how many orgasms a day?) and causal factors. What causes any sexuality but the magnetism between two people? Researchers' work serves only to reinforce their own heterosexually held values of superiority. Hence, they do not have any validity so far as explaining the phenonemon of the homosexual, his love or his sex, her love or her sex. They cannot know the homosexual's true subjective or psychic experience, and they refuse to recognize what the homosexual knows and feels is love—a love for someone of the same sex.

Who can say there was no love between Gertrude Stein and Alice B. Toklas during their years of togetherness, from 1907 to 1946, that ended only with Gertrude's death? Who can deny the love of W. H. Auden and Chester Kallman for the last forty years? Who will deny the truth of Radclyffe Hall's letter (found after her death) to Una, Lady Troubridge which said, "God keep you until we meet again . . . and believe in my love, which is much, much stronger than mere death . . ."? [14] These are examples of well-known or literary couples; there are thousands, nameless in our society today, who know the same union of love. The silent anniversary parties, not written up in society columns, are myriad. We know of countless homosexual love relationships, both male and female, that span from five to fifty years. Psychoanalysts who propound the "sickness theory" have failed to encounter or to admit the existence of such enduring love.

Lest we fall into the trap society has set for us, that is, the value judgment that only long-term relationships are valid and meaningful, we must make it quite clear that we do not believe the length of a relationship determines the quality of that relationship. Many heterosexual marriages, as with some lesbian and homosexual pairings, are simply *not* divorces. There are many such relationships that are held together, not by love, but by habit, possessiveness and insecurity. We have all known and walked in the field of loneliness, a universal feeling individually felt. Many couples after being together realize that they have grown apart, even grown bored, and that separation is imperative to individual growth in different directions. That does not necessarily mean that love ceases. Many homosexuals, both male and female, remain friends throughout their lifetimes and care deeply about each other, even when they have found other partners. There are also short-term relationships which are not "forever"; nor were they expected to be forever. This does not preclude the existence of love during the relationship and, many times, long after the relationship has ended.

Love, however, is not always reciprocal. Lesbians are many times stereotyped as predatory, masculinized women who prey upon young girls and seduce young women, or as sexually permissive and indiscriminate in their choice of female partners. Nothing could be further from the truth. Most lesbians are very hesitant about making an overture to a loved one unless it is known that she, too, is a lesbian or unless she indicates her own interest and willingness. Lesbian poetry is rife with lamentations of unrequited love, such as Del Martin's "Moon-Blink" written before her present eighteen-year love relationship, written when she was still seeking:

> The cave sound of the living dead
> Shattered by a woman's laughter,
> A black box nine by twelve
> Candled by the mirror in her eyes.
> Puppet feet learn to waltz
> With a shadow in a blue velvet robe.
>
> But the chameleon changes its color,
> Withheld arms embrace a bowling ball,
> The skies rain stars and alcohol,
> The chess men reach a stalemate.
> And a pale yellow begonia
> Lies marooned in a jungle of blue daisies.
>
> For blue daisies are not real,
> The moon is wrapped in a telegram,
> Gold imbedded in Idaho potatoes.

Hers were the halibut's eyes
And the flight of the peacock . . .
Mine the voice of the giraffe.[15]

Paul Goodman writes of an unrequited love that appears as an apparition in the poem "Long Lines" *:

I opened with my key, to my astonished joy
There in the room stood one I love, for whom I have
longed in my lonely exile, but I said perplexed,
"How did *you* get in?" in an interminable moment
I did not clasp him in my arms, and realized
that he was dead and that this was a ghost.
He said, "When you're dead too we'll be together
as we have failed. I love you, Paul," and was not
and I looked at the key that I was holding in my hand.[16]

The recurring theme of unrequited love in homosexual literature certainly indicates that both lesbians and homosexuals place value on and seek the fulfillment of love relationships. That so many are thwarted in their search or engage in promiscuous sexual contacts is due to society's sanctions against homosexual love. While heterosexual marriage is encouraged and glorified, society, on the other hand, discourages and makes it well-nigh impossible for male homosexuals to live and love together. Then, having driven them underground into a subculture held together on the nebulous basis of sex alone, society decries its practice. Promiscuity is thus the logical conclusion of an illogical premise. Until such time that homosexuals are allowed free expression of their nature it is impossible to determine if the homosexual is by nature any more promiscuous than heterosexuals under the same given circumstances and conditions. John Wiener speaks of his promiscuity and his love at the end of "A poem for the old man":

my beloved
who picked me up
at 18 & put love
so that my pockets
will never be empty,
cherished as they are
against the inside flesh
of his leg.

* Copyright © 1963 by Paul Goodman from *Hawkweed*. Reprinted by permission of Random House, Inc.

> I occupy that space
> as the boys around me
> choke out desire and
> drive us both back
> home in the hands
> of strangers.[17]

Woman to woman, man to man, we build our relationships by loving, by caring, without indifference. C.D. is now in his seventies. He and his lover have been together for over fifty years, caring for each other; though without covenant by the church or the state, their home is that of marriage, i.e., the union of love each for the other. They have extra sexual relations occasionally, openly within their relationship. They do no feel it is harmful, for they have found that when one of them returns to the threshold, that one is more giving than before, the will to love coming from the external, reinforcing the internal relationship. We give but to love and to want to love. We will to love, we will to live for love.

Love is a union, a partnership, a mutual adventure in growth, both individually and collectively, usually limited to no more than two people. Same-sex love unions cannot be defined in terms of heterosexual marriage, the mimicry of Mom and Dad, who have been the only models the homosexual has had. Both lesbians and male homosexuals have learned this the hard way, that is, to find a life-style of one's own, and to give it value toward life. As a partnership, there is always the question of male/female identity. Homosexuals, both male and female, are becoming increasingly aware of their ambisexual nature, that delicate balance between male and female components inherent in all human beings. This ambisexual poem by Renée Vivien is an early example in literature from this century:

> Your regal youth reveals the melancholy
> Of that Far North where mists efface all color.
> A need to quarrel wars with a need to weep
> In you who are grave as Hamlet, pale as Ophelia.
>
> Like her, you wander, lit by a lovely madness,
> Showering flowers, scattering bits of song;
> Like him you hide your suffering under pride,
> But your abstracted look betrays your pain.
>
> Smile, blonde sweetheart, or brood on, dark lover.
> Your ambivalence draws like a double magnet,
> Your flesh has a wax taper's chilly ardor.

My baffled heart is troubled when I watch
Your princely forehead, virgin's eyes of blue—
Now you are he, now she—and yet both together.[18]

A more contemporary example from the male viewpoint is this poem
by Paul Mariah, first published in *Colorado State Review:*

FROM BOTH SIDES

"Nero married Tigellinus as a woman and Sporus as a man."

Love, I have seen you
     from both sides.
          Lying
together as you do,
     male and female,
          with tongue
running from breast
     to taut nippled chest,
          from Eternal Cave
to tip of rod,
     running inside cave
          an inhabitant traversing
in strokes of measured
     in · ches   in · ches
          and tongue running
up sac, seam, head,
     engulfing flower
          and its stamen. The touch
of tongue from root
     to stem, from neck
          to torso and based
like statued liberty
     the phallus gestures
          upwardly, upmanly.
From full-mouthed breast
     to triangular temple
          of the Huntress, I,
lying between the two,
     am hunted, electric
          with love, discharge
with equal rite.
     I have seen you, Love,
          from both sides and
have been your man and
     have been your woman:

                                        I erect two temples
and lie between them
                        and Love, I have seen
                                        You from both sides.[19]

We can never absolve the total conflict as to what is masculine and what is feminine in each of us individually; we cannot even define those terms. We can absolve only what we have learned, what we have been taught, i.e., the role playing: butch-femme, master-slave, father-son, mother-daughter, mentor-student. Those false boundaries limit and inhibit each of us from being a totally free loving sexual human being in order to enter a partnership that is free enough to be able to grow as a union/toward a union. We stretch our minds beyond roles in order to grow, individually and collectively as a couple. To grow from impersonal beyond the personal toward transpersonal, each to the other, is an endurance test of any relationship. Most homosexuals are aware of and, indeed, in touch with the balance of male/female and accept it as a part of the total being. However, most heterosexuals deny and repress the inherent makeup of such a dual sexuality because society teaches, defines and directs them toward very rigid roles.

In heterosexual couples, the male is usually dominant and the female usually a lesser figure, a housekeeper who takes care of the children and the house, she who seldom has a voice in major decisions. Previously, homosexual couples often "played house" in this manner. Gay Liberation and the Women's Movement are now challenging the validity of all polarized roles. Male-female, masculine-feminine, man-woman, butch-femme—any use of these combined roles suggests to them concepts of aggression/dominance with or against passivity/dependency which they reject as being imposed upon them, as being unnatural to them. What they are seeking are new relationships: where each individual is respected and loved for her or his individuality; where one is equal to the other in decisions, in interacting both within the home and without, and in sex play, as a couple and as individuals. This is the new pattern that is emerging in homosexual pairings, and it is also appearing in the youth culture. Only through the inevitable change in awareness that the Women's Movement brings about and provokes will the heterosexual man come to understand the feeling of "togetherness" that comes from co-mutual decisions, that transcends ego, that brings two psyches and two bodies into one union. The power over impasse in decision making is granted by church, state, and society to the male, for the male, and is usurped by the male as head of the union—a union that thus depends upon inequality, or a togetherness that is not wholly together.

There are four faces of sex in each individual. Kinsey's scale allows for only two, heterosexual and homosexual. The four faces are: heterosexual, homosexual, autosexual, and asexual. Each of us as an individual contains all four faces simultaneously. The gears and spirals work and play at different speeds toward any given individual from another individual. Each face is double-faced with male and female components. These two-sided four faces are our sexual divided self, in R. D. Laing's terms, yet *united* in one body, one person, one individual. However, the social disorganization brought on in our society by urbanization and industrialization has so depersonalized people that it has greatly diminished the chance of encountering another united one in order to grow in depth toward a union.

With this schizoid complex society which we encounter daily, the social and other needs of the individual have increased. It is also becoming increasingly difficult for one person today to fulfill all the single needs of another person, be the needs social, personal, psychological, sexual or spiritual. How do *you* order about you meaningful relationships in order to fulfill *your* needs, individually or as a couple collectively? Yet the homosexual who is aware of the good within him or her takes pride in his or her social order and is today building a sense of community which the homosexual has never had before. Culture has forced homosexuals into a subculture which is gradually becoming a community where can be found security, mutual trust, companionship, understanding, loyalty and love between lesbians and male homosexuals, both individually and collectively, and separately.

The zaps, the demonstrations, the disruptions, the hostilities used by the blatant gays toward heterosexual society and all its institutions, which often appear to be destructive and offensive, are mere defense mechanisms in order to survive in a world which denies our beingness, our being permitted to love. Underneath these violent arrays, if any one will take the time, can be found a stillborn love, willing, waiting and wanting to be birthed, but rejected at all past turns.

Lesbians and homosexuals all seek love: to stand united with another one through the many faces of love, for love. Some have become so alienated from people because of society's strictures that they have lost touch with their worth and dignity as human beings and cannot love themselves, cannot accept themselves. Their values so negated, they lose the desire to live, because their desire to love has been forever thwarted. Some love, but their love is not returned. Others have found personal and abiding love as couples. Together we are learning to love each other as a community. These are all forms of homosexual love—woman to woman, man to man. But there is still another love—an unrequited love—the love the homosexual extends to the heterosexual world, from whence all of us came, which is yet to be returned.

The phenomena of love swarm about us in light energies, transforming states of inactivity and of apathy into states of immersed activity. We homosexuals and lesbians are already committed to exploring the phenomena with which we can construct a better world, a loving world.

NOTES

1. I Samuel 20:16–42.
2. Ruth 1:16–17.
3. H. M. and Nora K. Chadwick, *The Growth of Literature* (Cambridge [England] University Press, 1932), Vol. 2, p. 665.
4. Jeannette H. Foster, *Sex Variant Women in Literature* (New York: Vantage Press, 1956), p. 23.
5. *Ibid.,* p. 144.
6. *Ibid.,* p. 144.
7. H. Montgomery Hyde, *The Love That Dared Not Speak Its Name* (Boston: Little, Brown & Co., 1970), p. 1.
8. D. H. Lawrence, *Women in Love* (New York: Viking Press, 1960), pp. 472–73.
9. Foster, *op. cit.,* p. 17.
10. *The Songs of Sappho,* in English translation by many poets (Mt. Vernon, New York: Peter Pauper Press, n. d.), p. 15.
11. "The Loneliness of Radclyffe Hall" by Donald Webster Cory, *The Ladder* (magazine published by the Daughters of Bilitis, San Francisco), July 1963, p. 7.
12. "Commentary on Second Dialogue" by Frank A. Beach, in André Gide, *Corydon* (New York: Noonday Press, 1950), p. 188.
13. *Ibid.*
14. Una, Lady Troubridge, *The Life of Radclyffe Hall* (New York: The Citadel Press, 1963), p. 190.
15. "Moon-Blink" by Del Martin, *The Ladder,* May 1957, p. 19.
16. Paul Goodman, "Long Lines," *Hawkweed* (New York: Vintage Books, 1967), p. 122.
17. John Wiener, "A poem for the old man." *The Hotel Wentley Poems* (San Francisco: The Auerhahn Press, 1958), page unnumbered.
18. Poems of Renée Vivien translated by Abigail Sanford, *The Ladder,* October 1959, p. 15.
19. "From Both Sides" by Paul Mariah, *Colorado State Review,* Vol. 3, No. 3, Summer–Fall 1968, p. 34.

11

Love Relationships in the Life Cycle: A Developmental Interpersonal Perspective

David E. Orlinsky

Love is a word that has been so loosely used, and conveys so many different meanings, that simply discussing it has become a difficult undertaking. The ambiguity of the word "love" is no doubt amply illustrated by the variety of meanings imputed to it by the authors of this volume. Even at Agathon's banquet, however, the speakers who so long ago initiated the tradition of making learned discourses on love disagreed widely amongst themselves on the nature of their subject. Plato records, in his account of that *Symposium,* conceptions of love ranging from specifically sexual relationships to a vast principle of cosmic harmony, with many steps in between.

I

It does not seem out of order for us to start by examining the contexts in which we feel that use of the word "love" is justified or seriously intended, rather than a playful or a sardonic euphemism. As reader and author, we cannot lose much by getting clear on what we shall and shall not be discussing in the following pages. Beyond helping the semantic problem, we can also come to perceive the outlines of our phenomenon by charting the limits within which we legitimately refer to love.

To the modern mind, love has its fullest and richest meaning when used in reference to romantic, passionate, agonizing yet ecstatic love. This is "the real thing," as novelists, poets, dramatists, artists and composers have represented, praised and apostrophized it for centuries. "Falling in love" is experienced as a passive process, as a form of "possession" by some external force. "Being in love" is regarded as a transcendent state of self, emotionally intense beyond ordinary standards of good and bad or ordinary feelings of pain and pleasure. We normally associate this mode of love in America with relationships between young single men and women, and approve of it highly as the appropriate form of courtship for marriage. This association between romantic love and the process of mate selection is nevertheless a culturally variable factor. In Western Europe, from Tristan to Emma Bovary, romantic love was felt to be the appropriate form of the adulterous liaison. In ancient Greece, as Plato reveals, it was felt to be the appropriate form of homosexual love between a grown man and a young boy.

Seemingly opposite in psychological character, but no less truly regarded as love than romantic passion, is the tender, protective, nurturant attachment of parental love. In its most intense or purest form, it has been viewed traditionally as "a mother's love" for her nursling or dependent infant. We are inclined to admit, in these days of shared parental functioning, that a father may also feel this kind of love for his young children. Grandparents too may experience something akin to this toward grandchildren, if not as intensely as parents then at least less complicated by frustration-engendered resentments.

The reciprocal of parental nurturance as a form of love is childish dependence, which originally is often the quintessence of cuteness, charm and innocent bravado. Actually, it is necessary to be quite specific about developmental stages when discussing children's love, rather than generalize about a single category. The character of a child's dependence changes radically from infancy to the point at which it is diffused beyond immediate attachment to his parents. So, too, does the character of the child's love for his parents change, and the relative distribution of that love as between mother and father. I have found it useful to distinguish four stages (or, better still, "moments") of dependency in childhood: the physical or somatic dependency of the infant on his mother; the interpersonal dependency of the tot primarily on his mother, but secondarily on his father and other members of the family circle; the erotic dependency of the little boy on his mommy, and of the little girl on her daddy (the oedipal stage); and, finally, the cultural dependency of the juvenile upon his or her same-sex parent, and on surrogate adult models found in teachers and athletic, occupational or other real or mythical cultural heroes. The character of the child's love toward his parent is dominated in infancy by symbiotic acceptance, among tots by affectionate responsiveness, for the oedipal child by seductive possessiveness, and in the juvenile by hero worship or idealization. Love attachments between children also exist, sometimes from quite an early age. However, these tend to reflect the modes of love experienced first in parent-child relationships until later childhood (preadolescence), when they ripen into the mutual subjectivity and interdependence of intimate friendship.

Whether we may speak of friendship as a form of love is a more debatable matter. This is an area where we are inclined to draw a distinction between liking and loving. It is normal to like our friends; it is almost a matter of definition. But it may sound excessive, or slightly insincere, to say that we love our friends. Yet an immediate sense of protest arises here, for we feel that we do really love *some* of our friends. Those with whom we have shared intimate experiences and confidences over the years, whose lives and selves seem entwined with the meaning of our own, we feel we undoubtedly love. They may be few in number, compared to the many with whom we have positive social relationships, but they are the companions of our lives, our adopted brothers and sisters. In America we typically extend the category of "friendship" broadly, claiming and conferring it freely. It is clear that we do not love all those whom we call or who call themselves our friends. Some are little more than acquaintances, while for others we have only varying degrees of affection. Though we do not formally distinguish them by a special name such as "compadre," we nevertheless recognize a few people as intimate friends or life friends, and feel that love is not used metaphorically as pertains to them. Especially in late childhood, when intimate friendship first appears and we find ourselves chums, pals or buddies, the term love seems a legitimate usage. Most of the intimate friendships formed are between persons of the same sex, usually in the same age grade. It is asked if persons of opposite sex can be "just good friends." Individual instances show that they can, but these are relatively infrequent, perhaps because of the degree to which erotic feelings are sublimated in friendship. Usually only the homoerotic are sublimated to that extent. For obvious reasons, heterosexually oriented erotic feelings are retained unsublimated, and suppressed or expressed directly as circumstances warrant or allow.

We also recognize a form of love between persons of opposite sex that is neither intimate friendship nor romantic passion. It is most appropriately expressed between husband and wife in our society, but we recognize it as a quality of "emotional marriage" that may be absent from legal unions and present in stable extramarital or consensual relationships. Understood as an emotional rather than a legal relationship, this form of love may be called conjugal mutuality. It is overtly sexual and sensual, and plainly or honestly so; but it is that within a broader matrix of mutual intimacy, affection, domestic collaboration, and emotional commitment. By way of contrast, a transient sexual encounter or a purely sexual relationship between adults with little intimacy or affection is not considered a form of love. We may speak of "making love" in such contexts, but we recognize the phrase as a euphemism.

Several modes, qualities or types of love have been mentioned up to this point. Despite the manifest differences between them, in each case it seemed clear that "love" was appropriately used to describe the phenomenon. In reviewing the list, two general characteristics attract attention. The first is that the modes of love experience are patterned or organized in the form of two-person or dyadic relationships. When a person loves, he is participating in an interpersonal relationship, and he does so by fulfilling one of the roles defining that relationship. This may seem obvious but its implication is none the less important: *love experiences occur in socially patterned relationships, and can be understood adequately only in terms of the person's participation in such relationships.* Conjugal love occurs in the setting of a spouse-spouse relationship. Intimate friendship is a chum-chum relationship. Romantic love involves a lover-lover relationship. The several kinds of dependency love, each complemented by a mode of nurturant love, occur in different forms of the child-parent relationship. Thus, a strictly individual psychological analysis will fail to do justice to the forms, dynamics and functions of love experience.

The second common element that strikes one's attention is the fact that different love experiences are regularly, rather than randomly, distributed over the life cycle, from infancy through adulthood. Every stage of growth apparently has its own proper form of love. In our own culture, the sequence of types of love experience through the life cycle occurs in this order: (1) *symbiotic acceptance,* in the infant; (2) *affectionate responsiveness,* in the tot; (3) *seductive possessiveness,* in the oedipal child; (4) *idealization,* in the juvenile; (5) *intimate friendship,* in the preadolescent; (6) *romantic passion,* in the youth; (7) *conjugal mutuality,* in the mature adult; (8) *somatic nurturance, personal nurturance, erotic nurturance,* and *cultural nurturance* successively in the parent, as his or her children grow from infancy to emotional independence. Some of these forms, such as intimate friendship or conjugal mutuality, appropriately endure beyond one stage of growth in the life cycle; other forms, such as dependency love, often endure inappropriately and provide a basis for "neurotic" involvements. Yet *each stage in the life cycle is marked by the onset or emergence of a new form of love experience, and the form of love which is closest to a person's "growing edge" at any given time in his life is the form that is most absorbing and exciting to him.* Love involvements which continue past the stage of their initial emergence may be richly rewarding but they normally do not hold the center of stage in a person's interests. A newly emergent form of love, reflecting the growing edge of a person's involvement with others, is very much in the foreground of his concerns.

A general relationship may be perceived thus far between love experiences, interpersonal involvements, and stages of personal growth through the life cycle. What is the specific nature of the connection between love, involvement and growth? We have also emphasized the diversity of experiences which are legitimately labeled as love. What is the underlying unity that justifies the use of a single conceptual category for these diverse experiences? Before we turn to these substantive problems, however, a few more strictly terminological problems deserve attention in sharpening the limitations we have imposed on the concept of love.

We often use the word "love" to apply beyond the sphere of immediate human relationships. We speak of a love of God, of country, of personal objects (e.g., one's home), of natural beauties (e.g., the sea), of an activity (e.g., sailing), of a pet animal, and so on. Are these usages legitimate, and in what sense? How do they affect the thesis that love experiences are (a) socially or interpersonally patterned, and (b) related to personal growth through the life cycle? I think we may agree that these usages, though often euphemistic, are in certain cases quite legitimate. The religious man does experience a love of God, and the patriot a love of country, though the ordinary man may regard the usage as simply a manner of speech. Similarly, a child or a lonely man or woman may genuinely love their pet animal, though many pet owners have rather more casual feelings toward their wards. Admitting these cases, however, I would argue that even when legitimate or serious, the use of the term "love" with respect to nonpersonal objects or concepts is a *derivative* and not a primary mode of reference. By this I mean that each type of love experience is formed *initially* in a personal relationship, after which it may be transferred or extended to objects or concepts of a nonpersonal nature. The clearest evidence of this extension from the personal to the nonpersonal sphere in love is the tendency we have to personify the nonpersonal, to relate to objects as if their (to us) distinctive characteristics amounted to a virtually human personality. A man's boat or car may be his "mistress," but only if he perceives "her" as a being with personality. A woman's home may be her alter ego, her intimate companion, only if she perceives it as a living personal being capable of emphatic responsiveness in sharing and reflecting her moods and memories.

Extensions from the sphere of personal relationships, which are the primary referents of love, to the secondary nonpersonal sphere may be made by analogy (simple substitution) or by symbolic transfer. A lonely woman's poodle may be her substitute child, and she may lavish a genuine if often distorted parental nurturance on it. A child's dog may be his "best friend," especially if the child is isolated from others of his age. The sincerely religious person's love of God tends to be modeled on worshipful idealization, as does the patriot's love of country—as the concepts of God the Father and fatherland suggest. These are examples of analogic extension or simple substitution from the personal to the nonpersonal spheres of love involvement. Love of the sea, the mountains, or of particular activities tend to be more complex symbolic transfers of love from the formative models of personal relationships. The symbolic transfer differs from analogic extension in that the former involves the mediation of an intervening associational link between loved person and the loved object or concept.

Without taking up space for more detailed argument and exemplification, we may summarize simply by noting the distinction between the primary sphere of *personal love relationships,* and a derivative or secondary sphere of *nonpersonal love attachments.* The primary love relationships include the modes of love experience that are most significantly distributed over the life cycle, and it is in them that we must search for the specific connections between love experience and personal growth.

II

Let us reexamine more closely now the alignment between types or qualities of love experience, interpersonal relationships, and life cycle stages. These have been grouped together in the table herewith. In the

LIFE CYCLE STAGES, LOVE RELATIONSHIPS, AND QUALITIES OF EXPERIENCE

Life Cycle Stage	Relationship Roles (a) (b)	Modes of Love Experience (a)	(b)
I. Infancy	(1) Nursling –(8) Nurse	Symbiotic acceptance	Somatic nurturance
II. Early Childhood	(2) Tot –(9) Tutor	Affectionate responsiveness	Personal nurturance
III. Middle (Oedipal) Childhood	(3) Little boy–(10) Mommy or Little girl– Daddy	Seductive possessiveness	Erotic nurturance
IV. Late (Juvenile) Childhood	(4) Follower –(11) Model	Idealization	Cultural nurturance
V. Preadolescence	(5) Chum – Chum	Intimacy	Intimacy
VI. Youth	(6) Lover – Lover	Romantic passion	Romantic passion
VII. Adulthood	(7) Spouse – Spouse	Mutuality	Mutuality
VIII. Parenthood	(8–11)		

first column we have listed eight stages of the life cycle extending from infancy through the later phases of parenthood. Obviously, life does not end with the completion of parenthood. The number of stages differentiated is largely a matter of analytic convenience, rather than a reflection of necessary facts of nature. Continuity, if anything, is characteristic of the life cycle as a developmental process. Whether one distinguishes three or twenty phases depends essentially on the fineness of discriminations that must be made in dealing with the problem under discussion. The eight we have specified here generally accord with, but are not identical to, the divisions suggested by Erikson in *Childhood and Society* and by Sullivan in *The Interpersonal Theory of Psychiatry*.

The second column presents the roles by which love relationships are patterned. The role a person takes in a relationship should not be confused with the person who participates by taking the role. A role is an expected pattern of activity and experience, a segment of the relationship itself. Love relationships are composed of two role segments, listed separately under (a) and (b) in column two. A person participates in a love relationship by taking one of the roles in it, and engaging in the expected activity and experience together with someone who appropriately takes the reciprocal role. If a person can find no one to take the other role, he cannot act on or experience love feelings. In all cases except the nursling infant, the person involved in a love relationship also has other roles which involve him in other relationships. No matter how significant his love involvement may be to him, a person is more than can be encompassed in his love relationship (or in any other relationship). The different consecutive roles one takes in love relationships through the life cycle are numbered in column two in sequential order: (1) to (4) are dependent roles characteristic of childhood; (5) to (7) are equal, interdependent roles characteristic of adolescence and adulthood; (8) to (11) are dominant nurturant roles characteristic of parenthood.

The third column lists the modal or predominant quality of love experience which normally accompanies participation in each of the roles in each of the love relationships. Typical experiences listed under (a) and (b) in column three correspond to the roles listed under (a) and (b) in the second column. For example: the typical expected experience of the tot in a tot-tutor relationship is affectionate responsiveness; that of a lover in a lover-lover relationship is romantic passion. In actual occurrence, however, the expected quality of experience emerges in various degrees of purity and of intensity, depending upon a number of particular circumstances.

We see in the table that the two role segments of certain relationships are similar, and their corresponding love experiences are parallel, while in other relationships the two role segments differ. The former may be termed *symmetrical* love relationships, and the latter *complementary* love relationships. Symmetrical love relationships normally obtain between persons who are peers in age, status, and power; complementary love relationships exist between persons who are different in generation and power, and whose roles in the relationship are rather sharply differentiated.

The patterns discernible by inspection of the table suggest that more than a chance connection exists between love relationships and the developmental sequence. The thesis I will advance is that *each love relationship is a medium or vehicle of personal growth;* that *it is through participation in each love relationship that one progresses to the next stage of psychological development in the life cycle.*

One grows as a person through loving, though not only in this way. As one becomes a new and different self through this experience, he also becomes ready to engage in a new and different mode of relatedness to others. Love relationships are not merely pleasant or edifying but essential experiences in life, "growthful" in the same generous sense in which travel is "broadening." They are in fact necessary links in the process of personal growth.

It should be understood that I am using the concept of the life cycle in a psychological as well as a cultural sense, as a sequence of developmental changes through which a person normally passes in the course of his life. These changes are in part framed by physiological maturation and interpreted by cultural categories, but they represent a ladder of cumulative experiences for each individual in the culture who passes through them. An individual's progression, we should note, is not an automatic function of chronological aging. It is popular currently to conceive of development in terms of problem solving or achievement, but I prefer to view it as a psychological *unfolding* that proceeds now quickly, now slowly, according to the experience of the individual and what he makes of it. A person can actively seek certain experiences or avoid them, but he cannot make them happen. Though it takes time to engage and master the experiences requisite for personal growth, and a person ages as he grows, it is also true that a person may cease to grow though he continues to age.

It is also important to understand the sense in which the phrase "personal growth" is intended. Psychological development may be studied at varying levels of functional specificity or generality. In terms of specific functions, an individual may be conceived to grow in intellect, in social competence, in moral judgment, or in emotional maturity. The most general level at which an individual can be considered is *as a total person*, experiencing and relating to others and to himself. *Personal growth*, or development at this most general level, *involves the progressive differentiation and integration of a person's basic images of himself and others, and of his basic capacities for relating to himself and others.* Thus, our thesis states that a love relationship is a vehicle of growth for the individual considered as a total person, a way in which he extends his basic images of and capacities for involvement with others. I do not propose that specific functions such as intellect or conscience develop by this process. As in the use of a microscope, processes visible at one level of conceptual magnification may not be evident at others.

To gain a fuller appreciation of the role played by love relationships in personal growth through the life cycle, it is necessary for us to take a larger perspective. I have said that love relationships constitute a medium or vehicle of personal growth, but not the only one. *It is in fact necessary to distinguish two alternative modes of personal growth: individuation, or growth in the complexity and integrity of self; and communion, or growth in the complexity and integrity of personal involvement.* (The term "communion," which was also used by David Bakan in *The Duality of Human Existence,* does not fully convey the sense of this concept; some alternative but also unsatisfactory terms are "harmonization," "synergization," and "universalization.")

A person grows through an alternating, dialectical emphasis on individuation and communion. Between each successive phase in which individuation predominates, a phase of communion must occur. Similarly, between each successive phase in which communion predominates, a phase of individuation must occur. To establish a *new* mode of relatedness with others, one must first become in some ways a new self; to develop a new aspect of oneself, one must be drawn out into a new mode of involvement. The circularity apparent in this proposition is only apparent. The actual pattern of growth resembles a spiral more than a circle: a cycle which shifts progressively in position from one recurrence to the next. The first phase of a person's growth as a viable organism is in somatic communion (symbiosis) with his mother within her womb, and the first phase of individuation is accomplished in the processes which result in birth. That first step of individuation makes possible a second, new form of communion: the somatic dependency of the infant nursling on the somatic nurturance of the mother. Thus the alternating cycle of communion and individuation continues, at each point adding a new dimension to the person's experience of and capacity for involvement with himself or others.

Love relationships are the specific interpersonal forms of personal growth through communion. The participant in a love relationship becomes personally involved with the one with whom he shares that relationship, in such a way that their common union subordinates their separate individualities. The person becomes a participant in the literal sense, part of a larger, more inclusive whole. In love one ventures out beyond one's established self, to feel and do new things in exploring the new ground defined and made safe by the supportive force of the relationship. The old boundaries of the self are dissolved in the relationship; a new openness and fluidity of experience occurs between the two partners. They reveal to each other, and satisfy in each other, needs which define the growing edge of each. In effect, they establish a bond of exchange in which what each most wants of the other, the other wants most to do with him.

By way of contrast, the interpersonal forms which mediate growth through individuation are relationships of contest, conflict, and dominance. Rather than seeking a mode of involvement or harmonization with the other, the individual seeks a mode of distinction and contrast. Instead of dissolving ego boundaries in a relaxation of tension between partners, individuation leads to a sharpening of ego boundaries and a heightening of tension. Each of the phases of individuation is essentially a phase of self-assertion.

The process of individuation utilizes the assertive or aggressive energies of the individual, just as the process of communion utilizes his erotic or attractive energies. However, the self-assertive aggressiveness of individuation is no more intrinsically destructive than the binding eros of communion. Aggression and eros both have constructive and growthful, as well as destructive and regressive, potentialities. Normally, under optimal circumstances, both are constructive in tendency. Pathologically, under sustained adverse circumstances, both can be destructively expressed. Those who align aggression with destructiveness and eros with constructiveness, as did Freud, share in a serious conceptual error. Destructive impulses are aroused when either mode of personal growth is seriously warped or impeded, and it is initially directed against the damaging or frustrating agent, though like other feeling impulses it may be generalized to others. The motive of destructiveness is thus revenge: emotional or physical sadism, aiming to torture and humiliate, in the case of erotic destructiveness; passive or violent rebellion, aiming to transcend or obliterate, in the case of aggressive destructiveness. Love which has gone sour is no less a hostile force than self-assertion that has been thwarted too long.

The ideas set forth in this section should give some indication of why it is that we found the several types of relationships which we recognize as love, distributed in a regular pattern over the life cycle. The reason is that these love relationships form an integral part in the sequence of experiences which produce personal growth in the individual. Love is indeed a growth experience in the normal case, giving rise to "growing pains" as well as pleasurable excitement. Alternating with periods of personal growth in which self-assertive behavior is predominant, each of the distinctive love relationships is a step in development which the individual takes as he passes the cultural mileposts that mark the path of the life cycle.

III

Two questions now remain to be considered, the answers to which will extend and clarify our conception of love. First, how does a love relationship actually contribute to the personal growth of its participants? If love experiences are an integral part of growth through the life cycle, we have yet to specify the internal dynamic of this process. Second, how can we explain the different forms or qualities taken by love relationships at different points in the life cycle? We have claimed there is an underlying unity to the different manifest patterns of love relationship, but we have yet to say what that unity consists of and why it is so diversely manifested.

The answers to both these questions lie within the love relationship, i.e., in what takes place between and within the participants. All relationships, as Homans and Blau have argued, can be conceived as forms of *exchange* which are entered into by individuals. It is the kind of values exchanged and the rules governing the exchange that distinguish one type of relationship from another. The values which people seek and offer vary greatly. In the narrowly economic types of transaction, money is exchanged for material goods or services. Broader social relationships more often involve the exchange of such interpersonal values as esteem, compliance, companionship, advice or help in performing a task. Even the most personal relationships can be conceived as transactions in which the values exchanged between partners pertain to their deeper emotional needs.

The exchange of deeply personal values between partners is the core dynamic of the process that takes place within a love relationship. *Each person involved in love normally brings to the relationship qualities or characteristics which are essential to the personal growth of his partner.* It is the possession of these mutually needed qualities—more precisely, the apparent possession of these and the promise of their availability— that first attracts two people to each other. It is the actual presence of these qualities of response that feeds and sustains the love relationship. The activities and responses by which each person consummates his attraction is precisely what fulfills the growth need of the other. Under normal or ideal circumstances, what I most want to do or be with you is what you most need from me to stimulate or facilitate your growth as a person, and what you most want to do or be with me is what I most need from you. To the extent that this condition of reciprocity is fulfilled, a love relationship may be said to exist.

The process of exchange can be represented schematically in a diagram depicting the contribution of each partner to the other (see the figure below). We here represent Person A and Person B, the two partners in a love relationship, acting together. Within each person we have

The Cycle of Exchange in Love Relationships

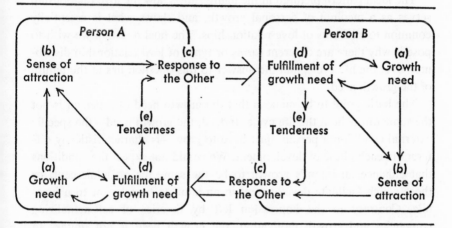

distinguished: (a) *a growth need,* defined in terms of the external conditions required for the development of new experiences and capacities; (b) *a sense of attraction,* directed toward those who appear to possess or embody the qualities that would satisfy the growth need; (c) *a response to the other,* aimed at engaging the other in a desired form of intimate behavior; (d) *a pleasurable sense of fulfillment,* originating in the satisfaction of one's growth need by the response of the other; (e) *a feeling of tenderness* or caring, a concern for the other based on gratitude for the pleasurable fulfillment received from him.

Two things are important to note about this schema. First, *there is a state of reciprocity or balance in the exchange between the two partners: the "natural" response of each toward the other provides the conditions which fulfill each person's growth need.* I shall illustrate this state of balance with some examples in a moment. Second, *there is within each partner a dual feeling-impulse shaping his response to the other: a sense of desire or attraction, and a sense of tenderness or concern.* The desire is "egocentric," and its nature is determined by the person's growth need, reinforced by pleasurable fulfillment. The tenderness is allocentric or "altruistic," and results directly from current and past experiences of growth fulfillment through the responses of others toward oneself. These two subjective strands of the love impulse correspond roughly, I think, to what Freud described as the sensual affectionate "currents of libido." They also parallel the traditional conceptions of love as "eros" and "agape."

The ideal pattern pictured in the figure shows how the love relationship serves as a medium of personal growth, and shows what is essentially common to all forms of love relationships. The final question we wish to pose is why there are different forms or types of love relationship distributed over the life cycle, and the answer to this question lies in the nature of the growth need.

The basic point to be made is that the growth need of a person is not the same throughout the life cycle. Indeed, the growth need—the specific external condition a person must have to grow—is characteristically different in each phase of development. We would not expect the conditions that enhance an infant's growth to be the same for an adolescent, or those which facilitate development in an adult to be relevant to a juvenile. Contrary to the impression left by theories of self-actualizing tendencies and growth motivation, the growth need is not unitary in quality, or even a substantive disposition. Often a need which originally is a growth need (e.g., the need to be nourished as a nursling) continues as an important motivation after it is no longer primarily relevant to the growing edge of personality. Then it may be called a maintenance need, in contrast to a growth need. The growth need of a person is defined functionally rather than substantively. When the function which the needed external condition completes is emergent or newly developing, it defines a growth need. When that same function is well established and integrated with the person's other functions, it defines a maintenance need.

The reason, then, why there are different modes or types of love is that different growth needs are salient in each of the developmental phases of the life cycle. The growth need of the infant nursling is *satiating stimulation* (sensory as well as nutritive). The growth need of the parental "nurse" (typically and most intensely, the mother) is *satiable needs*. The healthy infant provides its mother with satiable needs, and the normal mother provides her infant with satiating stimulation. Their growth needs are reciprocal (in this case, complementary) and their exchange is balanced. Each starts with that need and the capacity to be attracted or drawn to the other. Each experiences an expanding sense of attraction and of tenderness toward the other as that growth need is pleasurably fulfilled. In this way the dynamic exchange within the love relationship reaches a peak of intensity and as the emergent function defining the growth need in each becomes more routine and less salient, the exchange intensity declines. By this time, the child is no longer an infant nursling, but a dependent tot with a sense of living as a separate self. As the tot reaches toward greater competence and autonomy, the condition he needs to facilitate his growth is *guiding support*. The parent no longer functions primarily in the role of nurse, but is now more a tutor whose growth as a capable nurturant person requires evidence of *responsive development* in her charge. Again, in this second love relationship, the normal parent (still, in our culture, primarily the mother) provides her dependent tot with the guidance and support he needs, and the healthy tot manifests in return the responsive development that confirms and fulfills the personal nurturance of his parent.

In each period of the life cycle when personal growth proceeds by communion, the growth need of the individual is satisfied through involvement in a love relationship. The distinguishing characteristics of the love relationship are determined by the reciprocal growth needs of the participants: the type of person to whom one is attracted; the form of intimate contact which is desired; the kind of responses made to involve the other in the dynamic process of exchange. In the four asymmetrical love relationships (nursling-nurse, tot-tutor, little boy-mommy or little-girl daddy, and follower-model) the growth needs of the two partners are different because each is in a different phase of growth through the life cycle. In the three symmetrical love relationships (chum-chum, lover-lover, spouse-spouse) the growth needs of the two partners are parallel because each is in the same phase of growth through the life cycle.

The scope of this essay does not allow us to discuss further each of the growth needs, or the many interesting implications of the exchange model. These will be explored in greater detail in a forthcoming publication. However, I hope that I have already sufficiently demonstrated here that thinking of love in a developmental interpersonal perspective makes this important and complex phenomenon clearer and more comprehensible. It should be apparent, for example, that discussing the qualities and characteristics of love *in general* is for most descriptive or analytic purposes a source of considerable confusion. Although love relationships are similar in dynamics and function, they are markedly different in both form and content. Each type of love relationship involves its participant in a distinctive experience. Unless we intend to compare the common features of these different modes of love, we ought to train ourselves to state explicitly the specific type of involvement to which we have reference. What is true of romantic love is not necessarily true of conjugal love, much less of parental love. It is pointless to elevate one type of love relationship to a position of special honor, and to ignore or degrade the rest. It is no more than personal bias. I end as I started, by laying emphasis on how we talk about love. The manifold experience of love is too important to be subjected to careless study.

12

The Love Effect

Theodore H. Blau

During the nineteenth century, love was considered, together with electricity and heat, to be a "weightless imponderable" (Rabkin, 1969). Social scientists have neglected love as an area worthy of intensive exploration (Bloom, 1967). There is a tendency to avoid dealing with positive affective phenomena and to direct interest and effort toward human discomfort (disturbance, distorted behavior, illness, wrong, the unacceptable, etc.). Perhaps love as a behavioral phenomenon has been neglected because it is considered a "good" or acceptable response. This tendency is, of course, not universal (Ard, 1970).

Early theoretical formulations put love and hate in opposition to each other (Caruso, 1968). Freudian theory related love to life (Fromm, 1968). This position has been restated in modified form more recently (May, 1968). Freud's position, embellished by current analytic writers, proposes that "being in love" represents narcissism in the adult sphere. Current writers propose that the love phenomenon is an adolescent state and that when it occurs in maturity, represents a regression (Fornari, 1967). Love, as seen by Adlerians, was pretty well limited to sexual interaction (Ansbacher, 1967).

Opposition to the love-hate continuum of the traditional analysts, as well as the concepts of Lorenz, are represented by the view of the neo-analysts (Fromm *et al.*, 1968; Fromm, 1969). Klein has suggested that love parallels gratitude (1967). The suspicion that the love phenomenon is not integral to marriage is supported by research in Mexican rural communities (Maccoby, 1968), where the family interpersonal activity can

151

be vicious. Current writers propose that a stable marital interaction must include a capacity to hate as well as love (Charny, 1970; Goshan, 1967; Groh, 1968). There is some evidence that more of the love phenomenon is necessary where economic ties are of little importance in a marriage (Coppinger and Rosenblatt, 1969).

Social scientists associated with the humanistic movement propose that love is essential to self-actualization and the complete self (Stewart, 1969; Buhler, 1967; Martin, 1967).

The phenomenon of love is formed and shaped in childhood (Winnicott, 1968; Evans, 1969; Groth and Holbert, 1970; Lindenauer, 1969; Masters and Tong, 1968; Niles, 1967). This shaping by cultural factors seems to continue into adulthood, at least for women (Nataraj, 1968; Kephart, 1967; Kunz, 1969).

The enormous interest in group training and encounter meetings during the past decade is frequently associated with the concept of man's need for love (Dunnette, 1969; Stoller, 1968).

Ellis (1969) clearly suggests that healthy extramarital relationships include *love enhancement,* quite distinct and apart from a drive for sexual variety. Behavioral engineers consider love phenomena of sufficient significance that they have been writing about "installing repertoires of love behavior in subject" (Homme *et al.,* 1968).

The arts have paid the greatest amount of attention to love. The results have contributed much to aesthetics and entertainment. Clues from art media as to cause and effect of love phenomena have been at best vague.

Some behavioral scientists attribute prime merit to the personal experience as a means of understanding love. A personal experience can be stirring or therapeutic. These experiences can stimulate or guide a search for understanding. If we are to go beyond limited individual and group experience, cause-effect sequences must be explored. If we seek to create, communicate, modify and control the phenomena of love, an outline or structure of the effect must be developed. This structure can then be tested against a variety of data, including the personal experience. Through the ages, the experience of love has been known and described, but not successfully delineated. Such attempts are worthwhile, and the current presentation should be viewed as simply one more attempt.

The data source of this description of the boundaries of love is psychotherapy. The psychotherapeutic experience is an open-ended, relatively unlimited interaction whereby personal experience can be viewed in a fairly systematic way, experientially as well as longitudinally. Psychotherapy is a growing, enriching, learning, experimental experience for the doer as well as for the receiver.

I can recall only a very few people with whom I've worked in psychotherapy, usually on a limited basis, who never discussed their own perceptions of love. Inevitably, in the long-term, awareness-seeking context, the experience of love, as it is perceived and sensed by the individual, emerges.

Characteristically, the word "love" is used easily and indiscriminately. When asked, "Please tell me what this means to you," responses are often clouded by discussion of the *object* of the love experience, the *source* of the love experience, the *expected benefits* or *losses*, and, more rarely, the individual's affective response to the experience. These reports do very little to clarify the limits or borders of love, not so much because they are personalized descriptions, but because they are vague or evasive. Interaction about the love experience, as one might find in group therapy, seems to go along easily and superficially as long as no one asks, "What do you mean?" When this occurs, the response may range from interested but unproductive interaction to violent confrontation. One culture-laden characteristic of the love experience that seems to be consistent is a tendency for all to agree about its positive benefits. There is an assumption that "love is good."

When people speak of love, they may refer to fond affection, but the current discussion will be directed to the more strongly affective experience which tends to come upon us intensely rather than to grow gradually. This Love Effect is characterized by excitement, a heightened state of positive affect, warmth, a need to give or share, a seeking for closeness with the love object. There are touching needs. In the absence of the love-producing object, there is frequently a condition of yearning. This is manifested by preoccupation—even obsession—with the love-producing object, the interaction, past experiences, future expectations. A variety of physiological occurrences, mostly pleasing, accompany these reactions. There may be overt sexualization of the interaction—physically or ideationally. When the interaction is disrupted, there tends to occur a perception of sudden and intense panic. Truly, the Love Effect is a stirring, powerful experience.

In order to pursue the delineation of love, I would like to propose a hypothesis as to the cause of the Love Effect and then present some clarifying data gleaned from the psychotherapeutic interaction. It is proposed:

The Experiential Phenomena of the Love Effect results when the hoped-for, wished-for but unbelieved or unaccepted self is seen through the eyes of another.

Such a definition seems sterile, exudes no warmth, does less than stir. Perhaps, however, it can clarify. The hypothesis states that in order to experience love, one must possess some sort of self-image, limited or broad, conscious or unconscious. It is the image of what a person would like to be, how one would hope to be seen, or acts that one would like to perform. This ego ideal which most humans seem to have can be conscious, preconscious, or totally unconscious. One would have to assume that such an idealized self-concept is based on a variety of growth and developmental experiences, identifications within and without the family, the cultural expectancy, and from experience itself. It would not have to be very specific since most people seem to have a good deal of flexibility in their self-concept and are willing to change and modify this in accordance with pressures and opportunities that are presented within the environment. Mass media have probably speeded and intensified development of this ideal image in the contemporary developmental pattern.

There is, apparently, some guilt about this self-concept since most people when asked, "What would you like to be?" respond with a certain degree of discomfort. This may be based on the second criteria necessary for the Love Effect—that *one does not believe that one deserves the status of the ego image which is much desired.* Preliminary to the Love Effect, one often finds that an individual is given to understand that he has some particular value and, much as the individual may wish to have this value, his immediate response is disbelief. Thus, in order to be "in love," there has to be a certain degree of contrast or dissonance of self *vs* other reality rating. One wants to be a certain thing, but one believes that the capability doesn't really exist.

The Love Effect is liable to occur at any time that another individual (or even inanimate object) gives evidence that the individual in question is acting in a manner which reflects the ideal image. The love experience requires an external object—a person, an animal, a thing. From this object there must be a symbol, a statement, a posture, an expectancy that the ego ideal is seen, identified, or appreciated.

For the love experience to develop, it is necessary that the ego ideal be questioned, not believed, by the individual experiencing the Love Effect. The external love-producing object could not be effective if what it represented were fully accepted within the self. This tends to account for the "thine alone" concept in the love experience. Once the fantasized ideal self is met externally, the individual becomes self-reinforcing by thoughts or tokens related to the external object which produces the Love Effect.

Now that the process has been presented, some examples of how this very complex human interaction develops would seem appropriate.

Conditions Under Which the Love Effect Develops

Mother Love. When a child is born, emotionally he is pretty much of a clean slate. The early experience is that of survival. Nourishment, warmth, the tender loving care that comes from a mother, is of critical importance in producing a total human creature. All of this necessary attention directed to the child creates an aura of "you are the most important (or only) creature in the world." Any child who feels or is shown during the first year or two of life that he is not a most important creature is likely to be an incomplete adult. Parents who attempt to interpret reality to their children at too early an age may produce a child who is eventually able to relate to other humans only in emotionally limited terms. It all starts, however, with the greatest of all love offerings: "You deserve to live."

The child loves the mother because he is given to understand, "You are a great thing in the world." There is very little specification or delineation. The perception tends to be total. The child is treated as important and powerful, to be given the greatest care and tenderness. All of this, of course, comes to a fairly sharp halt when childhood training begins.

The child is generally disturbed by the parent's attempt to instill eating, sleeping, and toilet habits contrary to the child's natural rhythm. This is where the most powerful form of love begins to be tempered with dependency. When the mother first attempts to toilet-train the child, the child is usually puzzled, frightened, enraged. It is not too long before the child realizes that he cannot effectively control the situation by holding his breath, refusing to eat, withholding the bowel movement. These and other childish maneuvers soon cease to control the parent. The child begins to experience the frightening awareness that the parent is in control. This is the initial dependency perception. This is the first connection of love and dependency. If, at this point, the parent interpreted only reality to the child, the adult love experience in our culture would be limited. The mother, however, will continue for five, ten, twenty or more years to meet the fantasy expectations of her child. She will limit the child yet continue to encourage him to believe he is special and that all will be well. The process of growth and development of a child toward maturity in our culture is a gradual increase of reality testing and a decrease in fantasy support. This, with reference to our definition of the Love Effect, indicates that the child will less and less be supported about the worth of self in fantasy. It is not long before the child begins to understand that he is not total or magic.

One occasionally sees a three-year-old child standing in the front yard gesturing at the sky at sundown. The child is aware that at a certain time, the sun goes down. The gesturing is the acting out of the fantasy of controlling this phenomenon. The child is "making the sun go down." It is rare to see this among five-year-olds. By this age, reality testing is fairly strong; sometimes painfully so. A seeking for support of fantasy begins and the conditions are set for the Love Effect.

As development progresses, mothers often continue to tell their children that they are the smartest one, the strongest one, the sweetest, the toughest one, the meanest, the cleanest, the dirtiest, and other appellations that, at one time or another, are meaningful in support of or opposed to the child's growing ideal image. This is groundwork for the Love Effect, even in a family where the parents are extremely hostile. The five-year-old child may hear the father talking about a prize fighter on television. "He's the meanest, toughest guy going. He's really nasty." The child can then seek a reinforcement for a particular kind of early ideal image by stuffing a live frog down baby sister's mouth. The father is just likely to say, "You are the meanest, nastiest thing there is." The child's feeling in relation to his father's response is love, despite the fact that the father may punish the child severely. The concept that love is always a positive experience is simply not supported by clinical experience. Some people seem to feel loved or lovable when they are knocked down the stairs.

Mothers or mother surrogates serve significant roles in the early development of children. Mothering and mother love seem effective in direct relationship to the helplessness that exists in infancy. Mothering conducted past the twelfth or thirteenth year in the child's life can be less than helpful. No human of reasonable intelligence could be satisfied or fulfilled with mother's love after this age. Middle-class folkways and television notwithstanding, mothers ought to find other areas in which to be worthwhile after their children reach puberty. When the unreality support from mother to child continues into maturity, both parties are likely to find themselves in an emotionally limited or deprived state. The Love Effects known as "crushes" which are part of the childhood development are alternates or extensions of the fantasy support usually provided by parents.

Those children who are raised without benefit of mother love are probably able only rarely to experience the Love Effect. This situation is commonly found among orphans. Whether these people are fortunate or unfortunate is a complex question. Inability of the orphan to experience love or ability to experience only diluted forms is possibly a result of the pressure placed early in the orphan's life to face reality about the self and the self's unworth. The orphan is someone no one wants. The fact that the parents deserted the orphan through no choice of their own is inconsequential. The child still feels deserted and unwanted. This is a harsh reality.

If adoption occurs early enough, of course, the situation can be remedied. After two or three years of age, however, the youngster has adjusted to the fact that he is unwanted and faces this as a reality. Gestures of love and warmth are ordinarily rejected through avoidance, evasion, or refusal. The orphan can be a youngster seen as superficially mature, able to take responsibility, to accomplish difficult tasks with energy and application, and a "joy to behold," unless you try to create a Love Effect in such a child.

When orphans and children adopted after the first year of life mature, they have a difficult time making close object relationships where the Love Effect is likely to be a part of the interaction. Since they have a sharp and painful reality view of the self as an unwanted object and protect themselves through this view, the idea of somebody wanting them or seeing them at a level beyond their own view is frightening, dangerous, and unacceptable. Mates of orphans sometimes say, "There is no way to get to him." If someone were able to set off the inner awareness of "you are wanted," the love experience would occur, since it would certainly be a fantasy desired but unbelieved to the orphan. Because he was bruised early in life, the orphan is well guarded and unable to allow an emotional approach to be made. For all practical purposes, orphans have a great deal of difficulty acknowledging and experiencing the Love

Effect. They suffer as a result of this experience because they cannot participate in this marvelous fantasy. On the other hand, they are spared the pain of facing reality which eventually occurs in the waning phase of the love experience. Depending on the solidity or fragmentation of the ego structure, this phase can range from discomfort to devastation.

Object Love

As the human being grows and develops, it is possible to experience both mild and intense forms of the Love Effect where objects rather than humans are involved. Although much simpler and usually less intense than the human interaction, the Love Effect resulting from identification with or attachment to an object follows the basic formula of the ideal self brought into a temporary or quasi reality by a stimulus external to the self.

One often sees the phenomenon at work when children participate in fantasy play. A little boy gesturing, pointing and muttering in his backyard while wearing a leather holster and a plastic gun, may well be involved in a love experience. It is not so much that it is "his gun" as that the gun represents an actualization (no matter how temporary) of the wished-for, hoped-for self-image. "Powerful, controlled, feared, kindly law man, able to do and be" is an image almost every youngster has sought.

Moving a little further on the developmental scale, we find that youngsters can attach themselves to such things as bicycles, model airplanes, and boats that they have constructed, as well as a wide variety of fantasy play equipment currently available on the toy market. Children fondle and cuddle these objects. They take them to bed. They think about them intensely and frequently. They want to take them along when the family goes for a ride. A child certainly has a Love Effect in relation to these objects, since the objects demonstrate a hoped-for self that in reality does not exist. The child knows that this ideal self is not real, but, during the time that the interaction takes place, it is very close to reality and the child tunes his language, his gestures, and his energies to the fantasized self-image.

Adults are not deprived of the opportunity of experiencing the Love Effect with inanimate objects. People attach themselves to their automobiles, selecting a particular vehicle and firming their identification with such an object on the basis of their hoped-for self. To be in love with a car is to be someone we want to be, but feel we probably aren't. The vehicle in some way helps us to be our ideal self. The tremendous popularity of sports cars and convertibles suggests the kind of self-image sought by so many in our culture.

It is said that some women love their fur coats. There is reality in such a statement. In some way, this measure of affluence and worth demonstrates a body image, a social status, a self-concept much desired, but inwardly questioned. When the fur coat goes out of style, the love ceases. The object no longer serves as a stimulus for the Love Effect.

Infrahuman Sources

A pet offers an opportunity for a child to experience a powerful Love Effect. One observes children playing with dogs and cats, mice, toads and frogs, hamsters, even beetles and ants. The interaction may start on a relatively objective, observational basis. This tends quickly to become highly personalized. At this point, the creature becomes "a pet." A pet is simply a love object in which the individual invests some of his inner needs and cravings. As a result, to a larger or lesser degree, an individual can have a Love Effect from the closeness, licking, running, squeaking, sound making, cuddling, and other behaviors found among infrahuman species. It is common enough to hear a lady call her poodle "Son" or "Lover" or "Honey." Uncountable hours of dialogue occur between human beings and animals. The animals serve as stimuli for the perception of the hoped-for, wished-for self that the individual doesn't believe he or she is. One need only observe a human who has a close attachment to an animal to see the astonishing degree to which a wriggle, groan, scratch, shake, slobber, or grunt can be interpreted as a very personal attachment and demonstration of some specialness on the part of the owner.

The commonality of these phenomena illustrates the degree to which human beings reach for the Love Effect and the tremendously reinforcing power of such an effect. Such reinforcement is intermittent and variable and thus, very powerful. An occasional Love Effect is sufficient to keep humans actively directed toward arranging for a recurrence of the phenomenon despite the aftereffects and limitations of the phenomenon.

The Human Interaction

The most complex Love Effect and apparently the most powerful seems to occur in the person-to-person relationship. It can occur at any time that one person sees evidence from the behavior of another person that leads him to believe he is being seen in a manner similar to the way he would like to be. This can apparently range from the perception, "You are great, you are fantastic" to "You're the scum of the earth." The ideal image need is likely to govern the occurrence and the intensity of the Love Effect. This can account for the people in therapy who describe themselves as being deeply in love with intensely brutal, hurting people.

Because of the complexity of human interaction, there is opportunity to pick, choose, request, or arrange modifications of an interpersonal interaction. Thus, the conditions for the Love Effect can be changed to intensify or deintensify the experience. This tends to be a regular part of a love interaction. Depending upon the adjustment or balance of the individuals involved, each participant may choose a variety of ways of revitalizing the Love Effect as it wanes. The use of clothing, special words, stirring of guilt, creating of jealousies, underscoring and sharpening dependencies are but a few ways of revitalizing the Love Effect. This revitalization is necessary if the effect is to continue by the very nature of the causal sequence, the brightening of a fantasy into perceptual reality. This can be sustained for only a limited period of time and has a natural tendency to wane. The magical ideal of "love forever" is quite an impossibility. It is amazing, however, to observe the degree to which the Love Effect can be continued, revitalized, reintegrated, reexperienced, and extended despite its very temporary nature.

Phases of the Love Effect

The popular concept of "love forever" exists as a part of the cultural lore. Fairy tales often end ". . . and they lived happily ever after." This is taken to mean that they *love* happily and forever. Such a thing in all probability rarely happened. The Love Effect must be replaced by other interactions or the effect, and possibly the relationship, will disintegrate. The conception that love is forever and the exciting volatile interaction will never cease is one of the most destructive fantasies perpetuated by the mass media of our culture. The Love Effect itself is powerful in bringing people together. It does not last, and strong expectation can lead to devastating feelings of worthlessness in waning phases of the Love Effect.

The initial phase of the Love Effect has already been described. A hoped-for self is discovered in the activity of another person, and all the suppressed and repressed wish, need-yearning is released. The fantasy is, for the moment, fulfilled and a surge of emotional strength, feeling of well-being, excitement, and positive turgidity occurs. This phase is fevered, it is volatile, it is exciting, it is wonderful. Many people are frightened of this initial phase and avoid and evade anything which might set off the reaction. Sometimes, the longer submission to the volatility is put off, the more intense the effects. Depression, self-destructive acting-out and other negative reactions can result from evading this sought and expected human interaction.

As a relationship continues or as time simply passes, a series of panics seem to occur. These may occur early in the relationship based on the individual's fear of being involved in a love experience and may participate a running reaction. Panic that occurs after the Love Effect has occurred seems to be based on a sudden awareness of reality—"I know who I *really* am, and the love-stirring object no longer sees me in the magical way." The waning of the Love Effect leads to panic and then to rage. At this point, the Love Effect may be reinstituted by a variety of the mechanisms noted previously. The Love Effect may resurge to an equal or greater extent than the initial experience. As time passes, there again will be a lessening of the effect with a tendency for panic and rage to occur. At this point, the relationship may be severed, particularly among those whose fear reaction is early and intensely self-protective. The sudden change from excitement to despair can be intolerable. Some writers see suicide as both a logical and absurd response to the loss of a love object. The relationship is terminated because of the inability of one or both partners to tolerate the stress involved in continuing or revitalizing the Love Effect. The intensity of negative reaction depends on the degree to which the Love Effect is substantiated or buffered by such factors as mutual interests, affection, harmonious activities, sexual compatibility, and loneliness-reducing experience.

Much depends on the manner in which the Love Effect wanes. By manner we should more specifically say the suddenness or a combination of the suddenness and the kind and number of substitutions for the effect itself. In many ways, the Love Effect is like an addiction. The strong passive-dependent personality needs, common to both substance addiction and the Love Effect, indicate that the symptoms will depend upon the suddenness and intensity of withdrawal. The degree to which the individual has a passive-dependent personality structure will also influence the depth of the Love Effect as well as the intensity of the symptoms on withdrawal.

People talk very much about "falling out of love." In reality, they experience a withdrawal of the necessary components of the Love Effect, and they become aware, suddenly or gradually, that the stimulus source is no longer strong or available. The more acutely aware the individual, the more acute the withdrawal symptoms. Simply stated, it is proposed that the Love Effect is very much like a narcotic or substance addiction. In the presence of the substance, there are feelings of euphoria, worthwhileness, greatness, fullness, richness, capability, action, warmth, tenderness, peace, and the intense feeling of wanting to do something tremendous and being capable of this. By the same token, under conditions where alcohol is withdrawn from the regular drinker or heroin is withdrawn from the hard narcotics user, the sudden withdrawal is followed by depression, somatic symptoms, disorganized thinking, sleeplessness, confusion, searching for substitutions, and sometimes destructive acts. The individual from whom the Love Effect has been withdrawn suffers a similar response.

In long-range relationships, the Love Effect tends to be a more and more occasional experience. Positive, reality-oriented interactions based on sexual experience, warmth exchange, mutual dependency, and other affection ties create a less volatile but more secure interaction. If a marriage contract is established as part of the experience, the economic and social interactions may sustain the relationship during periods when the Love Effect wanes.

The phenomenon of the Love Effect is one of the most powerful of all human experiences. We have no data to support the existence of such an effect in infrahuman species. The response to this effect can be extremely positive or negative. It is originated and engendered by cultural values and conditions under which learning takes place. It is a proper but long-neglected area for study by behavioral scientists.

REFERENCES

Ansbacher, H. L., "Love and Violence in the View of Adler." *Humanitas*, 1966, 2 (2), 109–127.

Ard, B. N., "Love and Aggression." (In *Handbook of Marriage Counseling,* Ard and Ard, eds. 1968.

Bloom, M., "Toward a Developmental Concept of Love." *Journal of Human Relations,* 1967, 15 (2), 246–263.

Boyd, H., "Love Versus Omnipotence: The Narcissistic Dilemma." *Psychotherapy: Theory, Research & Practice,* 1968, 5(4), 272–277.

Buhler, C., "Human Life Goals in the Humanistic Perspective." *Journal of Humanistic Psychology,* 1967, 7(1), 36–52.

Caruso, I. A., "Life and Separation." *Revista de Psicoanalisis, Psiquiatria y Psicologia,* 1967, No. 5, 26–33.

Charny, I. W., "Marital Love and Hate." *Family Process,* 1969, 8(1), 1–24.

Coppinger, R. M., and Rosenblatt, P. C., "Romantic Love and Subsistence Dependence of Spouses." *Southwestern Journal of Anthropology,* 1968, 24(3), 310–319.

Dunnette, M. D., "People Feeling: Joy, More Joy, and the 'Slough of Despond.'" *Journal of Applied Behavioral Science,* 1969, 5(1), 25–44.

Evans, S., "For Love or Money." *Journal of Emotional Education,* 1967, 7(4), 156–158.

Fornari, F., "Notes on the Relationship to the Adolescent Object." *Rivista Di Psicoanalisi,* 1966, 12(1), 49–59.

Fromm, E., "Konrad Lorenz' Theory of Aggressiveness." *Revista De Psicoanalisis, Psiquiatria Y Psicologia,* 1968, No. 9, 5–16.

Goshen, C. E., "A Systematic Classification of the Phenomenology of Emotion." *Psychiatric Quarterly,* 1967, 41(3), 483–495.

Groh, L. A., "Interhemispheric Integration of Identity Relationships." *Psychiatria, Neurologia, Neurochirurgia: Journal of the Netherlands Society of Psychiatry & Neurology,* 1968, 71(2), 185–191.

Groth, N. J., and Holbert, P., "Hierarchical Needs of Gifted Boys and Girls in the Affective Domain." *Gifted Child Quarterly,* 1969, 13(2), 129–133.

Homme, L., Baca, P. D., and Cottingham, L., "What Behavioral Engineering Is." *Psychological Record,* 1968, 18(3), 425–434.

Kephart, W. M., "Some Correlates of Romantic Love." *Journal of Marriage and the Family,* 1967, 29(3), 470–474.

Lindenauer, G., "A Matter of Respect: The Importance of Communicating Love." *Journal of Emotional Education,* 1968, 8(2), 68–75.

Maccoby, M., "War Between the Sexes in a Mexican Rural Community." *Revista De Psicoanalisis, Psiquiatria Y Psicologia,* 1966, No. 4, 54–76.

Martin, A. R., "The Changing Image of Mental Health and Mental Illness." *American Journal of Psychoanalysis,* 1967, 27(1), 13–24.

Masters, F. G., and Tong, J. E., "The Semantic Differential Test with Borstal Subjects." *British Journal of Criminology,* 1968, 8(1), 20–31.

May, R., "The Daemonic: Love and Death." *Psychology Today,* 1968, 1(9), 16–25.

Nataraj, P., "Perception of Love by the Married and Unmarried Women." *Psychology Annual,* 1966–67, 1(1), 68–70.

Niles, E., "The Effectiveness of the Vicarious Sacrifice Unit for First- and Second-graders in Teaching and Understanding the Concepts of Six Key Words." *Character Potential,* 1965, 3(1-2), 45–50.

Rabkin, R., "Affect as a Social Process." *American Journal of Psychiatry,* 1968, 125(6), 773–779.

Sadler, W. A., "Play: A Basic Human Structure Involving Love and Freedom." *Review of Existential Psychology & Psychiatry,* 1966, 6(3), 237–245.

Sappenfield, B., "The Primacy of Narcissism." *Psychological Reports,* 1969, 25(2), 428–430.

Stewart, R. A., "Transcendence of Opposites." *Psychology,* 1969, 6(2), 62–64.

Winnicott, D. W., *International Journal of Psychoanalysis,* 1967, 48(3), 368–372.

13

Melding of Personal and Spiritual Values in Love

Billy B. Sharp

A bashful young Southern man had dated a young woman for quite some time. He was in love with her and wanted to marry her. But every time he tried to propose, he became terribly nervous and the words just wouldn't come out. He tried to say "I love you; will you marry me?" in all kinds of romantic settings—under the stars, under the flowering magnolias, on the living-room sofa, on a moonlit drive—but nothing worked. Finally, in almost complete desperation, he decided to write out an elaborate proposal and read it over the telephone. After several days of concentrated effort he was ready. With great expectation, he dialed his girl friend's telephone number. Just as she answered, a strong gust of wind blew the written proposal from his hands. Almost paralyzed with fright he blurted out: "I love you; will you marry me?" Then came the long-awaited answer: "Yes. Who is this?" The young man felt what he considered to be love, but he could not understand it and the subsequent actions which followed from it.

A young wife, shortly after her marriage, very casually asked her husband, "Why did you marry me?" His response was this: "I decided it was time for me to marry. You were attractive and available." At first, the young wife was disappointed and angry, but later she decided that impulsive action may well be an essential ingredient of love.

Love and Its Ingredients

Just what is love? What are its essential ingredients? There are as many answers to these questions as there are people who love one another, because each person functions with numerous definitions of the term "love." We can arbitrarily say that love has both personal values and religious values, so we have three terms to work with:

1. Love.
2. Personal values.
3. Religious values.

Let's try to create some working definitions and some suggestions as to how the three entities are dynamically related.

Love is probably the most personal act within our lives and the word may well be the most personal symbol within our language. Everyone has his own definition of love and his own feelings about the act or acts which it includes.

The feelings and actions of love are always in constant and continuous flux. They vary as one's assessment of himself and of others changes. For example, simple mortal love might be described as caring for yourself to the extent that you can then also care for others, and then attempting to weave together this caring in meaningful ways to form constructive relationships. ("Love thy neighbor as thy self.") This definition implies that there are internal and external aspects of love and different levels of each. With this definition, one can differentiate between human love and spiritual love, or natural and supranatural love.

The basic difference between the two types of love, theologically speaking, and perhaps psychologically too, is that God does not have to first love himself in order to love other objects. God, as distinguished from humans, apparently does not have to learn how to love. Theologically, this style of love is frequently referred to as *agape*.

The Cycle of Mortal Love

The absolute of spiritual love requires no maturation process; therefore, it remains constant, hopeful, and comforting at all times. Human love, or mortal love, however, is constantly in a state of flux and is directly related to emotional and physical maturation, and personal and societal needs and values. It cycles rather directly but sporadically in an ever-widening circle which includes dilemma, anxiety or tension, resolution, satisfaction, and comfort. This might be called the basic cycle of mortal love—something which requires living and learning.

The maturation process can perhaps be most easily seen if we use a formulation expounded several years ago by Fred Kuether and Herbert Holt.[1] Kuether set forth the idea that there are three distinct levels on which man can order his experience.

The Magic Level

The earliest of the levels is called by Odier the magic level.[2] The basic fact about man on this level is his complete helplessness. He must have someone to feed and clothe him, and many feel that he must also have tender, loving care. Infants exist on this level.

This magical existence conditions a certain psychic phenomenon which must be recognized if emotional development is to be understood. During this period, if an infant has a good mother, his needs will frequently be anticipated and fulfilled. If the needs are not anticipated, the infant can fret or cry and the loving mother will come with the answer to his need. With such repeated need satisfaction, the infant soon learns that he is the center of his universe.

Speaking experimentally, life on this level can be organized around four basic propositions:

1. I am the center of the universe.
2. Mommy and Daddy are here to meet my needs. (They are not people, they are objects.)
3. Everybody is my friend. (Everybody is an object, a source of need satisfaction.)
4. Things will not change.

This level of existence is a very pleasant one for the baby and the mother. If a person could have his wishes fulfilled, he would remain on this level forever. Here the infant is the god of his universe, and a mere cry will get him whatever he wants or needs. Children are reluctant to leave this level of existence, and it becomes a retreat for older children, adolescents, even adults, when conditions—either internal or external—become extremely painful.

Although this magic level is wonderful and satisfying, the human being will eventually, if not blocked by conditions, develop to a level where he realizes that he can do some things for himself, and that his parents are concerned about him. At this point he must give up the absolute dependency of the magic level. He now finds himself in a universe where he can bargain for what he needs, do things for himself, and pay (with dependency) for those things he cannot do for himself—or fall back to the magic level.

Black and White Level

The second level is the black and white level. It is organized on four basic propositions:
1. The world is black and white. (There are no grays. I must stay on the white side.)
2. People are for me or against me.
3. If I stay on the white side, I will win. (I will get what I want.)
4. If I win, things will stay as they are.

This is the level which most people experience a majority of the time. It is the level most characteristic for our present-day society. My three-year-old daughter moved from the magic level to the black and white level recently while we were sitting at the breakfast table. "Daddy, I don't want to be three," she said.

Existential Level

There is another level of living. Kuether has referred to this as the "holistic" or "existential" level of being. The individual progresses gradually from the magic to the black and white level of being when he discovers that he has some individual strength and can do things for himself, and that his parents are concerned about him and that he can bargain with them. There is another discovery man makes when he moves into the existential level of being. This is the discovery that he no longer needs his parents—or any substitute for them—in order to survive. In effect, he separates himself completely from those around him and begins to experience himself as an individual human being. There are only rare moments when man finds himself on the existential level.

Four propositions are basic to living on the existential level:
1. I am myself.
2. You are yourself.
3. We are both human beings.
4. Life is full of constant change.

On this level man accepts himself as he really is, others as they are, and he is aware that constant change is a part of life. He can participate more fully in the happiness and satisfaction of the present because he realizes that things will change very soon. He also can take the frustrations and pain in stride because he knows those too will soon change. He realizes that each state of being has its purpose. He also knows that there is a state of nonbeing, a state completely different from his own living existence. He knows that his body eventually will die. What happens after that he is not able to predict.

Moving from One Level to Another

An individual, as he matures, experiences in each of these levels love at its apex, and only realizes what he is missing when he contacts the next higher level and has satisfying experiences above and beyond what he originally thought possible. This does not imply that a person passes through the first two levels never to return again emotionally. We bounce from one level to another, but when we return to a lower level we then know the enjoyment and satisfaction we are missing from whence we came. We also are experiencing an alienation from a greater value which has been available to us at the higher emotional level. It is at this point in time and emotional space that psychological need separates temporary personal and absolute spiritual values, and we become consciously aware that something of value is missing in our lives. When this happens and we are consciously aware of the emotional void, we are exiologically alienated. In other words, in these times and spaces personal and spiritual values are not melded in love, but are separated by personal needs and choices.

There are any number of reasons why this can happen, but let's just select two and examine them more carefully. At the existential level we love whether or not we receive love in return. This emotional state is difficult to maintain on a constant basis. There are times when to get what we want we must trade off—we must become involved in bargaining and negotiating. When this happens we move back to the second level, or more specifically, to human need, not spiritual love. Perhaps the essence of love when we are standing on such shifting sand as this would be to not feel guilty about our alienated state, but to be responsible to it and committed to changing it. I recently listened to two professionals talk about a consulting arrangement. They were unable to enter this state. They couldn't talk about money. They felt that the "love level" had to be maintained at all cost. Consequently, no change could take place, and no growth, communication, or expanded love was possible.

Another factor which contributes to a movement from higher to lower levels is what might be called a "rightness zone." One of our basic human needs is to be right. If any one of us truly felt on both the conscious and unconscious level that our life-style was wrong, that feeling would be adequate motivation for change. But what happens is that a person is only as flexible as his rightness zone is wide. Once a person's behavior through deliberate process or happenstance extends beyond his rightness zone, he has difficulty accepting objects and actions in the other world and must retire from the existential level where "I am me" and "you are you" to the black and white level where "you are either for me or against me."

Relationships of Personal and Spiritual Values

There are many other reasons why a person moves from a higher level to a lower one, but I think these two are adequate to illustrate my point. I think we can see that the melding of personal and spiritual values in love is an ever-flowing river which involves constant change. At any point where personal needs or values motivate a person to move from a higher level to a lower level of emotional living, the togetherness becomes alienation and the degree of love is lessened in direct proportion to the alienation. But if a higher level of emotional living has never been reached, then the identical life-style would be a melding of spiritual and personal values in love. So the same actions and feelings at one point can be love almost at its essence, and at another point, in theological terms, could be referred to as original sin. Original sin in this sense is not a moral act but a conscious, deliberate *inaction* which by choice alienates one from the spiritual values which he knows (using "knows" in the Hebraic sense, which includes experience) and is unwilling to achieve. On the other hand, a deliberate decision to bridge this gap is a move toward love through melding personal and spiritual values. Another way to say this is that in our circle of love, it is at this point where the resolution of the dilemma is accomplished and a temporary state of comfort and ecstasy is enjoyed.

Nowhere is the maturation of love more beautifully expressed than in I Corinthians 13 (RSV).

If I speak in the tongues of men and of angels, but have not love, I am a noisy gong or a clanging cymbal.

And if I have prophetic powers, and understand all mysteries and all knowledge, and if I have all faith, so as to remove mountains, but have not love, I am nothing.

If I give away all I have, and if I deliver my body to be burned, but have not love, I gain nothing.

Love is patient and kind; love is not jealous or boastful; it is not arrogant or rude. Love does not insist on its own way; it is not irritable or resentful; it does not rejoice at wrong, but rejoices in the right.

Love bears all things, believes all things, hopes all things, endures all things.

Love never ends; as for prophecy, it will pass away; as for tongues, they will cease; as for knowledge, it will pass away.

For our knowledge is imperfect and our prophecy is imperfect; but when the perfect comes, the imperfect will pass away.

When I was a child, I spoke like a child, I thought like a child, I reasoned like a child; when I became a man, I gave up childish ways.

For now we see in a mirror dimly, but then face to face. Now I know in part; then I shall understand fully, even as I have been fully understood.

So faith, hope, love abide, these three; but the greatest of these is love

NOTES

1. Frederick C. Kuether and Herbert Holt, "Levels of Living" (Paper read at IV International Congress of Psychotherapy, Barcelona, Spain, 1959). See also Frederick C. Kuether, "The Images of Man and Their Religious Significance," chapter in *The Ministry and Mental Health*, ed. Hans Hofmann (New York: Association Press, 1960).
2. Charles M. Odier, *Anxiety and Magic Thinking,* translated by Marie-Louise Schoetty and Mary Jane Sherfey (New York: International Universities Press, Inc., 1956).

14

Love and Creativity

Lowell G. Colston

While I was giving thought to the theme of love and creativity, I happened to be driving in my car, listening to music on the radio. By a remarkable coincidence the first tune which I heard after switching on a favorite station was "You're Nobody 'Til Somebody Loves You." The rather striking congruence between the theme of the song and that of my thoughts immediately caught my attention. Despite the triteness of the lyrics and the obviously sentimentally romantic intentions of the lyricist, the song was pointing beyond itself to a basic truth. To put the theme positively: "You become somebody as you love and are loved." Love calls us into being. As a dynamic mass of protoplasm with a myriad of unrealized potentialities, each person is stimulated, prodded, supported —in many ways disciplined—by those who love him to become a person who is, in turn, creative.

Thus, love is the power which creates personal values. More than that, love is the vital and motivating force in the creation of social inventions. Social ethics, for example, is redeemed by love. Interpreting love as an intensely subjective preoccupation with truth, Sören Kierkegaard said: "Purity of heart is to will one thing: the good." [1] For him single-minded devotion to truth and commitment to creating "the good" was the loving thing. No one could conceivably hope to have the best of all possible worlds. Love, for Kierkegaard, then was the disciplined act of deep involvement in what is really worthy of such intense concern. This is the only way any degree of the true essence of the other becomes appropriated. Apart from such absorbing interest, realization of the good is not possible, because truth reveals itself to the "pure in heart."

Joseph Fletcher also makes a case for the creative power of love in his *Situation Ethics.* One of Fletcher's critics has jibed, "Love slithers through his works like a greased pig." Nevertheless, despite the obvious complaint that one cannot get a firm hold on what Fletcher means by love, the underlying assumption is valid. "Love is the only measure," says Fletcher. "This love means, of course, a social attitude, not the romantic emotion that the word has come to connote in popular literature . . . it is a personalist devotion to people, not to things or abstractions such as 'laws' or general principles. Personal interests come first, before the natural or Scriptural or theoretical or general or logical or anything else." [2] This personalist base is regarded as the measure of whether an action is good or not; thus, for Fletcher love for persons becomes the norm for social and ethical behavior. The direction is positive and creatively imaginative rather than negative and reductionistic as moral and legal interpretations of social behavior are seen to be.

Love as a meaningful term has fallen into modern disrepute. Rollo May, in his brilliant treatise on the relationship between love and will, asserts that both of these concepts have become the problems rather than the answers to the predicaments of our day. They have become problems precisely *because* they have been offered in the past as *the* answers to life's struggles and uncertainties.[3] Yet disputes as to what was really loving and what was appropriately willing have raged to the point of a confusing din. For example, love has been such an elusive will-o'-the-wisp to people who have based their worthiness on whether or not they have achieved it that it has become sadly disillusioning. To some the word "love" has been regarded as a deceptive façade for a subtly controlling and manipulating force employed by the clever or the more powerful. To others love has seemed a disheartening illusion attained by "story" people who do not actually exist, but are the figments of fictionists' imaginations. Yet, May declares, love remains the decisive force in all personal and social relationships, and he seeks to restore its central meaning.[4]

Love and will may tend to block each other. When will reigns, the tender feelings may be lost. A man whose son was arrested for participating with a gang in a destructive act of vandalism was not only terribly embarrassed, but deeply chagrined about his son's behavior. When he visited the youth in the local juvenile detention center, he expressed considerable surprise and puzzlement. After reviewing his hopes and plans for his son, he asked earnestly, "What do you want, son?" The boy answered quickly, biting his lip to control his feelings, "You, Dad." The chastened father put his arms around the boy and silently nodded his head in stunned recognition of his son's meaning.

On the other hand, love may block will. In the hippie movement, for example, love is regarded as indiscriminate. Rollo May rightfully sees the attitude displayed as a reaction against the manipulative will of the previous generation. The "immediacy, spontaneity, and honesty" in relationships are emphasized as implied indictments of the manipulative love and sex of bourgeois culture.[5] However, love requires encounter of person with person, spirit with spirit, in depth over a period of time.

Conflict is inevitable in such depth encounters. Creativity and growth are generated by the self-revelation coming out of conflict. One encounters the other in conflict so both experience potential creative transformation. However, such encounter is an act of choice and will in a responsible relationship. One must "care" what happens to the other and be deeply affected by that happening. Not to know anyone intimately in depth is really not to know anyone! To know one in depth involves commitment to him in the exercising of choice and will in a responsible relationship. Furthermore to know another in depth is to experience conflict out of which the growth potential of each is in some sense actualized.

Now that we have introduced a few notions regarding the meaning of love, we need also to be more specific about creativity. *Creativity is the process of assimilating, testing, organizing, and giving structure to what is exploding into consciousness.* Carl Rogers offers this definition: "My definition of the creative process is that it is the emergence in action of a novel relational product, growing out of the uniqueness of the individual on the one hand and the materials, events, people or circumstances of his life on the other."[6] Abraham Maslow says: Creativity in self-actualizing people is "openness to experience, more spontaneous and expressive, relatively unfrightened by the unknown dichotomies resolved into unities, relative absence of fear, greater wholeness and integration, self-acceptance."[7]

Harold H. Anderson has observed: "Creativity, the emergence of originals and individuality is found in every living cell. . . . We are just beginning to think of individual differences in a moving, changing, progressing, interacting way—a way we are beginning to call dynamic. . . .

In children creativity is universal. Among adults it is almost nonexistent. The great question is: What has happened to this enormous and universal human resource?" [8]

One possible answer is: It has been dammed up by the constricting devices of a technological culture, which is depersonalizing and dehumanizing in its net effect.

Arnold Toynbee has said: "Potential creative behavior can be stifled, stunted, and stultified by the prevalence in society of adverse attitudes of mind and habits of behavior." [9] I submit that such adverse attitudes are generated by resentment and hate. "Adverse habits of behavior" are the direct output of resentment.

Empirical studies tend to verify the thesis presented here: Love generates creativity. J. H. McPherson, in a study of the effect of environment on creativity, found: "A scientist's creativity is the result of a fortunate combination of intellectual characteristics, emotional dispositions and *a climate that is favorable for him.*" [10] (italics mine) The relevance of the findings of the above-quoted study for discerning the relationship between love and creativity is clearly evident in the conclusion the researcher drew: "A scientist who is able to use the major mental factors effectively, and who is problem-centered, spontaneous, and independent may thrive in a supportive and stimulating environment, but flounder in a hostile climate." [11] Here we see an empirical documentation of what Toynbee had postulated in a philosophical vein; potential creativity can be shut off in a hostile and destructive environment. In a situation of basic mistrust, parents of children, and vice versa, employers of employees, etc., creativity in any of its possible dimensions does not flourish. Love, which includes faith and trust, creates the climate conducive to creative endeavor.

Writing on the nature of creativity, Rollo May further elaborates on the theme: "Actual creativity I define as the process of bringing something new into birth. Creative persons are the ones who enlarge human consciousness. . . . Creativity is the encounter of the intensely conscious human being with his world." [12] Creativity is the encounter and engagement with the other at such depth and significance as to expand and stretch the personal consciousness of both. A creative transformation takes place in both so that they do indeed become new creatures.

Wellsprings for Creativity: Parental and Family Love

One striking conclusion that may be drawn from Walter de la Mare's collection of the early memories of men who had become regarded as performing creative acts was that most of them had intimate and stimulating relationships with their mothers.[13] The mother-child relationship seemed to be the spark that set fire to their imagination and probably effectively set boundaries for explorations which forestalled endless frittering.

For one notable example, Sigmund Freud's relationship with his mother is cited in Ernest Jones' classic biographical study of the famous psychoanalyst. The story was told that once in a pastry shop an old woman had encountered Freud's mother shortly after the birth of Sigmund, saying that she had brought a great man into the world. The proud and happy mother was impressed with the prediction and firmly believed it. "Another effect of the mother's pride and love for her firstborn," says Jones, "left a more intense, indeed indelible impression on the growing boy. As he wrote later: 'A man who has been the indisputable favorite of his mother keeps for life the feeling of a conqueror, that confidence of success that often induces real success.' This self-confidence, which was one of Freud's promising characteristics, was only rarely impaired, and he was doubtless right in tracing it to the security of his mother's love." [14]

Freud's creative genius undoubtedly was nurtured in a relationship which he himself drew upon to understand what he was later to describe as the Oedipal phenomenon. He attributed the development of his "sentimentality," which his biographer, Jones, interprets as passionate temperament, to his mother, who represented to him the "pleasure principle." She gave him the security to be the imaginative, sensitive, freethinking person which he became. His father represented to him the "reality principle." Although he was also described as kindly, affectionate and tolerant, he was recognized by Sigmund as being just and objective.

Creativity depends upon the development of sensitivity and the capacity for objectivity and organization. It is surely not unreasonable to assume that these facets are inextricably bound together in a decisively crucial interaction.

Insights of varying degrees of significance in all areas of life break into our consciousness with surprising force and brilliance at times. Undoubtedly we can say that they depend heavily upon an encouraging environment, wherein the child's sensitivities are given warm support. On the other hand, we can say that a "growth hindering" can occur when a cold, unloving mother or weak, ineffective father leaves the child floundering and unable to differentiate what he is experiencing. Some kind of innate struggle often keeps him from failing completely but usually does not save him from serious impoverishment. True, whatever frustration the child encounters may irk, goad, or inspire him to greater effort. However, fulfillment rather than frustration helps him become differentiating as to what is effective and what is not. He becomes wise— that is, truly discerning—only as he can assimilate what he may potentially learn from both his defeats and his victories.

In a study of "personal soundness in graduate students" which was a segment of a survey of creativity and psychological health, a charting of life-history factors associated with soundness was given. Unsoundness is seen to be inhibitory to creativity, soundness as conducive to creativity. Among seven factors which were considered as indicating the chief differences in life history between subjects rated high on personal soundness and those rated low were "image of the father as a respected, successful person," "affection and close attention from the mother," "presence of other siblings and positive relations with them," and "sexual expression."

> Many of the High subjects were closely controlled at home; but the general picture was of a mother who was loving without being seductive, and solicitous without being demanding or overprotective. Or perhaps it would be more correct to stress the fact the mothers of low subjects *were* generally reported as seductive and demanding.[15]

The subjects which were rated high tended to be able to make a responsible break with the family circle after their graduation from high school. Those who were low had difficulty making the break, and many remained dependent, especially on the mother.

The relationships with siblings, which form a part of the prototype for later relationships with others in the community, was friendly among the subjects rated high. Thus, these subjects learned role taking in the family which set patterns for creative interaction in the community. The students rated low in personal soundness had fewer positive and more frequently distorted relationships with siblings, consequently they tended to be ill at ease or defensive with peers in the community. Their patterns of behavior were thus more compulsive and lacking freedom and spontaneity. In sexual expression, both highly rated and low rated subjects seemed to be slow in achieving sexual expression with other people. However, the Highs differed sharply from the Lows in the capacity for forming enduring sexual relationships with women. Ninety per cent of those rated high compared to 45 per cent of those rated low had established enduring sexual relationships. Many of the Highs reported difficulty in sexual adjustment during the first year of marriage but they also reported they were able to solve the problem and stabilize their relationships. On the other hand, a number of the Lows were either homosexual or sexually quiescent.

The researchers concluded from the study as a whole: *"Soundness is a way of reacting to problems, not an absence of them."* I would add: A "sound" way of reacting to problems is prerequisite to creativity. Intelligent love frees a person to use his intelligence.

In relation to intellectual tasks, for example, there are two ways data reaching personal consciousness can be handled: (1) they can be given structures and formulated into plans or concrete entities or (2) they can, through fear, be rejected and blocked from contact with other data which have already been appropriated, a profound emotional blockage may prevent material from reaching consciousness at all.

On the whole the study just quoted tends to validate the thesis: Parental and family love—which includes engagement in depth encounter, encouragement of responsibility, strong and dependable models for identification, supporting and accepting attitudes, giving expressive leadership, etc.—creates an environment which stimulates and facilitates creativity. "We can speak, therefore, of the development of a personality 'slanted' toward creativeness and maintaining this slant—and slanting more and more determinedly—unless pushed violently back into some other slant through adverse circumstances." [16] The "slanting" favorable to creativity occurs in early stages of development as the child is learning to create and inevitably takes place in a total personal and social context. The child may learn to create from parent surrogates rather than natural parents, but his creativity will thrive in a total climate of love which actually motivates him to actualize his potentialities.

Love as a Stimulus to Personal Greatness

Encounters which expand personal consciousness open us up to our potential for creativity. The willingness to act on the ideas which emerge from such encounters and the courage to risk the consequences of the action are factors which contribute to personal greatness. Greatness is not in popularity but in singularity, when singularity means the originality and uniqueness of a creative life-style. How can we describe such a life-style? Various phrases have been used: the capacity to be puzzled, awareness, spontaneity, flexibility, openness to new experience, no boundaries, divergent thinking even sometimes foolishness, yielding, abandoning, letting go, being born every day, discarding the irrelevant, ability to toy with elements, change of activity, hard work, composition, decomposition, recomposition, change of pace, integration, being at peace with the world, harmony, honesty, humility, good sense of humor, integrity, inner maturity, skepticism, courage, boldness, faith, willingness to be alone. Perhaps numerous other phrases could be added to the list. Yet all of these require love which provides security amidst insecurities, to enable the person to tolerate temporary chaos; gives consistency to the person, in the face of many incongruities; and lends meaning to his existence, which is the critical factor, enabling him to tolerate ambiguities.

Although a number of Abraham Lincoln's biographers tend to cast aspersions on the character of the love which Mary Todd held for her "man of the ages," no one can doubt the tremendous influence both she and his stepmother, Sarah Bush Lincoln, had upon his life. Her discreditors saw Mary Todd as a hot-tempered, ambitious, shrewish, social climber who used Lincoln to get what she wanted. Others, especially the Edwards', her sister's husband and in-laws, regarded her ambitions as a mark of her strong character. Carl Sandburg notes, for example:

> In the Edwards' circle they believed there were clues to her character in a remark she passed at a fireside party one evening. A young woman married to a rich man along in years was asked, "Why did you marry such a withered-up old buck?" and answered, "He had lots of houses and gold." And the quick-tongued Mary Todd in surprise: "Is that true? I would rather marry a good man, a man of mind, with a hope and bright prospects ahead for position, fame, and power than to marry all the houses, gold, and bones in the world." [17]

Whether or not the story was apocryphal, it was passed along as true by the Edwards family as typical of the woman who was to become the wife of Abraham Lincoln.

One biographer of Abraham Lincoln depicted his wife Mary Todd as an outspokenly critical woman who pushed and cajoled Lincoln to attain the honor and social position she really wanted for herself. Another speculated if Lincoln had married Ann Rutledge he probably would have experienced more personal happiness in his marriage but indisputably at the price of his great creative impact upon history. Perhaps all of this is idle speculation. The fact is Lincoln *did* marry Mary Todd and she *did* become a driving force to his career.

Sandburg tells of a conversation in a railroad boxcar between Lincoln and Henry Villard, a newspaper reporter. They had crawled into the boxcar to get out of a thunderstorm, and, amused by the ludicrous picture of himself sitting awkwardly huddled with Villard at his side, Lincoln "rambled on" about becoming U. S. Senator. "I am convinced that I am good enough for it," Sandburg quotes him as saying, "but, in spite of it all, I am saying to myself every day: 'It is too big a thing for you; you will never get it.' Mary (Mrs. Lincoln) insists, however, that I am going to be Senator and President of the United States, too." [18] Then apparently extremely amused at the incongruity of the present situation and the commanding position of the White House, he roared with laughter, and choked out the improbability of it, "Just think of such a sucker as me as President!" Yet, it was to happen! And immediately after his election, he paid homage to his wife by saying to her jubilantly, "Mary, we're elected." Whether her ambitions for him were born out of *eros* or *agape,* they were interrelated in what must be called creative love. His expanding consciousness unbelievably to him eventually included the world and history and the realization of a manifest destiny.

Not everyone can achieve the personal greatness of an Abraham Lincoln, obviously. The rare person whose charisma and the kairos come into conjunction—whose personal gifts of intelligence, leadership, etc. are available at the right moment in history—of course achieves a level of creativity hardly possible for most people. However, my purpose here has been not so much to create a hero image who is to be emulated as a model of creativity but to show how he recognized (and I underscore) that in great measure he was also fulfilling the hopes and faith of Mary Todd, who believed in him from the time of their earliest meeting. Who knows what he may have become, teamed with a woman of lesser drive and social ambition than Mary Todd Lincoln?

The kairos or the right time for the creative act to occur presupposes a climate of acceptance of the creative spirit at work. This means the effective acts of creation are the work not only of the one who initiates but also those who respond. "If the people have no vision the prophet's genius, through no fault of the prophet's own, will be as barren as the talent that was wrapped in a napkin and was buried in the earth. This means, in turn, that the people, as well as the prophet have a responsible part to play. If it is incumbent on the prophet to deliver his message it is no less incumbent on the people not to turn a deaf ear. It is even more incumbent on them not to make the spiritual climate of their society so adverse to creativity that the life will have been crushed out of the prophet's potential mesage before he has had a chance of delivering it." [19] One way to protect the status quo, thus sanctioning the mediocrity and spiritual degeneracy of a culture, is to squelch and stifle any outburst of creativity. Conversely, the way to give vitality, freshness, and spark to a culture is to heed and ponder the prophet's message. In fact as Toynbee insists, "to give a fair chance to potential creativity is a matter of life and death for any society. This is all-important, because the outstanding creative ability of a fairly small percentage of the population is mankind's ultimate capital asset, and the only one with which Man has been endowed." [20]

The people see the prophet's life as an extension of their own and as giving articulation to their hopes. However, if they do not really hear, they rise up and slay their prophets before their message is really understood. A culture then degenerates and literally dies of its own hand. The love and acceptance of the people are required for the prophet to perform his creative action.

Love as the Impetus to Creativity in Relationships

Love is creative in the sense that love is the force or power which underlies what we intend to make happen. Rollo May says love and will are interrelated and are interdependent in efficacy. He shows how love and will can block each other. Will can be manipulative; love can be generalized and dissociating. They function together to plumb the depths and meaning of interpersonal relationships.

Quoting James Baldwin's prophetic hope for effective transformations in race relations through a new consciousness, May says: "Both love and will are ways of creating consciousness in others. To be sure, each may be abused: love may be used as a way of clinging, and will as a way of manipulating others in order to enforce a compliance." [21] Nevertheless, the expression of love is a way of producing change in others, of expanding and deepening consciousness in ourselves and others.

A woman in her early forties sought counseling because she suspected that her husband was "having an affair" with a younger woman. She insisted on "checking out" her suspicions because, on the one hand, she believed she "really didn't want to know the truth," but, on the other, she had never doubted the soundness of their, then, twenty-year marriage. When her husband finally confessed to her that her suspicions were, in fact, true, she was crushed. Following the counseling session in which she reported her husband's confrontation, she spent the whole night talking with him. "I simply was not conscious of him in many ways," she acknowledged at a subsequent counseling session. "I can see now that our life together has been rather dull and unimaginative. We did the same old things and followed the same old patterns for years. Not that I am happy about what happened but I have learned a lot about myself and about him." "How can people be so insensitive?" she continued in condemnation of her former state of unconscious behavior. "The only thing which makes me mad about him is that he would let me be that way. Why couldn't he tell me before how he felt about the humdrum life we were living? I thought he was satisfied. Then along comes this gal and she gets him interested in a lot of different things. I am interested in those things, too, but I didn't think he was. At any rate, we have developed a new appreciation for each other and I think we are breaking out of the rut." This is an indication of how a pattern of clinging dependent and manipulating relationships between two married people was being changed. They were beginning to create a new consciousness in each other. The task remaining would be arduous. Not all evidences of the clinging character of their love would be removed. But their awareness of each other and of the increased consciousness in both was evident.

Helmut Thielicke speaks of the creative power of love as *agape:* "Agape is not a response to 'loveworthiness' which is already there; it is rather the creative cause what produces this 'loveworthiness.' " [22] Using the analogy of the photographer's art in employing catalysts to bring the picture into view, Thielicke describes a similar effect of the lover on his beloved. Whether or not the analogy does justice to the complex process of calling the other into being, it illustrates the creativity in love as intentionality. The development of the capacity to perceive possibilities and to reach out to remake, to form and re-form, not as manipulation—to make what is there what I want it to be—but as creation to bring out what is there to become what potentially it is.

The real being of a person is always being brought into existence by the people who love him. Furthermore the value of a person is at a very different level from his useful value. Consequently, a marriage does not cease to exist when the other person is no longer important. Love discerns abiding qualities in the other that no utilitarian norms can either validate or invalidate. A person appropriates this meaning of love only if he allows himself to penetrate to the depth of the other's essence in unconditioned self-giving.

The Creation story in the Old Testament symbolizes God's action, in love, of giving formal structure, power, and vitality to transform the chaos into a universe with infinite creative possibilities. Men of faith see this continuing activity as the hope of man in creative transformation and renewal of the systems he creates and which, in a real sense, create him.

Dietrich Bonhoeffer has given expression to what he believed the New Testament to be saying regarding creative love. He put it in terms of what he called "concrete formation." What was meant, Bonhoeffer affirmed, was not the act of forming ourselves, or setting up programs, plans, policies, etc. to shape the world, but the act of God's love becoming incarnate in our midst. Love which is embodied in interpersonal relationships is generated by our responsiveness to God's initiative. Our responsiveness to love creates love within us, and opens us to the creative possibilities which we, in turn, form concretely in our own being. At the same time as we offer ourselves in love to our neighbor, we call him to authentic humanity. "Now there is no more pretence," says Bonhoeffer, "no more hypocrisy, or self-violence, no more compulsion to be something other better and more ideal than what one is. God loves the real man." [23] In the assurance of that love, the "real" man engages in creative acts. He is called and he calls others into being. Love is the originating power of creativity and finds its fulfillment in what man actually *does* for man.

NOTES

1. Sören Kierkegaard, "Purity of Heart," in Robert Bretall (ed.), *A Kierkegaard Anthology* (Princeton: Princeton University Press, 1951), p. 271.
2. Joseph Fletcher, *Moral Responsibility* (Philadelphia: Westminster Press, 1967), p. 34.
3. Rollo May, *Love and Will* (New York: W. W. Norton and Co., 1969), p. 13.
4. *Ibid.*, p. 16.
5. *Ibid.*, p. 278.

6. Carl R. Rogers, "Toward a Theory of Creativity," in Harold H. Anderson (ed.), *Creativity and Its Cultivation* (New York: Harper and Bros., 1959), p. 70.
7. Abraham Maslow, "Creativity in Self-Actualizing People," in *Creativity and Its Cultivation,* p. 85.
8. Harold H. Anderson, *Creativity and Its Cultivation* (New York: Harper and Bros., 1959), p. xii.
9. Arnold Toynbee, "Is America Neglecting her Creative Minority?" in *Widening Horizons in Creativity,* ed. by Calvin W. Taylor (New York: John Wiley and Sons, 1964), p. 3.
10. J. H. McPherson, "Environment and Training for Creativity," in C. W. Taylor, *Creativity: Progress and Potential* (New York: McGraw Hill Book Co., 1964), p. 130.
11. *Ibid.*
12. Rollo May, "The Nature of Creativity," in *Creativity and Its Cultivation,* pp. 57, 68.
13. Walter de la Mare, *Early One Morning in the Spring* (London: Faber and Faber, 1935).
14. Ernest Jones, *The Life and Work of Sigmund Freud* (New York: Doubleday and Company, Inc., 1963), p. 6.
15. Frank Barron, *Creativity and Psychological Health* (Princeton: D. Van Nostrand Co., Inc., 1963), p. 60.
16. Gardner Murphy, *Human Potentialities* (New York: Basic Books, Inc., 1958), p. 141.
17. Carl Sandburg, *Abraham Lincoln* (New York: Harcourt, Brace and Company, one-volume edition, 1954), pp. 69, 70.
18. *Ibid.,* p. 143.
19. Arnold Toynbee, "Is America Neglecting Her Creative Minority?" in *Widening Horizons in Creativity,* ed. by Calvin W. Taylor (New York: John Wiley and Sons, 1964), p. 3.
20. *Ibid.*
21. Rollo May, *Love and Will* (New York: W. W. Norton and Company, Inc., 1969), p. 309.
22. Helmut Thielicke, *The Ethics of Sex* (New York: Harper & Row, 1964), p. 32.
23. Dietrich Bonhoeffer, *Prisoner for God,* ed. by Eberhard Bethge, translated by Reginald Fuller (New York: Macmillan Co., 1954), pp. 148 ff.

15

Love, the Human Encounter

Everett L. Shostrom

Introduction

There is nothing in life that is so important as love, yet psychology has paid little attention to this vital area of human concern. As Maslow has said, "Particularly strange is the silence of the psychologists. Sometimes this is merely sad or irritating, as in the case of the textbooks of psychology and sociology, practically none of which treat the subject. . . . More often the situation becomes completely ludicrous. [As a rule] the word 'love' is not even indexed [in psychological and sociological works]." (1954)

I suggest that the reason that the field of psychology has been silent on love has been the inability to give to this subject any sense of scientific respectability and clarity. This paper attempts to begin the task.

Love as Encounter

In this paper, I hypothecate that love in its experiential sense may best be defined as *authentic human encounter*. The human encounter is defined as two persons *grasping* each other in emotional *contact,* having genuine mutual *concern* for the welfare and fulfillment of each other, and experiencing each other with attitudes of honesty, awareness, freedom, and trust.

Love defined as encounter may be placed in a frame of reference in which there are three elements: Self, Other, and Context. Love, it is posited, exists only when (1) *all three* of these elements are present,

(2) when none of these elements are *distorted,* and (3) when there is awareness of all three elements in the *here and now.*

In this paper, I wish to discuss the nature of love as the experiential human encounter and then to discuss in detail the means by which distortion of this human encounter may take place. Finally, I wish to discuss love developmentally showing how distortions may occur in the various stages of growing up.

Means of Distorting the Encounter

Three means by which love may be distorted are by transference, denial, and projection.

Transference is defined as the *distortion* of encounter. An example is in the therapeutic situation when a patient sees a therapist as a father figure, a brain washer, a devil or a judge. Here it is possible he is distorting the here-and-now reality of a genuine encounter with projections from the past. Likewise, if the therapist sees the patient only as a therapeutic label, as a schizophrenic, an obsessive, an anxiety neurotic, he also is distorting or oversimplifying the patient, and real encounter is lost.

Denial is a second means by which distortion of the human encounter takes place. By denial we mean the refusal to admit the three essential elements of the encounter: the Self, the Other, or the Context. If one denies that *he* is "being there" in the moment, if he denies the *other's* "being there" or if he denies the reality of the situation, encounter is not present.

Examples are:

1. Denial of self: Refusal to believe the truth of one's own deepest feelings and expressing instead a socially acceptable comment. Ex.: Saying, "I *like* you," when one really feels *dislike.*
2. Denial of the other. Ex.: "You don't understand." "You can't mean that."
3. Denial of the situation or the "now." Ex.: You always make fun of me (reference to past). You will think I am silly (reference to future).

When denial is not present, one is really "there" and confronts the other. The following are examples of actualizing encounter:

1. Self: "I really am *afraid* now—I feel it deep inside me."
2. Other: "I really like you. I mean that!"

3. Situation in context: "I really am aware of what's going on now. We are saying good-bye to each other!"

All emotions contribute to encounter, whether positive or negative. A special form of denial most commonly seen is that of hostility. By hostility I mean an attitude of negativity which makes no contact with the other. Sarcasm or the "silent treatment" are examples. Anger, on the other hand, is a *contact emotion,* since it is mixed with caring, it makes a direct encounter, blocking the barrier between the two persons involved.

A third means by which distortion of the encounter develops is through the mechanism of *projection.* Projection may be negative in the sense that it is a form of transferring negative dimensions of the self onto another. This is commonly understood. Less commonly understood, however, is projection of a "positive" nature. This occurs when one projects or gives the other the power that really exists in oneself. For example, to give another in an encounter the power of "teacher," "judge," or "wise one," is to give away one's own worth or ability. Thus, encounter is not *mutual* and it is therefore distorted.

Developmental Deficiencies in Loving

It is hypothesized that love can be seen in a developmental context and that given sufficient love in various stages of growth, one can then encounter adequately as a mature adult. The distortions of the encounter, however, are also usually learned in these stages of growth. Four stages of growth in loving are proposed:

1. *Affection* (Ages 1–6)

Affection is a helping, nurturing form of love. It involves the unconditional giving or *agape* type of love that characterizes the love of a parent for a child. It is hypothesized that affection is learned during the first six years of one's life, and that the quality of affection one receives during this period from one's parents in part determines the degree to which one can be affectionate later on in life.

2. *Friendship* (Ages 6–12)

Friendship is defined as a peer love based on a common interest and respect for each other's equality. Friendship is a love which has a "chosen quality." Friendship first develops between the ages of six and twelve, prior to adolescence, and is usually strongest between members of the same sex. Little boys like little boys, and little girls like little girls. In love and marriage, friendship means doing things together, sharing common interests, recognizing each other's uniqueness and individuality.

3. *Eros* (Ages 13–21)

Eros is the romantic form of love which includes factors such as inquisitiveness, jealousy, and exclusiveness as well as sexual or pure carnal desire. Eros first develops during the teen years when sexual maturity begins. In our culture, often the basis for selecting a mate is "romantic love," an experience of strong elation in which the individual feels "this is it."

4. *Empathy* (Ages 21 +)

Empathy is a charitable altruistic form of love which is expressed by a deep feeling for another person and a unique human being. It involves compassion, appreciation, and tolerance. The capacity to be truly empathic requires maturity and this capacity increases with age.

It is posited that given inappropriate training or trauma in any of these stages of growth, a person would develop distortions in the ability to love in an authentic manner as an adult. Transferences, denials and projections would distort such ability to love.

Mate Selection

I would now like to turn to a special form of encounter which takes place, usually between the ages of eighteen and twenty-five. These are the "mate selection" years, when love and mate selection become temporarily synonymous.

Complementary Pairs

Winch (1953) in his research has shown that most "attraction" is based on mutual need fulfillment. He concludes that "it is more fruitful to conceptualize lovers as being distributed along a continuum of exploitativeness" (p. 100). Others have had similar ideas about love and

THE MANIPULATIVE PAIRS

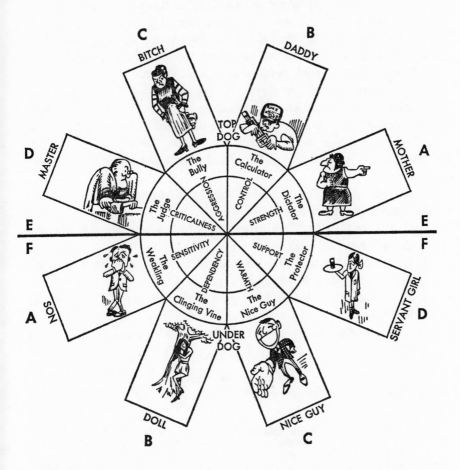

From *Man the Manipulator, The Inner Journey from Manipulation to Actualization,*
copyright Everett L. Shostrom, Ph.D., Abingdon Press, New York & Nashville, 1967.

complementariness. Freud distinguished between "narcissistic" and "anaclitic" love. One who loves narcissistically chooses a love object who corresponds to himself, what he once was like or wishes he could be. The anaclitic lover seeks a person who can tend or protect him. Jung suggests that introverts are attracted to extroverts. Mittelmann also writes about reciprocal patterns in marriage (1956).

All of the above led the writer to be impressed with the fact that love and manipulative patterns are very closely related. Thus, in relating the four basic types of pairings found in Winch's research to my own manipulative types, I found that they were very much parallel. The result may be pictured in a figure in which it will be noted that there are four basic complementary love pairings. They are described as follows:

A. Pattern A is the "Freudian Pair" where there is an anaclitic relationship of a protective and dominating wife and a weak and passive son.

B. Pattern B is the "Ibsenian Pair" of a strong calculating daddy-husband and a passive, doll-like wife.

C. Pattern C is the "Thurberian Pair" of a bitchy, aggressive wife and a nice-guy humble, weak man.

D. Pattern D is the "Shavian Pair" of a Pygmalion-type master and a servant-girl wife who serves his every need.

It will be noted that each of these basic patterns of "manipulative pairs" have roots in the writings of Freud, Ibsen, Thurber, and Shaw. A more detailed description of characteristics of each of these pairs follows.

THE COMPLEMENTARY PAIRS

A. "Freudian Pair"

MOTHER	SON
— 1. May appear more intelligent than him. A DICTATOR.	— 1. Likes her to "stick up for him." A WEAKLING
— 2. Plays dominant parent role.	— 2. Plays *submissive*, compliant son.
— 3. Plays nurturant role, cares for him, provides wants, gives service.	— 3. A passive, *receptive* little boy.
— 4. Is tense, active, CONNIVING with him.	— 4. Plays IRRELEVANT or WITHDRAWS.
— 5. Appears to need to "save" weaker "son."	— 5. Feels strong woman has what he lacks.
— 6. Projects aggressive and sexual impulses onto "son" and "controls" him.	— 6. She blows up and he "sits and takes it."
— 7. Feels "motherly" and may select younger man to "help."	— 7. Looks to her for orientation, guidance, direction.

— 8. Dominates him on an asexual basis—on my good nature.

— 9. Was more likely closer emotionally to father, who was stronger than passive mother.

— 10. Primary feeling expressed is HOSTILITY.

— 8. May seek "playmates" for purely sexual relationships but remains devoted to stolid wife.

— 9. More likely had a passive father, with whom he identifies.

— 10. Primary feeling expressed is APOLOGIZING.

B. "Ibsenian Pair"

DADDY

— 1. A "CALCULATOR" who does thinking for both of them.

— 2. Is *dominant;* likes her to lean on him.

— 3. A protective, *nuturant* parent.

— 4. Is controlled with little spontaneity. CONNIVING.

— 5. Is "mothering" and wants to care for her the way he was cared for.

— 6. Is controlling and molding. A Pygmalion.

— 7. Advises and directs wife on all matters.

— 8. Sex is an expression of power— he is a "knight-hero" with romantic illusions.

— 9. More likely also had a "master" father whom he could never please.

— 10. Primary feeling expressed is DEMANDING.

DOLL

— 1. Is tearful when left alone; a CLINGING VINE.

— 2. Is *submissive,* passive dependent little girl.

— 3. Is *receptive;* sees husband as protector and provider.

— 4. To get her way, WITHDRAWS and uses crying.

— 5. Has strong need to be taken care of; little domestic skill.

— 6. Says, in effect, "Treat me with gentle care; I am so brittle and fragile."

— 7. Often interested in material possessions.

— 8. Surrenders to being possessed by him sexually.

— 9. More likely a product of a marriage where she dreamed of being to father what mother was not.

— 10. Primary feeling expressed is SUBMISSION.

C. "Thurberian Pair"

BITCH

— 1. Is *dominant,* expressive, decisive. A BITCH.

— 2. Has receptive need for his and others' attention.

— 3. Is energetic, frank, openly displays feelings, BLAMING.

— 4. Sees self as "enthusiastic."

— 5. My father is often my model; I may not be sure of my femininity.

— 6. Loves to fight, argue, and angers easily.

— 7. Uses love conditionally to reward or punish.

NICE GUY

— 1. Is submissive NICE GUY.

— 2. A beloved jellyfish who *nurtures* her need for assertiveness.

— 3. Is "humble," PLEASING and PLACATING.

— 4. Appears fearful, hurt and dislikes anger.

— 5. After being pushed, may reactively respond, but ineffectually.

— 6. Derives vicarious satisfaction from watching her "blow off."

— 7. May become a "Don Juan" with a few drinks.

— 8. Aggressively demands sex, saying, "Be a man so I can be a woman."

— 9. Identifies with mother who was assertive and dominant, but had close bond to father which she had to deny.

— 10. Primary feeling expressed is CRITICISM.

— 8. A Good Boy who does his sexual duties by her.

— 9. Learned from his own father the model of being "nice." Survival meant submission.

— 10. Primary feeling expressed is WARMTH.

D. "Shavian Pair"

MASTER

— 1. Is JUDGE: self-assured, somewhat frosty and BLAMING.

— 2. *Dominant,* more intelligent, more informed.

— 3. At a deep level is dependent, *receptive* person.

— 4. A master expecting and demanding service.

— 5. Sees women as subordinate and role of wife as inferior.

— 6. He is a Pygmalion and at work to "improve" her.

— 7. Likes culture, money, books, plays, music, power.

— 8. A king and a firm disciplinarian in sexual matters.

— 9. Was, as a child, dominated by "Germanic" father and strong mother who was "possessed" by father.

— 10. Primary feeling expressed is DOMINANCE.

SERVANT

— 1. Plays PROTECTOR when his covert dependence and weakness appears.

— 2. Is *submissive,* may have humbler origin, less "academic."

— 3. *Nurtures* his dependence while remaining servile.

— 4. A very capable person, capable of making her own way.

— 5. Often chooses "helping" profession like nursing, a PLEASER and PLACATER.

— 6. Has energy, zeal, resourcefulness to render him personal service.

— 7. May be "more mature" than husband.

— 8. Sometimes feels like a "prostitute" or sex object for his need.

— 9. Usually the product of submissive father and aggressive mother. He is the "strong father" she never had.

— 10. Primary feeling expressed is PLEASING.

Symmetrical Pairs

In addition to pairings which may be described as "opposites attracting" and therefore are complementary, other researchers, especially Watzlawick, Beavin, and Jackson (1967) have stressed that other relationships develop because of their dynamic symmetry. That is, these authors stress that such partners mirror each other's behavior, and their interaction may be termed "symmetrical."

In our research, such symmetrical love pairings may be described as follows:

E. Pattern E is the "Albeeian Pair" of two strong persons, one of whom is usually a blamer and attacker, the other a conniver and controller. This is the "Top Dog Pair" and combines any pair above the center black line. The terminology comes from the writings of Edward Albee and his classical work *Who's Afraid of Virginia Woolf*. In this play, George and Martha both play an "escalating symmetrical game" with each other.

F. Pattern F is the "Lewisinian Pair" of two passive persons, one of whom is usually an avoider or constrictor, the other of whom is a pleaser and placater. This is the "Underdog Pair" and combines any pair below the center black line. The term comes from the writings of C. S. Lewis who in his *Screwtape Letters* satirically reminds us of the dangers of relationships in which we mutually try to please and cater to each other.

Actualizing Pairs

The writings of Maslow and others leads us to conceptualize Pattern G which we describe as the "Actualizing Pair." An examination of the items which contribute to this pairing shows a mutual respect for and an appreciation of one another. Also, each person in the pair is *both* active and passive, *both* strong and weak, *both* assertive and loving.

A more detailed description of the Symmetrical and Actualizing Pairs follows.

All of the items listed as belonging to the Complementary and Symmetrical Pairs are now being combined and standardized into a test to measure complementarity, symmetry and actualization in couple relationships. It is hoped that when this research is complete, we will have a measure of the degree of manipulative and actualizing dimensions involved in most love relationships today. This test is tentatively called the MATE (*M*utual *A*ssessment of a *T*wo-Person *E*ncounter).

A second test which measures the extent of distortions in love as encounter is the CRI (Caring Relationship Inventory). This test has been published (1966) and measures love in terms of the developmental stages described previously in this paper.

It is hoped that these two instruments are beginnings in the search to make the area of love a respected and fruitful dimension of psychological research.

THE SYMMETRICAL PAIRS

E. "Albeeian Pair"

ATTACKER	CONNIVER
— 1. Is BLAMER and ATTACKER of the other one.	— 1. Allows BLAMING and ATTACKING and then (he) (she) CALCULATES what's best.
— 2. Is verbally *dominant*.	— 2. Dominates by (his) (her) intellect.
— 3. (He) (She) thinks (he's) (she's) the boss.	— 3. (He) (She) controls by letting (him) (her) be the boss.
— 4. (He) (She) controls the relationship with volume.	— 4. (He) (She) controls the relationship with sarcasm.
— 5. (He) (She) is strong and knows the mate is also.	— 5. (He) (She) is strong and won't let the mate know (he) (she) is strong.
— 6. Competes with the other mate rather openly.	— 6. Competes with the other mate more covertly.
— 7. Is openly boastful of (himself) (herself).	— 7. Is covertly boastful of (himself) (herself).
— 8. Sometimes uses sex, or lack of it, to express hostility.	— 8. Sometimes sees sex as (his) (her) expression of power.
— 9. Identifies with (his) (her) dominant parent.	— 9. Identifies with (his) (her) more scheming parent.
— 10. Primary feeling is an "escalating" HOSTILITY.	— 10. Primary feeling is an "escalating" CRITICALNESS.

F. "Lewisinian Pair"

PLEASER	AVOIDER
— 1. Is primarily a PLEASER and PLACATER.	— 1. Is primarily an AVOIDER and CONSTRICTING person.
— 2. Wins over the mate by giving in.	— 2. Wins over the mate by refusing to play.
— 3. Controls by always being sweet and kind.	— 3. Controls by ignoring what (he) (she) doesn't want to notice.
— 4. Is very protective of the other's weakness.	— 4. Seeks out the other's protection.
— 5. Responds to the other's tears with kindness.	— 5. Controls the other by tears.
— 6. Ignores the other's "playing stupid."	— 6. "Plays stupid" well.
— 7. Makes "pleasing" the other most important.	— 7. Appears to please the other but more often avoids responsibilities.
— 8. Makes sex be "whatever the other one likes."	— 8. Avoids sex whenever possible.
— 9. Identifies with the "pleasing" parent.	— 9. Identifies with the "submissive" parent.
— 10. Primary feeling is to keep the waters calm.	— 10. Primary feeling is to avoid confrontation.

THE ACTUALIZING PAIR

G.

FEMALE	MALE
— 1. Sees the other mate as more a mature PERSON than a "man."	— 1. Sees the other mate as more of a mature PERSON than a "woman."
— 2. Is alternatingly dominant and submissive.	— 2. Is alternatingly dominant and submissive.
— 3. Is alternatingly nurturing and receptive.	— 3. Is alternatingly nurturing and receptive.
— 4. Gives and receives love easily.	— 4. Gives and receives love easily.
— 5. Enjoys his manliness and his sensitivity.	— 5. Enjoys her femininity and her assertiveness.
— 6. Respects his unique individuality as a person.	— 6. Respects her unique individuality as a person.
— 7. Enjoys a good encounter with him, either warm or not.	— 7. Enjoys a good encounter with her, either warm or hot.
— 8. Sexual expression is both mutual expression and passivity.	— 8. Sexual expression is both mutual expression and passivity.
— 9. Appreciates and identifies to some extent with both parents.	— 9. Appreciates and identifies to some extent with both parents.
— 10. Feelings are both strong and weak, loving and assertive.	— 10. Feelings are both strong and weak, loving and assertive.

Conclusions and Implications

The relationship between love defined as human encounter, love as developmental deficiency or achievement, and love as complementary or symmetrical need fulfillment may be thought of in the following manner:

Each person can be thought of as growing up with deficiencies in terms of certain forms of developmental love. This contributes to the attraction to and choice of certain complementary or symmetrical lovers or mate choices in the late teens and early twenties. Thus, most marriages at this critical choice time are "developmentally deficient choices." With increasing maturity, however, growth toward ability to encounter with risk and with ability to be warm, to be intimate, and even to be angry occurs.

Persons with developmental deficiencies in ability to love in the areas of affection, friendship, eros, or empathy may need assessment procedures and psychotherapy to (1) look at former choices to determine if there are any significant patterns in choices of significant love objects and (2) to discover which deficiencies may be present in love patterns. *Actualization therapy* or *encounter therapy* can then assist in development of new choice patterns and development of formerly deficient areas. Learning to encounter other human beings in groups appears to be the most adequate means available for making up for developmental deficiencies and for the discovery of actualizing interaction patterns.

REFERENCES

DiDominico, E., *"Some Theoretical Ideas on the Parental Relationships of Manipulative Pairs."* Unpublished, 1968.

Haley, J., *Strategies of Psychotherapy.* New York: Grune and Stratton, 1963.

Lowen, A., *Love and Orgasm.* New York: Macmillan, 1965.

Maslow, A. H., *Motivation and Personality.* New York: Harpers, 1954.

May, R., *Psychology and the Human Dilemma.* Princeton, N. J.: Van Nostrand, 1966.

Mittelmann, B., *"Analysis of Reciprocal Neurotic Patterns in Family Relationships,"* in Eisenstein, V., *Neurotic Interaction in Marriage.* New York: Basic Books, 1956.

Satir, V., *Manipulative Response Forms.* Unpublished, 1967.

Shostrom, E. L., *Man, The Manipulator.* New York-Nashville: Abingdon, 1967.

————, *Caring Relationship Inventory.* San Diego: Educational and Industrial Testing Service, 1966.

Watzlawick, D., Beavin, J., and Jackson, D., *Pragmatics of Human Communication.* New York: Norton, 1967.

Winch, Robert F., and McGinnis, Robert, *Selected Studies in Marriage and the Family.* New York: Holt, 1953.

16

Love and the Youth Culture

Al Lewis

As I write this article I feel at once apologetic and angry. Apologetic, because I have so little empirical evidence to work with; angry, that we have learned so little of what our young have to teach us.

If our attention is limited to cursing their cantankerous ways, jailing them for pot, and dragooning them into armies sent to foreign lands, we richly deserve whatever fate they may decide befits us.

This article is subjective and discursive. It is primarily based on my life experience as a fifty-four-year-old father of four, who has associated as a student, teacher and counselor with youth here and abroad. I feel closer to the young who want change than to those of my own generation who are complacent. My children have taught me more than books or schools. They personally introduced me to the "love generation." I thank them and the young people who have shared their lives with me.

In this article I will briefly examine the question of whether there is a youth culture, look at some of the issues which delineate the influence of the young on the nation, view their concept of love, and close with an example of love at work in the Brooklyn ghetto.

Strangers in a Strange Land

Who are these children (mine and yours), who have grown up strangers in our land? Periodical literature and the mass media have for the last decade been filled with cries of parental and establishment alarm over their attitudes and behavior. An English writer, Malcolm Muggeridge,

197

has dubbed them "a population stupefied with pot, allergic to any form of discipline or self-control, nomadic, promiscuous and indulgent. . . ." [1]

Their "underground" press has condemned us, the "over-thirty" generation, for the "gift" we have given them: pollution, war in Viet-Nam, sexual puritanism, love that is duplicity, politics characterized by a "credibility gap," schools that are "prisons," prisons that are "schools for crime." They are indeed, "strangers in a strange land."

"Who am I?" "What is the meaning of life?" Such questions haunt them, and us. These youthful Americans, inheritors of material wealth unprecedented in history and of an education unparalleled in depth and intensity, are in revolt. Hidden or open, this rebellion that can no longer be dismissed as the work of "outside agitators" has seeped deep into the root system of American society, down from the halls of Berkeley and Columbia ("Up against the wall, Mother F-----"), into the high school and even the grammar school classrooms ("Teachers aren't human").

Is it true as they say in the "youth culture" that we put love of things above love of humankind?

"Youth Culture"—Fact or Myth?

Is there a youth culture? Social science has not agreed upon an answer.

Musgrove, a British psychologist, claims the "psychology of adolescence" as an invention of psychologists that has "helped to create what it describes." [2]

Elkin and Westley [3] earlier maintained that the conception of a "youth culture" is a myth based upon biased selection of evidence.

James Coleman [4] in 1961 surveyed ten high schools considered representative of typical schools and communities. He concluded that the existence of an adolescent subculture was beyond dispute.

Jahoda and Warren [5] reviewing diverse references find:

> The entire controversy [about a "youth sub-culture"] seems to us to be about a pseudo problem. . . . Sub-culture is not a "thing" whose absence or presence can be verified; it is a concept that may lead to fruitful research, and does not exclude other conceptual guides. . . . It follows that such a group in society can usefully be studied from the point of view of what they have in common as well as from the point of view of what they share with the major culture.

Is there a "youth culture"? Maybe yes, and maybe no. Meanwhile it is a convenient label that I shall use with this understanding. "Youth culture" or not, there is plenty of action among the young that affects us all.

The Influence of the Youth Culture

Let us refresh ourselves on some of the salient issues of the past decade in which the young have been a major factor.

1. The young were a major factor in the 1968 elections. The Chicago demonstrations not only brought tens of thousands of young people to the "windy city," they sent Richard Nixon to the White House and Lyndon Johnson into retirement in Texas.

2. The rebellion of the young against the Vietnam war has profoundly affected the nation. Tens of thousands have been and are dodging the draft (Senator Fulbright estimated that over 50,000 of our most intelligent and sensitive youth are in Canada alone). Many draft board files have been rifled and destroyed, military installations and government buildings bombed and burned, officers "fragged" in the field, and millions have marched in massive demonstrations unprecedented in the history of this country.

Are our veterans really "returning"? How could they return to their old life styles? Consider the words of John Kerry,[6] a Vietnam veteran, testifying before the Senate Foreign Relations Committee:

> [We are determined] to undertake one last mission, to search out and destroy the last vestige of this barbaric war, to pacify our own hearts, to conquer the hate and the fear that have driven this country these last 10 years and more, and so when in 30 years from now our brothers go down the street without a leg, without an arm, or a face, and small boys ask why, we will be able to say "Vietnam" and not mean a desert, not a filthy obscene memory but the place where America finally turned and where soldiers like us helped it in the turning. . . .
>
> To attempt to justify the loss of one American life in Vietnam, Cambodia or Laos by linking such loss to the preservation of freedom . . . is . . . the height of criminal hypocrisy, and it is that kind of hypocrisy which we feel has torn this country apart.

This is an eloquent sample, among many, of the opposition of the young to hatred, violence and hypocrisy, that has influenced the majority of American people to oppose the war in Vietnam.

3. The young confront our society in a new way with the problem of drug abuse. They have used drugs as a new way to experience, a new answer to boredom, to the meaninglessness of their lives. The majority

of adult Americans drink alcohol and coffee, smoke tobacco, take aspirin, sleeping pills, tranquilizers, pain-killers and a host of other drugs prescribed and unprescribed.

Criticized by their parents, hounded and jailed by the police for the use of what seems to be a harmless drug, marijuana, they strike back with a condemnation of adult hypocrisy. And they are right. We adults, by our use of three to five mind-altering drugs daily, provide the "role model."

Joel Fort, a physician who worked with youth in Haight-Asbury, has written a searing indictment of adult society in his book on drugs. He spoke as an expert, but echoed the cry of the young when he said:

> Nothing more clearly reveals the overwhelming hypocrisy of American society than the massive, completely authenticated abuses of alcohol and the relatively scant public or professional attention given to this problem.[7]

It is difficult to admit, but the facts cannot be denied: it is the parent generation who are the real drug abusers, not the young. And it is the youth culture that has called it to our attention!

4. The sixties saw students discover themselves as "nigger," and shake the educational and political establishment to its foundations with demonstrations from Berkeley to Columbia. America became aware that a significant section of its young felt their educational institutions were irrelevant, authoritarian, dehumanizing. It is difficult to judge the total effect of their activity. The demands for "student power" have not resulted in much student representation on administrative boards, or influence on budgets, appointments or university government. But black study programs have come into existence on many campuses, joint student-faculty committees are in existence, and there is a growing awareness on the part of educators and public officials alike that changes must be made. Changes not only in higher education, but at the elementary and secondary levels as well. For all appearances, each new generation of our young are not only following their older brothers and sisters, they are going beyond them.

5. The youth have had a profound effect on American cultural values. Pop culture is probably for the first time determined by the young, with folk rock, acid rock, hard rock, poster art, light shows and whatnot on the psychedelic scene. I can remember when it was easy to find symphony and opera on the radio. Today, it is the music of the

young. Record sales are dominated by the young, whose musical heroes sell their platters by the millions. They not only control mass music, they use it to express their discontent with the status quo. Turn down the volume and listen to the lyrics. "All I want is just be free and live my life the way I want to be. All I want is just have fun and live my life like it just begun. But you're pushing too hard on me" (The Seeds). "Mr. America, walk on by your supermarket dream; Mr. America, walk on by the liquor store supreme; Mr. America, try to hide the emptiness that's you inside" (The Mothers of Invention).

In dress and food the young have also effected changes in the American life-style. Only a few years ago, long hair was forbidden in the schools, and cause for expulsion in many. Last month the Los Angeles Board of Education abolished dress codes. Today long-haired lawyers work not only in courts but in Governor Reagan's state offices.

Remember when organically grown food was only for adult "health nuts"? The young took it up—health food stores have flourished; million-dollar wholesale businesses have been built on it; and even "Mr. America's" supermarkets are carrying health food lines. Here too, "the times they are a-changin'," and the young have played a significant role in that change.

Whether scientifically distinguishable or not, the youth culture has marketedly influenced national life. Our youth search for a new way of life that puts people above property, the individual above bureaucratic organization, and human relatedness at the core of society. Central to that core is what they call "love."

Love and the Youth Culture

"We are determined to undertake one last mission," said John Kerry to the Senators and the nation that had sent him off to kill, "to search out and destroy the last vestige of this barbaric war, to pacify our own hearts, to *conquer the hate and the fear* that have driven this country these last ten years. . . ."

"I love me. Loving doesn't hurt, and hating isn't lovely," wrote a sixteen-year-old black girl in the Brooklyn ghetto, who attended a workshop I conducted.

"All you need is love," goes a line from the Beatles.

I have heard it used everywhere in conversations among the young, in my classrooms and out; and in a recent survey of college students, love and affection ranked at the top of their list. My conclusion is that the ethos of love is a dominant and dynamic factor in the youth culture. Let us explore some of the facets of its meaning.

Love as Rebellion

Implicit in the use of the term "love" in the youth culture is their rejection of current values and life-styles. As did Kerry, they reject "the hate and fear that has driven this country the last ten years," and the hostility and alienation they find in their familial relations. Statistical evidence of this is contained in the 1965 study of thousands of students from the eighth through the twelfth grade, made by Evelyn Duvall. She found that "less than half of them wanted their marriages to be 'like their parents.' " [8]

I found the same theme in most of the interviews I conducted for this article. Typical is the following statement by a twenty-one-year-old girl of lower middle-class origin with two years of college, now engaged in "a search for myself and for meaningful relations":

"We know that marriage doesn't work. I don't know of one older couple that is happily married. Most of our parents are divorced. We don't have anybody to respect. We don't have an ideal. We can't say, 'Well I'd like to be married and have a family like so and so,' because we don't know any so and so who has a good relationship."

And her male companion, twenty, son of an upper-middle-class family, added:

"It's all a drag, a hassle. People get together and they find they don't like each other and they stay together and hate each other. They don't know what love is, and maybe we don't either. But one thing is sure, we don't want to be like them."

Love has become a "mission" in their lives, because in too many instances they have not had it—not in their homes, not in their schools, not in the larger society. What they have for the most part experienced is alienation, hostility, and hypocritical lectures on a morality honored in the breaches. They are in rebellion against this model, freeing themselves to listen to their own expectations, to become the persons they want to be.

Love as an Experiential Search for Meaning

Flowing from their rejection of current values, I find a second characteristic: love as an experiential search for meaning. Having no models they can consciously internalize, they seek to create their own. As one interviewee put it:

"Well, it's like this: people don't like what it's been, but they don't know exactly what to do about it. We've got to find it out on our own."

And another interviewee in response to the question "What is love?" replied:

"You don't know till you've tried, trying is a part of the learning process."

So love is a matter of experience and experiment; it defines itself in the process. So they are off to learn to live with others, "make it" with others, sharing a bed for the night, living with another for a few days or a few weeks, then dancing off to another scene. In the process partners share their food, their household chores, their money. Hopefully, they come to know themselves and each other more fully as human beings.

Is this experimentation a scene of "free love" and mass debauchery? Perhaps among a minority. A few of those I interviewed, perhaps 10 per cent, separated sex and love. This minority saw sex as a natural need you had to fulfill, that might or might not be related to love. But for the majority, it was a matter of learning to love through sharing with someone you "grooved" with. It might or might not include sex. That depends on "time, place and condition." I found, as did Herbert Otto in his study of Communes [9] ". . . considerable sexual permissiveness . . . [but] a strong tendency toward interpersonal commitment in a continuing relationship."

Love as Inclusive

A theme I frequently found was the inclusiveness of love. Two quotations from my interviews will illustrate my point. The first interviewee, a twenty-year-old female, said:

"I think it [love] is a lot of things, respect, caring, wanting to share something with them. Respect for yourself and others."

Interviewer: "All others?"

"Yes, all others."

The second, a twenty-two-year-old male, said:

"I think one of the problems is that people confine their love to their families, the milkman, a few people. People walk down the street, and nobody smiles. You have to love people out in the street as well as those in the house. And you have to care enough about them to tell them."

Young people are relating across racial, status, socioeconomic and sex barriers in a way I was not accustomed to in my generation. Males and females relate as friends without sexual involvement, with members of other races on both a sexual and nonsexual basis, and easily, I have found, with members of the "over-thirty" generations who are understanding equals and not superiors seeking to "lay a trip" on them.

Love as Self-Love

Having rejected the models of their elders, open to experience in a new way, I find the young engaged in a search to find and love themselves. "You have to respect yourself before you can respect others," "If you don't like yourself, you can't like others," were statements made by many interviewees. Had they been to encounter groups where this theme is de rigueur? Two or three had. Had they read Erich Fromm? A few. But the ideas he has expressed might be considered a summary of most of their views:

> If it is a virtue to love my neighbor as a human being, it must be a virtue—and not a vice—to love myself. The love for my own self is inseparably connected with the love for any other being.[10]

Another aspect of this love of self is the concept of enjoying living. For them "life is meant for fun," to be joyful. Work is one aspect of this, a part of realizing themselves, a part of enjoying themselves. John is a young doctor, with "no interest in money, just enough to survive." His main interest is in a free clinic and a "professional life, not as an economic machine, but as a human being with medical knowledge to share." His attitude is typical of a growing number of young professionals—doctors, lawyers, social workers—and of nonprofessionals as well.

Love as Togetherness

Love for the young began with rejection of parental and societal models—running away from home. But they found no place to go. Earlier in the decade they huddled together in places such as Haight-

Asbury, and were driven from there by the authorities into communes and other cooperative living arrangements. Today they are involved with varying success in creating an "alternative culture": free schools, free clinics, underground newspapers, alternative radio stations (some listener-supported like New York's WBAI-FM; some commercially supported such as KTAO in Los Gatos, California), no-charge bus lines (example: the People's Free Wheel in Boston), a Movement Garage in Albuquerque, free stores. The problems of "togetherness" in this alternative society are manifold, and their outcome is not yet determined. But they represent the efforts of an active minority of the youth to make the word love "become flesh," to create a different way of life. At least one observer, historian Harvey Goldberg of the University of Wisconsin, maintains that this counterculture and its institutions must be viewed as "part of an epochal change sweeping American society." [11]

Love of Nature

Another feature of youth's love is a more reverent and loving attitude toward nature. Many have an awareness of natural beauty that leads them to go for long walks on the beaches, hikes in the mountains, to swim in the nude, to crowd a city rooftop to watch a sunset.

Born in a decade in which extinction by pollution has been discovered by our scientists, they are keenly aware of its dangers. Many see our way of living, the mad rush for profits and material possessions, as the cause, and give their support to various organizations working to protect the slender chain of life that sustains man.

They are cognizant, too, of man's need for nature to sustain himself psychologically. One young male interviewee, reared in the city, put it this way:

"I think we are related to everything around us, you feel it . . . like if anyone goes out into nature where there are trees and flowers, they feel like running and singing . . . like it's far out to be alive. I think we have too much concrete around us . . . in the city frustration bounces back and hits you all the time . . . and all those ignorant and selfish people that are around, they get hung up in the confusion. What we need to do is to drop them off in a forest or by a lake. Then they can express themselves more. People can't express themselves when they are surrounded by concrete. . . ."

According to Ashley Montagu, "Scientists are discovering at this very moment that to live as if to live and love were one is the only way of life for human beings, because, indeed, this is the way of life which the inner nature of man demands. . . . This is not a new discovery in the world; what is new is that scientists should be rediscovering these truths by scientific means." [12] And what is even newer is that our youth have put love at the core of their youth culture, and are trying to live by it and change the world through it.

The "Love Project"

What are some of the practical ways in which we can aid in the triumph of the ethos of love over the hatred, negativism and alienation prevalent in our lives? One example is the "Love Project" which began at Thomas Jefferson High School in the inner city of Brooklyn, New York.[13]

Jefferson is a school typical of many, including those in the white "middle-class ghettos" of America. Ninety-nine per cent black and brown, the average daily attendance is 60 per cent. Cutting of classes, dropouts, lack of money, drug problems, vandalism, theft, racial and political conflict, and overcrowded classrooms are a part of the daily life of the school. Is it a wonder that teachers, administrators and students alike become progressively dehumanized and hopeless in such an environment? All are trapped in a destructive cycle from which there is seemingly no escape. But sometimes in the midst of degradation and destruction there grows a new life, a new hope, a new promise. The love project is an example of the growth of new hope.

The Love Project began in November 1970, when a courageous teacher, Arleen Lorrance, acting chairman of Jefferson's drama department, attempted to break up a fight between two students at a student assembly in the school auditorium.

"Instead of yelling, 'Cut it out, man,' I grabbed this six-foot-two kid's hand as he ran by me in pursuit of the other fellow and said: 'Please don't go,' " said Mrs. Lorrance. The student stopped and looked at Mrs. Lorrance, and then continued on. "But the tragedy of the whole thing came to me because I realized he didn't have a choice," she continued. "He was living in an environment that said manhood is more important than principles and he had to go and get this kid because he had to prove himself. But the important thing is that he did not lash out at me physically or verbally. I reached out to him with love . . . and he, having to continue on to 'prove his manhood,' said almost gently, 'Let go of my hand.' " [14]

Back in the classroom, Mrs. Lorrance through tears shared her anguish with her students. They heard her and spontaneously at this moment "The Seekers"—an organization of teachers and students—and the Love Project were born. The Seekers work up "love" projects in which the entire 4,500-member student body and faculty are involved in giving and receiving gifts. The first project was to bake and distribute cookies to the entire student body and faculty. The next project involved the collection and distribution of thousands of books to students and faculty (the most requested books were dictionaries and entire collections of Shakespeare!). Other projects have involved baking and sharing bread with students of nearby Andrew Jackson High School in Queens, painting classrooms, and so forth.

Jefferson teachers Nancy Lapidus and Leo Spector joined in the repainting of the Little Theatre classroom. Some 300 students and faculty participated in the project. "Students flipped over the discovery of what can happen when one mixes colors; others got 'high' on the exotic shades. . . . The students saw this as a true act of giving and receiving. . . ." To quote Nancy Lapidus, "You could cut the love with a knife, it was so thick." [15]

Winston Churchill is quoted as having said, "People often stumble over the truth but they pick themselves up and hurry along as if nothing had happened." [16] What is the truth involved in the "miracles" taking place at Thomas Jefferson High School? Is it the same insidious germs of human cooperation that infected the now famous Hawthorne Experiments conducted by T. Elton Mayo of Harvard Business School almost a half-century ago? Is the Love Project an exemplification of the important finding of social science, that solutions lie in the "problem population" itself? I am strongly inclined to think so.

In March 1971 the Love Project came to the attention of the National Center for the Exploration of Human Potential, and leadership workshop scholarships were offered to Mrs. Lorrance and a student, Beatrice Leyba. In May by invitation of the Seekers and the principal, Margaret Baird, the writer conducted a Developing Personal Potential workshop for twenty teachers and administrators and an equal number of students at Thomas Jefferson High School.[17] Teachers, students and administrators alike reached out and experienced themselves and each other in a new way.

Jefferson principal Margaret Baird set an inspiring example by participating in the workshop, and later gathered and circulated to the entire school feedback from workshop participants. Here are some of the comments:

"These have been six delicious hours of life that reassure us of the fact that love really does work."

"The workshop has shown me that to love other people besides black people won't make me less black. . . . Loving doesn't hurt, and hating isn't lovely."

"This soft openness turned this hard-walled area [the school gym] into a love area. I'll never forget."

"I found the other half of me."

"Love works—the workshop is love. It is people, young and younger, sharing, caring, being, seeing, reaching, becoming. We became a we. We will go on together. We can reach out to others in our school. We can include and help them—help them be."

Marion Zack, a guidance counselor and head of the College Discovery and Development Program at Jefferson, wrote: ". . . the most important features of it for me, have been the warmth of greetings by the students with whom I shared this experience. It was unique in the sense that we were all very human together."

Nancy Lapidus, a young teacher, wrote:

"I began to see my students and colleagues as having a continuity in time that I had never seen before. After the DUE exercise,[18] I became close with a girl who had been in my class every day for a whole term. . . . She became three-dimensional for me and judging from her warm response since then, I think I became a whole person for her. I think this was typical for the others in the group.

". . . The value of the program, in my opinion, was that we were able to counteract, in only a few hours, the dehumanizing effect of large systems such as the educational system. . . . I would like to see this experience extended as widely as possible . . . as one of my students put it, 'so wonderful, it's beyond words'."

Arleen Lorrance, originator of the Love Project, said:

The workshop literally transformed people; they smiled, as a matter of fact, they laughed . . . and they [students, teachers and administrators] did this with each other . . . openly, freely, lovingly. . . . Students had come to experience a new dignity and now *wanted* to do their school work . . .

for themselves and not just to impress their teachers. And this was not just a momentary reaction. The workshop was held on the 13 and 14th of May and still today [4th of June] the work is flowing in . . . and at a highly creative level. Teachers began to relate to their students as younger friends instead of charges. . . . The students went home and shared the joy of their experiences with their friends and relatives. . . . It had a warming effect on those with whom they shared this new sense of themselves. Their friends and relatives, in turn, were anxious to have this shared with them. . . . Beyond this, they wanted to come and participate themselves. . . .

"A year ago these same Jefferson students were running through the halls kicking in doors," said Mrs. Lorrance. "During the recent street disorders in Brownsville, only a few participated. The great majority stayed inside and continued their school work."

The Love Project at Jefferson High School is going forward as a pilot project not only for the New York City School system, but for other schools. Ten teachers, students and administrators attended a six-week summer workshop in group facilitation and leadership conducted by the National Center for the Exploration of Human Potential. They are returning to their school to carry on the work they have begun with the support of their principal, Margaret Baird, and top officials of the New York City Schools. The Love Project and the Development of Human Potentials Program are an example of the application in practice of love as a creative and dynamic force that has the possibility of changing not only schools, but life in our society as well.

Writing this article was a learning and integrating experience for me. I hope it has been for you, my unseen reader.

In summary, over the last decade the young have been increasingly in rebellion, passive and open against the hateful, the negative, the "put down" of people in our culture. Their activities have deeply shaken us all. We adults, our defenses raised, have engaged in our own form of rebellion—"adult backlash." It is not easy to confront ourselves as individuals, far more difficult as a nation. In this rebellion, ours and the youth, I find a message pregnant with meaning; the young care, their elders care, too.

Love, caring, I find a dynamic force in the youth culture. Their caring started as a rebellion, a survival reflex. But "love will find its way," today as yesterday during the long eons of life's evolution on this planet. The young are reaching out for us. Will we give them our hand? Will we reach out, too? We have much to learn from each other. Can we together build and rebuild a better life that will ensure our species' survival? I believe we can.

NOTES

1. Malcolm Muggeridge, "Unresisting Imbecility," in *The Con III Controversy: The Critics Look at the Greening of America,* ed. Philip Nobile (New York: Pocket Books, 1971), p. 1.
2. F. Musgrove, *Youth and the Social Order* (London: Routledge, 1954), p. 2.
3. E. Elkin and W. Westley, "The Myth of Adolescent Culture," *American Sociological Review,* XX (1955), pp. 680–684.
4. J. S. Coleman, *The Adolescent Society* (New York: The Free Press, 1961).
5. Marie Jahoda and Neil Warren, "The Myths of Youth," in *The Young Adult: Identity and Awareness,* ed. Gerald D. Winters and Eugene M. Nuss (Glenview, Illinois: Scott, Foresman and Company, 1969), p. 35.
6. Quoted by William F. Buckley, Jr., Los Angeles *Times,* June 14, 1971.
7. Joel Fort, M. D., *The Pleasure Seekers: The Drug Crisis Youth and Society* (New York: The Grove Press, Inc., 1969), p. 36.
8. Evelyn Mills Duvall, "How Effective Are Marriage Courses," *Journal of Marriage and the Family* (May 1965), p. 97.
9. Herbert A. Otto, "Communes: The Alternative Life-Style," *Saturday Review* (April 24, 1971), p. 17.
10. Erich Fromm, *The Art of Loving* (New York: Bantam Books, 1956), p. 49.
11. Quoted from an AP dispatch by Ken Harnett, San Diego *Evening Tribune,* May 1971.
12. Ashley Montagu, *The Humanization of Man: Our Changing Conception of Human Nature* (New York: Grove Press, 1962), p. 112.
13. See Arleen Lorrance, "The Love Project: An experiment in the Use of Love as a Means of Reducing Hostility Between Teachers and Students." Available through The National Center for the Exploration of Human Potential, 8080 El Paseo Grande, La Jolla, California. See also Bert Shanas, "Violence is Turned into Peace by That Thing Called Love," New York *Daily News,* May 24, 1971.
14. Shanas, *op. cit.*
15. Quoted from Thomas Jefferson High School Newsletter, May 1971, edited by Arleen Lorrance.
16. Charles Hampden-Turner, *Radical Man: The Process of Psycho-Social Development* (Cambridge, Massachusetts: Schenkman Publishing Company, 1970), p. 185. See his discussion of the Hawthorne experiment for a thought-provoking analysis of some of the factors that may be involved in the Love Project.
17. The Developing Personal Potential program was developed by Dr. Herbert A. Otto. Based on an ego-supportive and life-affirming approach, the workshops are conducted in an atmosphere of love and caring. Further information is available through The National Center for the Exploration of Human Potential, 8080 El Paseo Grande, La Jolla, California, 92037.
18. Herbert A. Otto, *Group Methods to Actualize Human Potential: A Handbook* (Beverly Hills, California: Holistic Press, 1970), pp. 23 ff.

17

Function—a Dimension of Love

Carl D. Levett

When a woman says: "I know I love him," she is conveying a highly personal and individual feeling. Her love will be emotional and ordinarily subject to little rational assessment. There is no love meter for gauging the quality, intensity, or scope of subjective love feelings. Further reflection may produce additional revelations: "I don't know; there's something about him. I just feel it; that's all." The popular notion of love as "that indefinable thing" is treasured by many women who want to preserve love's mystique rather than have the "petals picked off the rose" for purposes of analyzing the blossom. Yet the moment the woman sheds her wedding gown, she is introduced to that vital dimension of function: how will she and her spouse behave within the boundaries of their relationship?

Function refers to performance: how the individual parts operate separately and together. The young bride and groom will be connected to historical patterns of behavior that affect their own person as well as each other. There will be effective and defective ways that they will administer their own and each other's needs which will severely test their personal and interpersonal awareness, self-discipline, and freedom to be themselves. Regardless of how attractive and sensually desirable each feels initially toward the other, they will ultimately be uniquely affected by the impact of these functional dynamics that either converts their loving to deepening and more meaningful involvement, or dissipates their positive sensitivities in disillusionment and despair. Although the love quotient may not be objectively measurable, the matter of function is verifiable.

The loss of communication, the increasing interpersonal tension and quarreling, the mounting evidence of unresolved problems, are matters that can be functionally identified. The dynamics of love and function in interpersonal compatibility would appear to revolve around a third vital force: the dimension of caring. For it is the denominator of caring that provides the mortar that binds the potentially affirmative forces of love and function in a common cause of human resolution of need and fulfillment.

Caring for the other, symbolically, can be conceived as a form of caring for one's self. "The better I treat her, the more she is likely to have available the functional wherewithal to treat me better." Since the energy of a human relationship springs from the hope that personal need will be met, and that the other person will be capable of interpersonal responsiveness, renewal of that energy involves interdependent caring. The realization of interpersonal hopes will tend to generate more will for preserving and building the relationship as more real satisfactions are experienced within it.

It is germane that in human relationships involving love and function caring that people attempt to use other people. If use by one person of another takes on the character of stripping the other of the state of humanness, then the using becomes perverse since it denies the other the natural and inherent qualities of personal identity. Under these circumstances, use becomes abuse.

The sexual area between husband and wife is an obvious arena for use and abuse that touches on love and function-caring processes. A husband has a grievous day at the office. His wife is not particularly responsive to his sexual advances. The husband crudely berates her: "I knock myself out all day long and what do I find when I approach you? You're as cold as an iceberg." What he demands is that she function as an object that releases him of his pent-up tensions regardless of her own natural inclinations. What she yearns for is for him to perceive her as a person entitled to her own separate set of sensitivities. Even if she is submissive to his demands, in order to placate him, it will become increasingly difficult for her to maintain positive love and function-caring attitudes toward him as long as the pattern denies her the means to be accepted as the human being she truly is—separate and unique.

It is also true that the concept of use can be affirmative. One person can use another for learning, for growing, for finding more friendship and love. Should the husband, who is so bound up with frustration, reveal his true state to his wife, he might discover that she can be responsive to using his openness in ways that consummate a more diverse and deeper level of human intercourse—that sexual involvement may eventuate, but on the basis of more expansive communication of personal feeling and need.

A human relationship is built, developed, and created out of the realities and ideals each person contributes. There may be principles and basic conceptual systems that can enhance and make a relationship function more effectively, but it is the two human beings who must ultimately establish the configuration and the innards of their mutuality. Their adaptability will be founded on each partner's past experiences and their capacity to research and repair the happenings of the moment. Their individual and bilateral processing will be the vehicle for building an interrelatedness unique unto themselves. A man may take his wife to the theater. She may believe that he should check his coat before the play begins. He may prefer to hold the garment in his lap. The difference in value considerations between her belief in social proprieties and his penchant for casualness may set off a series of diatribes that seriously impairs their having a compatible evening together. Any attempt by two individuals to design, research, and test interactional affiliation immediately introduces two distinct wills, two separate sets of values, beliefs, and need systems. Each will bring a relatively unmanageable unconscious life which plays deviously upon personal behavior and functioning.

The attitudes and definitions regarding the meaning of love, function, and growth that each person manifests in interpersonal exchanges will diverge as well as synthesize. The diversity of love tones are unlikely to be impressive: ranging from tenderness, affection, reverence, sympathetic understanding, warm attachment, devotion, desire, attraction, adoration, passion, lust, to ecstatic oneness. *In situ,* the love expectations may move from tenderness to passion, from reverence to sympathetic understanding—moment to moment.

Love tones between a man and a woman appear to encompass distinct areas of experience. A man may love a woman's gracefulness, her manual dexterity, her voluptuousness. A woman may love a man's voice, his sense of humor, his intelligence. The differentials in love tones will be unique to each pair. Whatever form, definition, and scope the love tones may take, the nature of its flow will fall into certain categories of stimulation: the physical, social, mental, sexual, emotional, and spiritual.

In general, love tones seem to flow in three directions: outward, in cherishing the other person or persons; inward, in being wanted and needed as a person; and interactionally, a mixture of inward and outward feeling. A fourth direction, sometimes considered somewhat esoteric and mystical, but well-known within the disciplines of liberal religion, psychology, and psychiatry, involves the love tones of experiencing a joy and delight of one's self. The search for life's real meaning within the larger context of creation has inspired more exploration, particularly by the contemporary generation, for an answer to self-loving: "Love thyself as thou wouldst another; love another as thou wouldst thyself." If a man or woman cannot love that which he or she truly is, will not such negative fancies betray a love-caring mode of functioning toward that person—the self? For when a man feels unworthy of love for his self, will he not resist another's love caring out of deference to his own conviction?

Each adult evolves a set of criteria and priorities for self and other person caring. "I don't want to talk about that," a husband says in resisting his wife's questions. In taking that position he is declaring his individualistic function and love-caring conceptions. Whether he is right or wrong in regard to his stand is less relevant than the manner in which he and his wife will process their love and function-caring interests. How each behaves in relation to the impasse will be the cornerstone for the construct of their relationship. Each will reveal an individual will in a process of constructiveness or destructiveness, controversial value and attitudinal systems, varying degrees of self-discipline, differing capacities for having, giving, or denying freedom of choice. It is within that climate that the two selves will interact and find channels for friendship and a reconciliation of differences, or lodge vicious and vengeful assaults on each other for control and mastery over the direction and outcome of their involvement.

The indices to functional growth, as an extension of love and function caring, are more easily interpretable in retrospect than through projection. Person expansion, release of potentials, personal development, are not as easily assessable as might first be conceived. It is difficult to evaluate functional growth in a moment of time inasmuch as little determination can be made regarding the ultimate value of any particular human experience. What might eventually prove growthful might temporarily appear regressive. A man makes a decision to leave college in order to accept a well-paying position which offers unusual opportunity for travel to foreign countries. It will take time for him to appreciate the significance of his choice in terms of personal and occupational growth. Yet, since a man behaves, in part, on the basis of trial and error, the slippage in performance can be considered reversible, most times, and re-formed into a renewal of growth. The life of any self-realizing individual will be peppered with examples of self-negating situations on the road to personal achievement. Although the diversions from integrated growth are infinite, so are the returns to the mainstream of functional resurgence. Growth becomes more a matter of long-term personal expansion, taking into account the effective processing of those inherent capacities that are available and the adversities that are bound to occur.

A man may grow in one area and concurrently suffer a loss of personal development in another segment of his life. An employee may be promoted to an important executive position. The new responsibilities make inordinate demands on his time. Whereas he formerly had opportunity to involve himself with family and friends, as well as time to enjoy the pleasures of physical activities—tennis, puttering in the garden—few of the familial and avocational pursuits are possible under the new regimen he establishes. His functional growth in the search for personal expansiveness in industry widens as his involvement in other personal areas narrows.

Love, function, growth-caring forces are in continual flux in relationships involving friends, parents and children, husbands and wives. How each person processes individual functional and growth values beyond the subjective feelings of love, becomes crucial in terms of the quality and outcome of the interpersonal experience.

Two women may seek a divorce. The first woman may love her husband even though he is functioning as a reprobate in his gambling, drinking, and carousing escapades. She may be affirmative in her love and function-caring relatedness to him. "I know Doug is unhappy within himself. I only wish there was something more I could do to help him." Douglas is at liberty to do what he chooses with his life. Apparently, Douglas has very little concern for love and function-caring relatedness to himself. Despite his wife's devoted love caring for him, she is totally ineffectual in helping him overcome his self-impugning behavior. "If he would just settle down, I know we could work things out together." His dysfunctioning systems begin to corrode her love and function-caring feelings toward him until his destructive behavior undermines her self-functioning. "I can't go on like this. I can't think straight anymore. I'm so impatient with the kids. You can take just so many tranquilizers."

Within this context, the more love and function-caring feelings she has available for Doug—with a paltry feedback to herself—the more depleted and empty she becomes. To maintain this pattern in the face of a growing disregard for her own well-being brings her to the point of crisis. She is now confronted with a dire choice: either she continues to bestow her love and function-caring sensitivities on Doug as she dies a little more each day—by virtue of personal exhaustion and self-annihilation— or she accepts letting her love and function-caring feelings for him expire in order that her love and function-caring sensitivities for her own person may continue to live. The essential nature of her detachment from Doug, via divorce, arises out of a resolution as to who best deserves her love and function-caring concerns. Once she chooses herself, she can no longer abide by the marital vows. Yet, even with divorce, there may be remnants of love-caring feelings that remain: "The funny thing is that in some ways I still love Doug even though we just can't get along together."

A second wife seeking divorce is married to a kind, thoughtful, uncomplicated, pleasant man. She describes the deterioration of her marriage on a qualitatively different level than the first woman. "It isn't that Jonathan and I argue, or fight, or don't get along. He's nice to me and all that. In fact, he's always trying to please me. There aren't any particular things he does that are offensive to me, but I find him a complete bore. Down deep I feel that there must be more to life than the drabness, the sameness, we have: knowing every morning in every way what the day will be with him. I really don't have anything against him. I suppose I love him in a special kind of way: more like a sister or mother maybe. But, since I've gone back to work and had a chance to meet other men, I know that I've got to live for more than just security. Maybe my working has helped me to realize that I can take care of myself now. I've tried talking to Jonathan, but he doesn't have any idea of what bothers me. Perhaps it was enough for me when we first got married, but it isn't now. Maybe I've changed some. I know that Jonathan has stayed pretty much the same. If I'm making a mistake, at least I'll have given myself a chance to find it out rather than just stay put and suffer inside, never knowing what I might have been able to give myself."

She is expressing love caring for Jonathan in this soliloquy but on a level which is irreconcilable with the passionate and fully functioning, male-female relationship she cherishes. The perception of her husband as an obedient and conforming "good boy" does not offer her hope for consummating her expansive feminine needs. The issue is not that Jonathan's functioning is inherently wrong; it is that it is felt to be wrong by his wife at this point in time. Whereas she has been using the years of marriage for growth caring of her own person, apparently Jonathan has stagnated in terms of his own development. The gap that exists between them is one of growth caring which has its impact on the levels of love caring and function caring that each requires. It isn't that her functional survival is in jeopardy in being married to Jonathan. It is rather that she cannot conceive of living more and better with him. Growth caring for herself and the opportunity to know and discover more of herself through the cutting edge of a fuller man-woman relationship demand resolution. Whereas divorce in the first case is predicated on the survival of self, in the second instance dissolution of the marriage arises out of a need for a completed self.

The variables of love, function, and growth caring present a challenge to parents regarding their child-rearing responsibilities. In the formative years, many mothers are capable of imparting a warm and relaxed responsiveness to their infant children: "Don't worry, little one; I am here." Such tender devotion may be sufficient to supply the infant's overriding security needs for closeness and reassurance in the earliest of years. It is when the infant moves into later childhood, prepuberty, and adolescence that the mother's functional and growth-caring capacities may be severely tested. The development of the child's potentials for self-discipline, self-management, self-sufficiency, and the processing of a more balanced dependent-independent relationship with the mother will require improvisation. Yet, the mother's personal functioning and growth potentials may be too deficient to provide for this dimension of the child's maturation. The mother may attempt to compensate for her sense of functional inadequacy by invoking more "loving care." This may be symbolized by: "Can't you see how much Mommy loves you; why do you make it so hard for Mommy?" If a mother with these limitations has an offspring who demands a high order of functioning from her, there can be a serious loss of relatedness between the two. The feeling on the part of the youngster that the mother is bankrupt as a source of functional learning and growing can result in a commensurate loss of rapport and an impoverishment of interpersonal communication, dependency, and trust. The child's insecurity in the mother's incapacities may activate a more frantic effort by the youngster to work things out without mother as a way of dealing with the exigencies of function and growth. The mother's loss of influence may prompt her to give unlimited freedom to the child as the only recourse to not aggravating a situation which is already felt to be beyond the mother's ken. The child's freedom can revert to outright license and pseudo independence without a paternal figure present who would intervene and confront the mother and youngster with the unreality of the unsupervised functioning.

A very different form of interactional function and growth pattern may appear between mother and child. Within this frame of reference, the mother is prideful of her own self-sufficiency and actively engaged in "bettering" herself. Love caring for her child is entangled within a compulsive kind of function and growth-caring design for living. The mother is warmly responsive to the youngster when she observes that the child is identified and motivated toward self-sufficiency and self-improvement. If the child is relatively passive and dependent in temperament, the mother's overdrive may be beyond the offspring's capacity to absorb. Warning signals of imminent maladjustment may appear at those times when the mother attempts to pressure the youngster into premature activities and involvements. Disturbed feelings of personal inadequacy and failure may accrue for both as the child defines the mother's despair in terms of a negative self-image. The anxiety of constantly disappointing mother, by not measuring up to her functional and growth ideal, may translate itself on the part of the child into regressive, hostile, or resistive patterns. In not being able to catch up with mother's functional and growth expectations, the youngster is likely to wallow in feelings of personal nonworth. The mother's frustration will tend to be expressed with only her fantasied love-caring ideals in mind: "I can't do a thing with that child, she'll eventually drive me to distraction."

Love, function, growth-caring patterns that realize fuller human potentials, are not readily acquired in homes, communities, and societies which breed a large measure of distortion, contradiction, spurious values, and pernicious behavior. This is not to imply that superior love, function, and growth-caring forces do not exist in various quarters and levels of communal and contemporary life. It is a kind of educational sophistication that is unlikely to be found in abundance. It occurs when the function caring of one person allows the other the dignity of being that which he or she is: a living, changing, evolving entity—separate and unique. The conditions drastically alter from the man-machine relatedness as the chemistry of interhuman drama unfolds within the extensive and emotional feedback experiences of two people catalyzing the dynamics of their separate existences. The interpersonal pulsation becomes the means for transforming personal perceptual worlds into newly realized vistas of discovery that break down archaic ideational barriers and escalate higher levels of humanization. These higher forms of learning can only occur if free-form functioning becomes the basis for interrelatedness in contrast to programming and performance demands on each other.

A wife may be standing over the kitchen sink preparing to wash the supper dishes. Her husband is lounging in the living room reading the evening newspaper. The wife says to herself: "Just look at him. You'd think he'd at least have some consideration. Here I am, knocking myself out all day like I was a maid, and he doesn't have the decency to even offer to help with the dishes. Wait until he asks me to do something for him. I'll show him."

Within her internalized dialogue she has not yet established room for interpersonal communion. What exists for her is an already erected conception of what the husband has to be in order for her to experience him in any love-caring way. Her love caring places an advanced demand on him: "What good is it if he can't offer without my having to ask?" Within such a pattern, the husband symbolically represents to her an automatically installed dishwasher. What she is loving is what she has established as her due: a mechanical device in the form of a husband—a machine that should automatically know what she is feeling and turn itself on and wash the dishes without her even having to flick the switch. This level of interaction is preordered, fixed, and lodged in an idealized and romantic framework which is suitable to having robot services continually available but which repudiates the process of interpersonal realization through mutual discovery of need and the establishing of reasonable, cooperative, and integrative ground rules for handling household chores.

The wife who expects automated responses from her husband may deign to ask her husband to help her with the dishes. In all probability, she will be expecting an answer that will, in advance, suit her and comply with what she has already decided that he should do to please her. If he says: "Gee, honey, I really don't feel up to it," she, very likely, will interpret this as a renunciation of his love-caring feelings toward her.

Only when she can ask openly and without any preordained demand, can he answer freely and in terms of the human being he feels himself to be at that moment. Granted that she will have to grapple with the frustrations resulting from the unknown outcome of her wish that he choose to help her. In her willingness to accept the propriety of his free-form existence, she is also promulgating the conditions for her own freedom of choice when he asks her for help. If either partner does accept doing and helping when the incentives and motivations are lacking—without freedom of choice—the remains of such processing can eventuate in only one state—automated living, by prescription. It might very well be that the husband chooses to help with the dishes even though he has little desire to do so. But the choosing will be his and not hers. The choosing will be his out of a self-realizing decision rather than one born out of fear of hurting her, personal guilt, or the threat of losing her love-caring feelings for him.

If both parties can allow the free-form ingredients of their functioning to provide the basis of relatedness, each can be truer to his and her own actuality. It is at this point that they will be confronted with a new world of tribulations but also the opportunity for functional growth. It is also at this very point that the preciousness and the essence of their humanistic processing can be preserved and allowed to resonate within the emotional and spiritual flow of the relationship—a dimension of love, function, and growth caring that can live that moment and be renewable each passing day.

18

Love and Life Goals

David G. Jones

"It's a damn sorry world. My whole life has been wasted. If I had it to do over again, I'd do it all differently. I did a lot for people, and nobody has ever done anything for me. What I am really bitter about is that nobody gives a damn!"

The speaker was a recently retired high school athletic coach from a wealthy New England town. Years before he had given up control of his life to the events and persons around him and he blamed those events and persons for his wasted years. He felt he had been enslaved and he was right. But as Ezra Pound once said, "A slave is one who waits for someone else to free him!" [1] The cause of his slavery lay within himself. Man must choose or be chosen for.

The real tragedy is that this waste of human potential does not need to happen to the coach or to anyone. We can, by our own efforts, control much of our lives. We do not have to be straws in the wind to be blown about haphazardly. We can become more autonomous, more free to recognize and choose among the alternatives open to us in our own specific situations.

The high school coach lacked two major characteristics of autonomy: love and the establishment of life goals. Life goals would have given him the clarification of what he hoped to accomplish. Love for self would have given him the self-knowledge to determine those goals and love with others, the courage to act on them. This chapter is an exploration of those two characteristics of autonomy and the effect each has on the other.

I. Love

Each of us needs the support and fulfillment that comes through loving ourselves and being loved by others. But as adults we are not dependent on other persons to initiate that love. Through our own efforts we can come to love ourselves more, and through offerings of love to others we enable others to respond with love toward us. "One is not loved accidentally. One's own power to love produces love." [2] Love toward either myself or another depends on proficiency in certain skills and attitudes necessary for depth relationships. I term these "love-arts." Proficiency in the love-arts can be developed.

Love has two foci: love for self and love for others. Love for self is that state of being in which I take seriously my own satisfaction, fulfillment, and security. Love for others is a relationship in which the other person's satisfaction, fulfillment, and security mean as much to me as my own. The two foci are intricately related. Likewise, the two sets of love-arts involved in each, though different, are dependent upon one another.

A. *Love for Self and Love-Arts*

> The love-arts related to the love for self are:
> 1. Becoming more self-accepting
> 2. Establishing personal growth goals
> 3. Gaining competence in the use of time
> 4. Being open toward growth and change

DIAGRAM 1. (The lists of love-arts contained in Diagrams 1 and 2 are not intended to be exhaustive but they are seen as primary.)

1. *Becoming more self-accepting* is the key love-art for the love of self. This is the key because it is at the base of all human striving, both in reaching for personal potential and in building depth relationships with others. It involves answering continually the question: "Who am I?" If I do not have some understanding and acceptance of my own identity I cannot enter into relationships with myself or anyone else. Maslow has stated, ". . . to a large extent [a person] can receive from the world, and give to the world, only that which he himself is. . . . A study of the innards of his personality is one necessary base for the understanding of what he can communicate to the world, and to what the world is able to communicate to him." [3] And as Emerson said, "What we

are, only that can we see." [4] We are far more than we know. Opening ourselves up to ourselves, expanding our self-knowledge, opens up both internal and external worlds not ever dreamed of before. *Becoming more self-accepting* involves the continual journey of exploration through previously undiscovered areas of our personality. These journeys aid and are aided by new personal discoveries about the external world. Each feeds the other. Both would be practically impossible without having or at least having experienced a supportive love relationship with another person.

Being self-accepting also involves knowing my strengths and resources. This can be brought about as simply as assessing my strengths from time to time. To assess my strengths I might ask myself: In what ways am I most creative? What turns me on the most? In what situations am I most comfortable? In what have I had the greatest success?

A periodical internal boasting session in which I admit to myself my areas of greatest strength and greatest self-pleasure can be helpful. Our modern Western Christian heritage has made such statements very difficult. We have inherited from our culture a false sense of humility which can cause us not only to deny strengths, but to bury them so deeply as never to be aware of them. We have been taught to be psychological dwarfs. A recent example of this occurred in a training group of public school teachers from a Bible Belt rural area. They were given an assignment to arrange themselves in order from the least important member to the most important member. *Every* person ran for the chair designated for the least important! What a disservice such persons do to themselves and the world by denying their potential resources. Of course, the temptation of such humility is that if a person does not admit to himself he has strengths, then neither does he have to admit to himself that he has responsibilities to use them.

A realistic assessment of my strengths usually turns up several weaknesses also. *Becoming more self-accepting* involves not only awareness of strengths but also the acceptance of my weaknesses. I need a healthy acceptance of my weaknesses not in the sense of not wanting to do something about them, but in the sense of not letting them block the use of my strengths. Too often fear of disclosure of my weaknesses causes me to use my creative energy in keeping hidden rather than in striving for personal growth. Acceptance of my weaknesses means not wasting energy on defending them.

To become more accepting of myself also means accepting both the maleness and femaleness within me. Only to the extent that we can accept the male and female that exists within each of us can we be in meaningful communication with a person of the corresponding sex. If I deny and suppress my femininity I will have little or no depth relationships with women. I had withheld tears in public for thirty years until I met a man who cried whenever the feelings within him determined it. Only then did I face into my own feminine needs to express tenderness and concern and to express myself without fears of being judged as unmasculine. I was amazed how my relationships and communications with women began to move to deeper levels. Likewise, if I deny my masculinity, a love relationship with another man will be practically impossible to achieve.[5]

Therefore, the love-art of *becoming more self-accepting* requires the ability to examine relationships of men and women who are important to me. As I uncover the models I hold of femininity and masculinity, I can explore realistically my feelings about them. One technique I have found useful is to describe how I imagine my mother and father to have been at my age and to compare myself to my images of them. My images can control me either by my using them as models to conform to, or by a tendency to overreact against them. But such models can be extremely helpful if I examine them in comparison with myself in order to uncover my own uniqueness.

Becoming more self-accepting is the primary love-art and the following love-arts are related to and dependent upon it.

2. The love-art of *establishing personal growth goals* is based upon the exciting work of Richard E. Byrd.[6] It is one of the most useful and necessary concepts in the realization of personal potential. Instead of simply coping with circumstances that threaten us, there is another way. We can decide in what ways we wish to become: in essence, to fulfill what we potentially are. The growth process is natural but it can be assisted by working consciously on goals we determine for our own individual growth.

One of the best methods for establishing goals is to examine situations of discomfort in which the use of personal abilities and resources are inhibited. This may include crises or provocative situations of all kinds. How do you respond to being controlled by others? How do you respond to physical affection? How do you respond to anger? These are the pressure points of life and provide excellent learning opportunities.

It can be very frustrating when my discomfort keeps me from using the abilities I know I have. For example, I am extremely uncomfortable when someone I love or respect is angry with me. My normal style of response is to retreat by either remaining silent or becoming very rational and objective. This rarely makes for a creative resolution of the tension. My personal growth goal within such situations is simply to relate my feelings to the other person as they develop, without rationalization and as spontaneously as possible.

One of the most helpful suggestions offered by Byrd is that of experimenting with an opposite stance. If a person can only speak cognitively, he might experiment by only expressing feelings. If a person is always a leader in interpersonal relations, he might attempt following for a while. Taking an opposite stance stretches behavioral skills. It also expands the available repertoire of behavior to be called upon when needed.

These personal growth goals can be worked on in any living situation. The danger is that people may feel manipulated if the experimentation does not also take into account the feelings of others involved and the appropriateness of the behavior to the task at hand.

3. *Gaining competence in the use of time* is the love-art on which I work the most.[7] It is probably the most frequently neglected skill in our culture.

A person who is time-competent lives fully in the here-and-now with a sense of the continuity of past and future. He is not burdened by guilts, regrets, or resentments from the past. His aspirations are tied meaningfully to present growth goals. He has faith that the future will emerge out of the present and is not therefore rigidly tied to future-oriented, overly idealistic goals. Nor does he allow fears of the future to inhibit present actions.

Every moment I allow myself to live elsewhere than in the present I am being time-incompetent. One of the best illustrations of time-incompetence took place in a training group of twelve outgoing missionaries. They were having serious difficulty. They did not want to be in the course. They had not known and did not like the others in the group. They were becoming more and more spiteful and punishing in their behavior toward each other. Tension and hostility mounted until one man finally exploded with "I can't stand any of you! I can't wait to get to Africa so I can love the natives!" His future goal could possibly always remain in the future. He had not learned to love in the present, only in the fantasies of his wished-for deeds *somewhere else*.

A divorcée I once taught has extremely strong feelings of resentment and anger toward her ex-husband. Having felt betrayed by one man, she has resisted any feelings of love or intimacy toward any other man in the five years since her divorce. Her regrets from the past are closing her off from expanding her own potential as a warm and caring person. She and the missionary both lacked proficiency in the love-art of *gaining competence in the use of time*. They are both wasting their lives by not allowing themselves to be what they actually want to be.

Fears of what people will think also can keep us from being more time-competent. I am most free to be spontaneous in those situations in which I most trust my strengths and resources without need for reassurance from others. Time-incompetence can keep others in control of me, through overconcern with their approval.

The moments I truly love myself are those times I am all there and not wasting my life through procrastination. When the pride-in-me is most evident I feel strongly moved not to waste my uniqueness by waiting until some later time to be me. If I cannot deal with anger today, the chances are that I will not be able to deal with it at some other, more convenient, time tomorrow. This love-art is directly linked to the establishment of life goals and will be dealt with again in that portion of this chapter.

4. Developing the attitude of *being open toward growth and change* involves both changes in me and changes in the world. Through stretching my vision and receptivity, it enables me to see truth as others see it. It is the ability to see truth (or at least parts of truth) in all things without having to fit everything into a closed, tight package.

Being closed to the needs, perception, and feelings of others is the main cause of the so-called "generation gap" society is now experiencing. The views of those under thirty are dismissed casually by a large number of those of us in the over-thirty group. A large company in Minnesota has gone on a billboard campaign to try to convince young men to get haircuts and young women not to wear miniskirts. This reactionary view is an attempt to return to the "good old days" of our culture, or at least to maintain the status quo. This view does not recognize the changes that are occurring in the world. On the other hand, young people under thirty have a tendency to dismiss the perceptions, experiences, and particularly the needs of those over thirty. Neither subculture seems to be able or interested in listening to the views of the other.

One of the best examples pointing out the need to be open to truth as other people perceive it comes from a story told by Margaret Mead of her experiences among primitive people. It involved a day when she was awakened by shouting and commotion from the other side of the village where she was living. Seeing a man coming from that direction, she asked what all the noise was about. He replied that a man had come from the next village and was preaching against the intrusion of foreigners and how everyone from the United States ought to be sent back where they came from. As soon as she was able she went to seek out this man from the next village who had created such a disturbance. She discovered much to her surprise that there had been no such person in the village that morning. Returning to her informant she asked why he had told such a tale. His reply was: "Oh? No man? Well, if he had come that's what he would have said!" To a person from the Western world he lied. But he had not lied from his own view of truth. His understanding of truth was "he would have if he could have." There are many cultures in the world today that hold similar views. We need to be open to views of other cultures or we close ourselves off from the world either by a superior attitude or by isolationism. We do not have a monopoly on truth. We can bring this love-art more closely to our daily lives by being open to the views of our spouses, our children, and our neighbors.

Being open to new ideas also enables us to be open to the changes occurring both in ourselves and in the world. It prevents us from seeing the world as static and change as merely an illusion. There is so much evidence of change in the world today that to be closed to it brings the danger of personal obsolescence. By developing proficiency in the love-art of *being open to growth and change* both in ourselves and in the world we can guard against that danger.

All of the love-arts described above are seen as necessary to the love of self. My proficiency in their use results in more personal creativity and the development of my uniqueness. Becoming more aware and more sure of my uniqueness gives me the courage to risk entering into love relationships with other persons.

In loving myself I gain the power of identity that is necessary before love for others is possible. Love for others involves the giving of self, but as Rollo May has pointed out, "One gives only if he has something to give, only if he has a basis of strength within himself from which to give." [8]

B. *Love for Others and Love-Arts*

Love for another person is a relationship in which the other person's satisfaction, fulfillment, and security mean as much to me as my own.

The love arts related to love for others are:
1. Being self-accepting
2. Being open in communication
3. Developing trust in others' strengths
4. Risking involvement in life
5. Enjoying the exploration of another's world

DIAGRAM 2

Love for another person involves demands. My five-year-old son loves his teddy bear but I am not always so sure he loves me, at least not in the same way. His teddy bear never complains, is always there when needed, can be left alone for hours or days at a time and not get angry or huffy. His teddy bear places no demands on him, but his father does. His father's love costs him more.

Love is a willingness both to place demands upon and receive demands from another person. It therefore takes strong trust in myself not to be consumed or overwhelmed by the demands of my son. But equally important is the confidence and trust I have in his strengths to receive the demands I place on him. The fear of hurting or damaging another person by placing what appear to be overwhelming demands on him has destroyed many love relationships even before they were developed.

Love for another person involves sharing control of myself. But placing control of my life in another person's hands involves certain risks. Indeed, one of the major aspects of love is my willingness to risk for another person. The risks in loving another lie in the fact that I do not know what the loved one's response will be, nor can I always anticipate my own future reactions.

1. The first and most commonly felt risk is that of rejection. There can never be 100 per cent certainty that the receiver will not reject my offer of myself. Rejection at the very least is painful, and can cause withdrawal from relationships through mistrust of others or of my own resources. If I become an isolationist in interpersonal relationships, it is likely that I will turn more inward and become more static in my

personal growth. Withdrawing from love relationships with others can be self-destructive. In order to risk the rejection I might receive in offering love, I need to have trust in my own strengths. Proficiency in the love-art of *being more self-accepting* makes this possible.

2. A second and more subtle risk in loving another person is that of acceptance. If I offer myself to another person and he accepts, this places great demands on me. It involves a commitment which demands an ongoing openness in communication. In many instances I have failed to move into a depth relationship with another person out of fear of the demands of such a commitment.

Such demands are always present even in the beginning of love relationships. An illustration of this took place in a church school class of ninth grade girls. The class was studying Christian love and what it might mean to them and their lives. They finally decided that Christian love meant "doing something lovable for someone you didn't like." The teacher suggested that during the week they might test out their concept. When they returned the following week, the teacher asked for reports. One girl raised her hand and said, "I've done something!" The teacher replied, "Marvelous! What did you do?" "Well," the girl said, "in my math class at school there's this glunky kid." The teacher said, "Glunky?" And the girl replied, "Yes, you know, glunky. She's got four heads and, she's all thumbs, and she's got three left feet, and when she comes down the hall in school, everyone says 'Here comes that glunky kid again.' She doesn't have any friends, and nobody asks her to parties, and you know, she's just glunky." The teacher said, "I think I know just what you mean. What did you do?" "Well, this glunky kid's in my math class and she's having a tough time. I'm pretty good in math so I offered to help with her homework." "Wonderful," said the teacher. "So what happened?" "Well, I did help her, and it was fun, and she just couldn't thank me enough, but *now* I can't get rid of her!" Commitment in love in the face of demands means a willingness to be open and honest in an ever-changing relationship. The demand on the ninth grade girl was to be open with the glunky kid about her real feelings. If she failed to do that she would fall into the trap of being patronizing, one of the worst enemies of love. The willingness to risk acceptance in a love relationship involves proficiency in the love-art of *being open in communication.*

The least successful group in which I have ever worked had been together for seven days. They were afraid of themselves, of expressing their ideas or feelings, of getting involved on even the shallowest level with each other. Finally on the seventh day one man blurted out, "I don't like any of you!" This was the first real expression of love in the entire seven days. He cared enough for the others to at least tell them he did not care. Being open in a love relationship does not mean expressing only sweetness and light. It does mean risking myself by sharing openly how I feel toward the other person.

3. Being open with another person brings about a third risk in a love relationship: that the other person might be hurt. It is based on the fear that the other person may be destroyed or damaged if I give myself openly. It is the fear that another person may not be able to stand up under an open expression of feelings whether positive or negative. The love-art necessary here is *developing trust in others' strengths,* which means trusting their strengths and resources as much as I trust my own.

A major criteria of a love relationship is allowing the other person freedom to grow. If I decide what is right for the love receiver by choosing to withhold pertinent information, it is patronizing of the other person's strengths. It becomes a manipulative relationship in which freedom becomes more and more remote and the relationship less meaningful.

4. A fourth risk in a love relationship is the possibility of being hurt through the loved one's loss of security or satisfaction. If I love another person I am doubling my chances of being hurt in this life. However, without a love relationship my chances for finding meaning, fulfillment, and happiness are practically nonexistent. The love-art of *risking involvement in life* involves risking the danger of pain through a loved one's pain. But not risking involvement brings the larger danger of personal stagnation.

To risk involvement in life is made more easy as I become less controlled by the fear of what others may think of me, and more able to act in harmony with my own intuition and feelings. Real involvement in life means the willingness to be perceived by others on the basis of my natural behavior, rather than attempting to put myself across as a particular type of person. Involvement in life also means the willingness to encourage natural behavior in others rather than putting pressure on them to act out my stereotypes based on such things as position, past experiences with them, race, or religion.

Proficiency in the love-art of *risking involvement in life* can be gained through the practice of all the other love-arts in day-to-day, real-life situations.

5. One extremely important aspect of love relationships involves the joy of sharing private worlds with another person. Proficiency in the love-art of *enjoying the exploration of another's world* is greatly enhanced by zest for new discoveries. Each person being a unique being can bring new insights, new ideas, and new philosophies into relationship with my own. Such discoveries sometimes delight and sometimes threaten, but rarely bore me.

The most successful technique I know for moving into such a walk through another's world is to ask another person what really turns them on and to reciprocate by telling them what turns me on. By this I mean sharing what is most exhilarating in our lives, of what we most anticipate doing or seeing or experiencing. Journeys have been quite varied and have described moments with a child, or abandonment to the beauty of sunsets, or the commitment to a job or a profession or community work, or the thrill of sexual relations. Sometimes, after only an hour's conversation with a new acquaintance, we know each other more deeply than some people we have known for years.

This love-art can be practiced anywhere: on a plane, on a bus, in a restaurant, or around the family dinner table. It can be an extremely exciting trip. What you are sharing together is what means the most to you in this life. This is a far more effective way to get to know people than the usual "what do you do, where are you from and how many children do you have" type of conversations so familiar to all of us. It can also open up more depth communications between members of families who normally do not share their worlds with each other.

The risk involved in this love-art is in feeling overexposed to another person. My private world becomes less private, my secrets less hidden, and my weaknesses more evident. To trust another person with myself is risky. He might use the knowledge of my weaknesses against me, he might ridicule things sacred to me, he might take too lightly my private world by giving it away to others, or worst of all, he might laugh at me when he finds out who I really am. The beauty and joy of a love relationship is developing such trust in a person that the fear of overexposure melts away. The sheer magnificence of the message of Jesus of Nazareth (not always the message of his followers) is that no matter who I am or what I do, God loves me anyway. This depth of love is possible between two human beings but it takes hard work to make it happen. It can begin with a simple journey through another person's world.

Love For Others	
Risks	*Love-arts*
1. Rejection	Being self-accepting
2. Acceptance	Being open in communication
3. Hurting the other person	Trusting other's strength
4. Being hurt by the other's pain	Risking involvement in life
5. Being exposed	Enjoying the exploration of another's world

DIAGRAM 3

II. Life Goals

"It has been one of the findings from the Human Potentialities Research Project that a systematic thinking-through and working-through of life goals and values is rarely undertaken by the average well functioning person *or the achieving person who has become established in his vocation or profession.* More often than not, if there has been an elucidation of life goals and if clarification has been sought in relation to personal values, such efforts have been haphazard, usually characterized by certain superficiality, and lacking in both depth and planned, systematic effort." [9]

To establish life goals is not an easy task. It is involved with the deepest questions a person must ask about himself and his world.

Questions such as What difference is my life making? Who am I, anyway? Am I using my gifts and talents for myself? What is my uniqueness? What is my responsibility to others? Are my feelings and behavior congruent? What assumptions do I hold about life?

Answers to these questions are elusive and difficult to reach. Proficiency in the love-arts is a prerequisite to the quest. Love of self provides the self-trust and self-knowledge necessary to establish life goals. Love relationships with others provides the support necessary to risk making a choice for one's life.

The establishment of life goals is an attempt to plan a more meaningful existence. Meaning occurs in a person's life when he realizes a moment of almost total satisfaction in who he is and what he is doing. The more we can live to the fullest of our potential within every moment, the more meaning we can discover for our lives.

Personal life goals can be divided into two different categories: (a) long-range goals, and (b) ongoing process goals.

(a) The average person generally thinks of long-range goals when the word "goal" is used: a higher position, a better-paying job, becoming president of a club, buying a bigger house, marrying and having a family, obtaining a college degree, etc. These goals are usually future-oriented and are seen as accomplishable. They usually are easily measurable by "I did it" or "I haven't done it." Most of us want more things, more comfort, more fame, but what we want *most* is more difficult to determine. One excellent method of establishing ultimate, long-range goals is to ask ourselves the question: "On the last day of my life what would I have had to accomplish in order to be satisfied?"

Establishing Long-Range Goals	
Dangers	*Love-arts*
1. Being future-oriented	Gaining competence in the use of time
2. Setting goals apart from personal feelings, needs and resources	Being more self-accepting
3. Being trapped by unfulfilling commitments	Being open to growth and change

DIAGRAM 4

In establishing such long-range life goals, three potentially powerful dangers exist:

1. The first danger lies in their future orientation. We can become so involved in dreams of the future that the present is ignored and wasted. The "future" in reality never comes.

Future goals must be related to present reality. An idealized goal can prevent realization of present potential. In one company with which I worked, one of the key vice-presidents fully expected one day to be president. His creative, normal behavior on the job became more and more immobilized as he tried to live into his image of what others would expect in a president. He took fewer and fewer risks and revealed less and less of his true feelings and ideas. His future goal blinded him to his present opportunities. Only when the president retired and he was passed over for the position did he realize the years he had wasted. He had become virtually a yes-man. The accomplishment of future goals must emerge out of present behavior. He lacked the love-art of *gaining competence in the use of time*.

Our public school system in the United States has created in our culture built-in tolerance to time-incompetence. We were made to deal with irrelevant facts toward a future goal through so many school years that our sense of the use of time as a culture has been dulled. When I finally received my high school diploma, a goal toward which I had worked for twelve years, I was quite surprised to find I did not feel any great sense of fulfillment. So to fill the void of meaningful purpose in my life I immediately established another goal for another diploma four years hence. This is not to say I am not happy to have those diplomas. But much of my life lacked relevance to the present experience of what was happening to me. If I could have tied together future goals and ongoing goals I would have learned much more, and used so much more of the potential I had. The danger of a future-oriented goal is that we can sell our lives for it without ever being aware of what we are doing. The love-art of *gaining competence in the use of time* is extremely important in establishing and accomplishing meaningful long-range goals.

2. The second and more subtle danger in long-range goals is that when a goal is finally reached, we may find we do not really want it or are not happy with it after all. A good friend of mine wanted to be known as an expert in the applied behavioral sciences in Africa. He and his family made many sacrifices to attain that goal. The main difficulty he found when he had almost reached his dream was that he did not *like* to work in Africa. Life began to drag for him until he got into related work in an entirely different area.

The subtlety of this danger can be seen in the fact that he fully believed it was what he wanted until he was almost there. What he had failed to do was to look deep within himself to discover his strengths, what he most liked to do, where he was most creative; and, just as important, to discover his weaknesses, what he least liked to do, what blocked his creativeness, and in what type of situations he had the most difficulty being motivated. Had he built his life around his known desires, strengths, and weaknesses, his future goal would have emerged out of him. What he did was to establish a specific goal based on strategy instead of self-knowledge. The love-art he most lacked was *being more self-accepting*.

3. A third danger in long-range life goals is that we may become

trapped in a future-oriented lifetime commitment that can cease to have meaning for us. In order to gain the freedom to risk establishing meaningful life goals we need the attitude that "nothing is forever." If we make a decision and it turns out to be a wrong one, we still have ourselves and our resources which can be applied in a new situation. If we have to give everlasting commitment to anything, reluctance should be expected to occur. The Roman Catholic Church is discovering that a person who takes a vow at twenty-five years of age may be a very different person who feels betrayed and trapped at thirty-five. Persons change. The world changes.

One of the great pressures persons face in our Western culture is that of *not quitting*. There are hundreds of thousands of people who are in miserable and nonproductive situations. But they will not leave until they "lick it" because our cultural values say that quitting and, therefore, quitters are "bad." This is reinforced by such well-known adages as: "Quitters never win, winners never quit." . . . "If at first you don't succeed, try, try again."

Dr. Seuss once wrote a brilliant article for the *Saturday Evening Post* entitled: "If At First You Don't Succeed, Quit!" His argument was that many people who are unsuited to certain situations foolishly refuse to give up. How much more meaningful and productive their lives could be if they were in a situation that inspired them to new creativity, rather than forcing them to hang on for mere survival. We need to be open to change and growth or we can lose our lives in doing meaningless tasks. I am not saying that it is always good to quit. But I am emphasizing the need to recognize the alternative of quitting which long-term commitments tend to make us forget.

Another example of a lifetime commitment is that of marriage. We take vows in marriage to a future commitment to live together as man and wife till death do us part. Certainly that vow is a clearly stated, long-range life goal. But as the statistics point out, the commitment to a future goal is not enough in at least 50 per cent of marriages. Marriage should be an ongoing *present* commitment to grow in relationship through openness and work, rather than depending upon a future-oriented vow to somehow produce a magic no one really expects. The same is true in any commitment to a long-range life goal. It must be tied to present, ongoing goals if it is ever to be truly and meaningfully accomplished.

After exploring the danger involved in long-range goals I feel it necessary to reemphasize the importance of establishing them. Long-range goals provide criteria for establishing ongoing, process goals. Both long-range and ongoing goals provide a sense of purpose in life. Commitment to that purpose brings a motivation that can bring about a greater use of our resources, all of which help us to become more of what we potentially are. The fear of a long-range or lifetime commitment has caused many persons to forgo *any* commitment and to flounder through the years. Commitment to goals are necessary for any of us to find meaning. But commitment must also be tied to present reality.

(b) Ongoing, process goals are those goals established for the present reality. They are the greatest guards against the dangers inherent in long-range goals. These are objectives we seek within our process of becoming. What we want to become can be determined by again asking ourselves the question: At the end of my life what must I have done in order to be satisfied? Or perhaps even better: If I were to die today, what would make me most unhappy not to have accomplished? In answering that question I establish my long-range goals. I must then ask myself the question: What am I doing now that will help me accomplish that, or doing now that will hinder me from accomplishing that? The answers to these questions give me ongoing life goals. Long-range goals may be in the form of attainment of personal growth: I want to be more open, more loving, more directive, less directive, etc. To set ongoing goals, ask the question: What am I doing right *now* to become more open? Much as the missionary who wanted to love in the future, we cannot be more open or more loving if we are not *now* in our present behavior working on it.

In the balance of things, what I am doing now must be what I choose to do or I wouldn't be doing it.[10] If I feel I ought to be more open in the future but am not now working on openness, then I need to reexamine my goals. I may be establishing goals out of some external moral imperative that I have not truly accepted. If I really wished I were more directive, I would be. If I really wanted to be somewhere else, I would be there. A long-range goal is far enough removed for us to live more comfortably with not doing anything about it and still justify our *wanting* to do it. The value in ongoing goals is that we cannot fool ourselves as easily. Ongoing goals force us to face into what it is we truly want and expect out of our lives. In establishing them we create for ourselves a learning climate for self-growth.

Personal growth goals are ongoing, process goals. All of the love-arts could also be ongoing life goals and the concept of them is based on the hope that they will be used in this way.

In order for ongoing goals to be used most effectively, only one, or certainly not more than three, should be worked on at any given moment. If too many goals are being worked on at any one time it becomes confusing, especially in attempting to analyze the results.

Working on process goals requires experimental behavior and any deliberate attempt at new behavior is hard work. It can be physically and emotionally tiring, sometimes a little frightening, but almost always exciting. There are risks involved in being experimental. I may fail. New, untried ways of acting sometimes produce unexpected reactions, while old behaviors, though not fully satisfying, at least have reactions to which I am accustomed. People may oppose me by bringing pressures to bear to make me act in the pattern in which they know me. But being experimental is imperative to my functioning as an autonomous person, a person who creates and guides the forces of change in the world around me.

III. Conclusion

A person is in charge of his life or he is controlled by internal or external forces to which he submits. At any point in my life, I can review my individual history with feelings of satisfaction or regrets. If I have regrets and have control of my life, I can act to change my situation. If I do not have control, I can only live with my regrets and hope that something will happen to make me more satisfied. I continually seek to gain more control over the forces of change that surround my life. Without that control I am subject to the accidents of fate.

Love and the establishment of life goals are not ends in themselves. They are means to the end of a more autonomous and meaningful life.

Love for self helps to develop strengths, confidence, and self-knowledge. Self-love enables me to build love relationships with others. Love for others gives me support, courage and empathy, and enables me to grow more in self-awareness and self-love. Having been loved by others paradoxically gives me the strength to stand alone if necessary.

Through love I gain the self-knowledge and the courage to establish life goals based realistically on my present and potential strengths. The establishment of life goals gives me the criteria I need to make the ongoing decisions of my life with a sense of purpose and accomplishment rather than whimsically and haphazardly. Definite life goals give my life direction, purpose, meaning, and commitment. It is through establishing life goals that I can put skin around my values and breathe life into them. Having ongoing, process goals gives me the sense of adventure that brings the realization that every day is the first day of the rest of my life.

Consequently, having life goals aids accomplishment, accomplishment increases my sense of personal strength which enables me to offer myself more in love for others, love relationships provide the support I need to accomplish more of my life goals. Love and life goals are inextricably woven together. Both are necessary for personal autonomy and both can be developed through proficiency in the love-arts.

NOTES

1. Ezra Pound, *Impact* (Chicago: Henry Regnery Co., 1960).
2. Erich Fromm, *Man for Himself* (New York: Fawcett World Library, 1967), p. 106.
3. Abraham Maslow, "Isomorphic Interrelationships Between Knower and Known" (mimeographed lecture, 1959).
4. R. W. Emerson, quoted by A. H. Maslow, *ibid.*
5. Frances G. Wickes, *The Inner World of Man* (New York: Frederick Ungar Publishing Co., 1938); Maslow, *ibid.*
6. Richard E. Byrd, *Creative Risk Taking Training Laboratory, Book of Basic Readings* (Minneapolis: Jones and Byrd, Inc., 1968), p. 19.
7. Richard E. Byrd, "Training in a Non-Group," *Journal of Humanistic Psychology,* Spring, 1967.
8. Rollo May, *Man's Search for Himself* (New York: New American Library, 1967).
9. Herbert A. Otto, *Group Methods Designed to Actualize Human Potential, A Handbook* (Beverly Hills: Holistic Press, 1970), p. 82.
10. Richard E. Byrd, *op. cit.,* p. 35.

REFERENCES

Allport, Gordon, *Becoming.* New Haven: Yale University Press, 1955.

D'Arcy, M. C., *The Mind and Heart of Love.* Cleveland and New York: The World Publishing Co., 1964.

Erikson, Erik, *Childhood and Society.* New York: W. W. Norton & Co., Inc., 1950.

Fabun, Don, *The Dynamics of Change.* Englewood Cliffs, N. J.: Prentice-Hall, Inc., 1967.

Heidegger, Martin, *Existence and Being.* Chicago: Henry Regnery Co., 1967.

Jones, David G., *Sentiency, A Workshop in Love and Life Issues.* Minneapolis: Jones and Byrd, Inc., 1968.

Maslow, Abraham H., "A Theory of Metamotivation: The Biological Rooting of the Value-Life." *Journal of Humanistic Psychology,* Fall, 1967.

————, *Toward a Psychology of Being*. D. Van Nostrand Co., 1962.

Sullivan, Harry S., *Conceptions of Modern Psychiatry*. New York: W. W. Norton and Co., Inc., 1953.

Tillich, Paul, *Love, Power and Justice*. New York: Oxford University Press, 1960.

19

Love: Reflections, Fragments, and a Method Designed to Enhance Love

Herbert A. Otto

It is one of the paradoxes of our existence that, although we know of our continuing need for love, we do not allow ourselves a full and ongoing measure of love—this quality which wise men and prophets of all ages have celebrated as the essence of being and the manifestation of God in man. Do we really accept the culturally fostered platitude that love comes but once or twice in man's life and then is most likely to end in tragedy, frustration, or monogamy? There is, of course, nothing wrong with love ending in monogamy if the quality of love continues to play a central role in the marriage, and does not become tarnished, attenuated, and excessively feeble or unrecognizable. Are we at a point in our development where we will recognize our need and accept the responsibility for *developing* and *experiencing* the love which we have within us as a lifelong regenerative force?

Love is an act of courage—it is daring to touch an ultimate—it is the ultimate touch. Being touched and touching a being.

In too many of our loves we too soon lose the courage to discover our many selves in the beloved. By closing these many doors of self-recognition, we deprive love itself of that vital quality where the beloved offers ever-new gifts and adventures.

240

Love is a process of unfoldment reaching ever deeper levels of the larger-than-self. It is a process of becoming ever closer to what we really are.

He who would be alive must ever partake of the pulsating stream of love. If we want to stay fully in touch with ourselves, we must be "in love" continuously with a friend, a child, a lover. The more we pulsate in this stream of love, the more we pulsate with life.

Why aren't we living the exuberant life-style of love?

I finally reached the conclusion that man's fear of himself—which expresses itself for the most part as fear and suspicion of his fellow man—is a major factor which keeps him both from actualizing his potential and from loving.

Loving is inseparable from leaving. Whomever and whatever we love, we must ultimately leave. This fear of leaving or being left keeps many people from loving.

Love is a climate marked by the appearance of changes in season—but the climate prevails.

In my work with healthy well-functioning people, helping them to actualize potential, I have encountered a disturbing phenomenon, which I have called the "love is too good for me syndrome." Over and over I find creative, productive people of both sexes who, once in love and thoroughly enjoying a deep and satisfying relationship, unconsciously begin to take steps and engage in maneuvers designed to destroy the relationship. It is almost as if these people are saying "I don't deserve this great pleasure, these wonderful feelings. I must stop it." It is currently my assumption that to accept so much love and pleasure would mean that the person must take a next step toward change and personality growth. Thus, the abortion of love and deep pleasure which rests on a very complex causality is at the same time a means of opting for the status quo—"I will not be changed by the experience of love."

A central question in our lives: "How can we be sensitive and open to the quick flash or sustained offering of love and caring given by another person, and give in return?"

We are all basically loving but we need to get rid of a lot of inner garbage first before love can reach all aspects of our being.

Too often love is the unlived value.

Due to the nature of our either/or thinking, we fall into the error of deciding "My love for this person is greater than for that person." This formulation is inaccurate. Can it be: "My love for this person is different from my love for that person."

Love is a peak event which need not be singular, which can occur often in our lives, but which for too many reasons we too often deny ourselves.

Love, then, is discovering among the flowers of the beloved the myriad buds of self, knowing that these too will open.

To love is to grow.

Multiple Love Relationships

Small children are capable of loving several children with great intensity and devotion. The pre-teen and teen-ager can let themselves experience different feelings and qualities of love toward several boys or girls at the same time. We as adults are prone to dismiss these manifestations of love as "teen-age crushes." However, another possibility presents itself: that man is capable of not only one but several loving and deep relationships at the same time, if he so wishes and has the freedom to do so.

Although we may not choose to admit it, the main characteristic of these relationships of children and teen-agers to several other age mates is an emotional involvement of considerable intensity, which invariably has some sexual overtones. Similarly, a loving, emotional involvement of varying intensity, quality, and depth at the same time with several persons is not only possible, but has been experienced by many adults. The familiar triangle situation wherein one person loves two persons at the same time but with varying and different qualities of love, has been described, often celebrated, in the literature of all ages. Certainly the experienced marriage counselor has come across many instances of persons deeply, responsibly committed in love to two individuals at the same time. "I love you, you as my wife (husband) but I love her (him) in a different way." How often have these words echoed through the divorce court?

The element of deep pain and struggle in the triangular love complex is often introduced by the mental construct, whether implicit or explicit, *that love and loving should be and can be only on a one-to-one relationship*. Inseparable from this mental set is the "love-as-ownership" issue. Seemingly a carry-over from male ownership of goods and chattels (women were legally considered to be chattel in many Western countries into the early twentieth century), love is seen as conferring ownership rights. "I love you, you love me—therefore I own (should have) *all* of your love" is accepted as a basic premise. Ownership and possession have been both the delight and despair of lovers throughout the centuries. However, it is exactly these mental constructs of ownership and possession which create the barriers and griefs on which love so often flounders. Owning or expecting to own all of another person's mature heterosexual love as one's lifelong due is one of the bases of contemporary monogamy—an institution which is in difficulty. (The large divorce rate and the even larger subclinical incidence of marital unhappiness which never reaches the counselor or divorce court is a clear indication of the deep-seated problems inherent in today's modes of married relating.)

When love is conceived as bestowing ownership qualities, that which we call "jealousy" emerges in clearer perspective. Jealousy is attributed in part to outraged property rights ("I own your love—you own mine"), and in part to the formulations "I must own, have, possess, *all* of your love and attention; otherwise you are not giving me what rightfully belongs to me," and "I am afraid of losing what is mine."

Another major element in jealousy and the process of love between two people is insecurity. At the very base of much insecurity is love starvation. Everyone is starved for love—few of us have enough love in our lives. If, then, we do let love come into our lives, we often have reached such a point of starvation that, like the hungry man, we must have all. We insist on total possession, even if it kills love. Suffering from love starvation, we deeply fear that there isn't enough to go around—for that has been our experience. We must have every bit of love the other person is capable of giving. Our own feelings of insecurity, based on love starvation, demand this.

When we feel insecure, we question: "Does the person I love really love me?" The answer we give ourself is "Of course he loves me *if he gives me all of the love he is capable of giving.* But if he gives even a part of this love to another, he does not truly love me." The deeper issues here are those of self-worth and self-identity. If a woman is not sufficiently secure and fulfilled by her status as a wife and homemaker, she may reach out and supplement her sense of identity and selfhood by incorporating considerable elements of her husband's identification (including his successes, values, viewpoints) as a part of her ego structure. Her sense of self-identity may become blurred through this incorporation process and at the same time there may be an awareness and resentment of what is going on. This symbiotic process of supplementing her identity by deriving part of it from her husband (or lover) leaves the woman in a vulnerable position. A threat of loss of the man (the possibility of his sharing his capacity for affection with someone else) undermines her sense of identity and contributes materially to the end product we call "jealousy." Happily, with the advent of Women's Liberation many women are now able to attain a new sense of self-worth and identity separate and apart from their function as wife and homemaker.

A woman or man may also supplement their sense of self-worth by a strong identification with the partner. The more solid a person's sense of self-worth, the less likely he is to succumb to petty feelings of jealousy. The greater our sense of self-worth, the less easily are we hurt by actions of the beloved *which we interpet subjectively* as indicating a diminishing of his love. When the sense of self-worth of one person becomes excessively dependent on the love of another person, the entire relationship is in difficulty. Love can and does make us feel more worthy, but this should be a by-product rather than the main product of love. Love can and does give us greater self-esteem, but this is a part of the process of love, not *the* process.

Identity in love also has another aspect. Most lovers report a simultaneous blurring and heightening of their sense of self. They feel their own identity more intensely at the same time that they experience oneness with the identity of the beloved. These pulsating changes are a part of the process of love. As the lovers temporarily merge their identities in the process of love, they emerge with new permutations and growth in their personality. In the merging of identities there is a cross-pollination as subtle nuances and factors in one person's being enrich the other. Again, if one person's sense of identity is excessively dependent for its definition on the beloved, the relationship is in difficulty. A heightened sense of identity emerges from the process of love—it is not the focus of love.

One of the main doubts of most men and women when confronted with the idea that a person is capable of simultaneous multiple love relationships centers around the belief that everyone has only a limited amount of love to give. This is true if we do not have enough love inputs and positive inputs, enough caring coming in. If we become participants in the stream of love, our capacity for loving is as limitless as our capacity for vital, creative living. In the final analysis, ecstatic living is inseparable from the free flow of loving.

To many, the notion of multiple love relationships is ludicrous, bizarre, *unthinkable*. This is precisely the point. *We are what we think of ourselves,* we are what we feel, we are our mental constructs, our vision of ourselves. Today we may not feel like it or may not be ready for a multiple love relationship. Tomorrow we may change. Or we may never change.

This, then, is my main point: I may not myself have the interest or need to enter into a multiple love relationship; but I can understand, accept it (and perhaps feel a little envious) when other people are involved in such a relationship. From my point of view, love is so rare and so precious that those who are able to share love should never be discouraged from the risk taking inherent in giving their love to more than one person. Love is too rare to discourage its sharing.

If we believe in monogamy, a major question with which we are left is: "Do we believe in only monogamistic loving?" Or, to put it differently, if we encounter a married person who has entered into a love relationship with several other single or married persons, what is our attitude?

Kinsey, Cuber, and other researchers have found that the lifelong monogamistic commitment is a pious fiction for many people. An exclusive sexual (and emotional) lifelong commitment to the marriage partner is the exception rather than the rule. Having a spur-of-the moment affair or sexual encounter of some sort at some time(s) during the marriage seems to be one characteristic of the contemporary union. The extramarital liaison is rarely openly admitted to, and rarely are its implications fully explored through discussion by both marital partners. However, this type of relationship has become institutionalized to a certain extent. It is often called "an arrangement" and one or both partners feel free to engage in other sexual relationships while exercising all due discretion. Many couples who *live* according to such an arrangement have grave difficulty accepting it, do not deal with it honestly, cannot come to emotional terms with it, and cannot discuss it.

The affair or sexual encounter of the married person in most instances seems to be an act of desperation, laden with guilt feelings and a nagging sense of transgression. It appears to stem from the unacknowledged realization that the love relationship with one person exclusively and for the rest of one's life is, for most people, an unsatisfactory compact. Implicit also is the fact that in many marriages, due to a multitude of factors, the interaction between partners opposes and stifles the development of individual potential and interpersonal growth. The partners, in fact, have an investment in maintaining the relationship as it is and where it is, however unsatisfactory this reality might be. Also, since people grow at different rates and in different directions, couples often tend to grow apart and outgrow each other while at the same time they attempt to prevent each other from growing.

A loving and sexual relationship with several persons simultaneously can be a means of personality growth and self-unfoldment and seems to meet a deep and present need in many persons. In many instances, the extramarital affair is a means of reaching out for further personality growth, for fulfillment, through an emotional and sexual relationship with a person other than the spouse. Sometimes it can also be understood as an act of desperation designed to maintain the marital equilibrium. ("I love my husband dearly but I had to do it—I couldn't stand our marriage the way it was any longer. Yet I don't want a divorce. My husband and I belong together.")

I want to make clear that I am not opposed to the institution of marriage. My interest is in exploring alternatives to monogamy, as I believe that the living, loving arrangements of man in a free society should be bounded only by the limits of his imagination and needs. I am very much interested in regenerating the institution of marriage so that it can become a more viable and workable structure.*

At various phases during most people's lifelong unfoldment and growth, there may be a need to have a loving and sexual relationship with more than one individual. Conscious acknowledgment and communication of this need may open a new dimension of freedom. When

* See Herbert A. Otto, *More Joy in Your Marriage* (New York: Hawthorn, 1969), and "The New Marriage: Marriage as a Framework for Developing Personal Potential," in Herbert A. Otto, ed., *The Family in Search of a Future* (New York: Appleton-Century-Crofts, 1970).

multiple love relationships have become socially acceptable to a greater degree than the acceptability today accorded to the institution of divorce, it is highly probable there will be concomitant significant gains in man's capacity to accept and love both himself and his fellow man. In a society characterized by estrangement, repression, violence, generation and credibility gaps, *all possible loving relationships must be fostered to reverse the course of destruction and to make man more human.*

"Commitment with Freedom"—A Credo

One of the central issues in any deep union between two people, and particularly in marriage, involves the areas of freedom, trust, commitment, and dedication. These concepts often are not static but developmental—they may expand, broaden, deepen or change as a result of the relationship or as a result of life experience. In too many instances internal changes in attitude or viewpoint concerning these central issues by the man or woman are never communicated to the other partner. The issues are not openly discussed until triggered by a crisis event. I consider it most important that a couple about to enter into a deep union of any type mutually explore these issues which are so central to the nature and direction of the developing relationship. Such avoidance is part of a universal human tendency to shun confrontation and exploration of the other person's values and viewpoints because we fear conflict and disagreement. Our need for love is so great that we let our fears of conflict keep us from coming to grips with the central issues of the relationship. Yet, resolution of these very issues can open us to new dimensions of understanding and caring and bring us the measure of love called for by our need.

To me, the essence of a relationship is capsulated in the Eastern maxim, "Commitment without chains." I believe in the absolute commitment of two people to each other in love, in caring, and in dedication to each other's growth. Yet I am deeply convinced that my love must have freedom within the relationship. For example, I would consider it an infringement on my beloved's freedom to say, "You must not have a sexual relationship with anyone else." I may have my wishes and express them—but wishes are neither imperatives, commands, nor rules. It is here that I must place the greatest possible amount of trust in my partner and our love. I trust my partner and our togetherness sufficiently to know that any relationship with another person, sexual or otherwise, is a part of the dedication and commitment of our love. It may be the result of various needs and causes within the mysterious being who is my love. I trust that whatever my partner does is done within the overriding framework of our love and with the preservation, maintenance, and continuation of our love in mind. In this sense, then, I must trust my partner's dedication to the centrality of our love and our commitment to each other. This is the freedom of responsibility—I trust my beloved to be responsible for the person she is and can be and for the creative unfoldment of our union. This to me is the freedom which we as lovers must have, to continue to grow in our love throughout the years.

Love: An Integrative Experience *

> We will be judged by what we have not done,
> by the love we have not shown.
> —HENRY DRUMMOND

The following can be read aloud as a means of beginning the experience:
Love is one of the most important elements in anyone's life. In contemporary Western culture, where estrangement from self and others has become a psychological epidemic in our times, love has never been more important. Love starvation, recognized and unrecognized, is at the basis of much interpersonal unhappiness and intrapsychic turmoil. As we cease to love ourselves and others, we die or join the living dead all around us—the zombies who move through life uninvolved, unfeeling, uncaring, clothed in the raiments of superficialty and strangled by their fatal commitment to the status quo.

This legion of the living dead suffers from the far advanced disease from which we all, to some extent, suffer: *We do not give to ourselves and to each other enough love to sustain the high level of vital functioning of which we are capable.* It is the purpose of this experience to help you to use your fantasy and imagination as a vehicle to bring more love to your being.

Love: An Integrative Experience can be either a dyad (two persons), triad (three persons), or a group experience in a small (seven to twelve persons) Growth Group. With some simple alterations, a person can also have this experience by himself. There are four distinct parts to this experience. Each part begins by letting the ideas, associations and imagination flow, then proceeds to verbal sharing and discussion, including formulation of action plans.

---

* Revised version of chapter by the same name from Herbert A. Otto, *Group Methods to Actualize Human Potential: A Handbook,* Holistic Press, 160 So. Robertson Blvd., Beverly Hills, California, 1970.

To maintain the element of surprise and spontaneity and in order for this method to be most effective, *you are urged not to read ahead but to finish one part of the experience before reading the next.*

This is a voluntary experience and no one is to be pressured to participate if you are in a group. If you do not wish to share your ideas, just say "I pass" and this will be respected by everyone. You should do this in the clear recognition however that verbal sharing of your ideas and thoughts could be a freeing experience for you. This experience takes approximately one and one-half to two and one-half hours, depending on the size of the group and other variables.

As previously mentioned, this method can also be used by a couple. The experience can take little time or a great deal of time, depending on the extent to which each member of the couple wishes to involve himself in the experience. Mood, attitude, and other factors will play an important part in relation to the length of time spent experiencing and may not necessarily affect results, whereas the quality and depth of communication will have much to do with the outcome.

PART I

Begin by taking five minutes silent time. Relax, close your eyes and let images and thoughts flow as you ask yourself one of the following Key Questions:

For use by couple: What has been the most loving moment in our relationship to date?

For use in group: What has been the most loving moment in my life?

As you share your answer, share as much detail as possible and try to recapture the feeling of that moment. If another loving moment comes to your mind, share this one also. It is best, however, to restrict this part of the experience to sharing of one or two loving moments.

Do not read ahead.

PART II

Ask yourself the following question: HOW AND IN WHAT WAYS CAN I GIVE MORE LOVE TO OTHERS? (This is based on the recognition that by giving more love to others, love will be returned in even greater measure.) Take about five minutes, close your eyes and in answer to this question let images and ideas flow in.

Now share the harvest of your imagination with your partner or group.

As a closure for this part of the experience, participants may wish to share *how they feel now* as a result of this experience.

PART III

Ask yourself the following question: HOW CAN OTHERS GIVE MORE LOVE TO ME? (What can they do?) Close your eyes and let the images and ideas come in. Take about five minutes to let your imagination unfold.

Now share the results with your partner or the group. Finally, answer for yourself and discuss the following with your group (or partner): IN WHAT WAYS CAN I INITIATE ACTION SO THAT MORE LOVE WILL BE GIVEN TO ME BY OTHERS? *Do not read ahead!*

PART IV

Finally, ask yourself the following question: HOW CAN I GIVE MORE LOVE TO MYSELF? (This is based on the assumption that we first need to love ourselves before we can love others.) Close your eyes and let images and ideas make their appearance. Let your imagination flow. *Take about five minutes for this.*

Following this five-minute period, *share the results with your partner or group.*

In conclusion—answer for yourself and then discuss with your partner or group the following: WHAT POSITIVE CHANGE AND ACTION IS INDICATED IN YOUR LIFE (if any) AS A RESULT OF THIS EXPERIENCE?

20

Love: Its Aspects, Dimensions, Transformation and Power

Pitirim A. Sorokin *

I. The Psychological Aspect of Love

Psychologically the experience of love is a complex consisting of emotional, affective, volitional, and intellectual elements. It has many qualitative forms. Each "shade" of love as a psychological experience has its own "color." [1] *In any genuine psychological experience of love, the ego or I of the loving individual tends to merge with and to identify itself with the loved Thee.* The greater the love, the greater the identification. The joy or sorrow of the loved person becomes joy and sorrow to the loving person. Genuine sharing of all the values of life follows. Sacrifice for the loved person becomes a sacrifice for the person himself.

In other words, *love as psychological experience is "altruistic" by its very nature;* whereas the opposite *experience of hatred is inherently selfish.* In a real love or friendship a friend is one who does what is good (or what he believes to be good) for another for that other's sake, and not because the friend gives him pleasure or is useful to him. Pseudo friendship, motivated by pleasure or utility, takes the other person as a means and not as the end value.[2]

Love is the justification and deliverance of individuality through the sacrifice of egoism. It rescues us from the inevitability of death, and fills our existence with an absolute content. . . . Sacrificing egoism and

* Excerpts from Chapters I and II of *The Ways and Power of Love,* by Pitirim A. Sorokin, Chicago: Henry Regnery Company, copyright © 1967.

251

surrendering ourselves to love, we find in it not merely living, but also life-giving power, and we do not forfeit our individuality (personality) with our egoism, but on the contrary make it eternal.[3]

More concretely, *love is the experience that annuls our loneliness;* fills the emptiness of our isolation with the richest value; breaks and transcends the narrow walls of our little egos; makes us coparticipants in the highest life of humanity and in the whole cosmos; expands our true individuality to the immeasurable boundaries of the universe.

Eliminating our loneliness and binding us by the noblest of bonds to others, love is literally a *life-giving force,* because as the studies of suicide show, an empty loneliness is the main cause of suicide, and because altruists live longer than egoists do.[4] Making us full-fledged coparticipants in the lives of others, love infinitely enriches our lives by the greatest and noblest values of all humanity. In this sense, it fills us with *knowledge,* because coparticipation and coexperience in the richest experience of all the generations of humanity—rather than only in one's individual experience—is the most efficient method of learning and the most fruitful way to truth and knowledge. In this sense, the love experience leads to a true cognition and *love becomes truth.*

Love beautifies our life because the love experience is beautiful by its very nature and beautifies the whole universe. To love anything or anybody means literally to immortalize the mortal, to ennoble the ignoble, to uplift the low, to beautify the ugly. Anything that one looks at through loving eyes becomes "lovely," that is, beautiful.

By its very nature *love is goodness itself;* therefore *it makes our life noble and good.*

Finally, *love experience means freedom at its loftiest.* To love anything is to act freely, without compulsion or coercion. And vice versa: to be free means to do what one loves to do. In this sense, *love and true freedom are synonymous.* Compulsion and coercion are the negation of love. Where there is love there is no coercion; where there is coercion there is no love. And the greater the love the greater the freedom. A person who loves all humanity is free in this human universe; a person who loves the whole universe is free in the whole world. A person who hates the world is the greatest of slaves—subjectively and objectively. Anything or anybody is his enemy, anything or anybody hinders him, opposes him, presses upon him, limits his freedom incessantly, at every turn, in every action, in every thought, emotion, or volition. The whole world, from inanimate objects up to his fellow men, becomes his prison filled with innumerable executioners.[5] Freedom is love and love is freedom.

The love experience is marked further by a "feeling" of fearlessness and power. Love does not fear anything or anybody. Where there is fear there is no love; where there is love there is no fear.

The fearlessness and freedom of love implies power. A person who is not afraid of anything is subjectively (in his own experience) and objectively a powerful person. He cannot be intimidated; he cannot be bribed; he cannot be beaten into subjection. All his energies are coiled up into the single power of love. Nothing in this coiled-up energy is wasted in inner conflicts and external friction; the whole of it is directed to one great purpose. And often the more it functions, the greater are the returns of the energies it generates in others; the more it expends itself, the greater are the returns that replenish its expenditure. In this sense it is a form of energy that is almost inexhaustible (like the energy of intra-atomic friction), an energy that sometimes actually grows through its expenditure. Herein lies the fact of the majestic, gigantic power of love and gentleness, of the power of the great incarnations of love like Buddha and Jesus, St. Francis and Gandhi. Even from a strictly "positivistic" standpoint, the influence exerted by these apostles of love upon the whole of human history far exceeds the influence of the mighty conquerors, rulers, empire builders, and seeming controllers of millions of soldiers and subjects. *The most effective and most accessible way to acquire the maximum of constructive power is to love truly and wisely.* The kingdoms built by the apostles of love prove to be more enduring than those built by hate and coercion.[6]

Finally, *the love experience is equivalent to the highest peace of mind and happiness.* Beginning with the somewhat puny *"peace of mind"* of Freudians and of our best sellers on "how to stop worrying," and the lollipop happiness of our dime-store hedonists and chamber-of-commerce utilitarians; passing through the short-lived "peace of mind" and "happiness" of contemporary sensual lovers; and ending with the unshakable peace of mind and unutterable bliss of an all-embracing, all-forgiving love, the love experience is the only experience that brings both of these graces of God—peace of mind and happiness—to their fruition. When love is slight and impure, peace and happiness are slight and fragile. When it is unbounded and pure, happiness becomes the ineffable *summum bonum.*

Such are some of the important characteristics of love as psychological experience.

II. The Five-Dimensional Universe of Psychosocial Love

As an empirical psychosocial phenomenon, love remains a many-dimensional cosmos. It has at least five "dimensions": the intensity of love; its extensity; its duration; its purity; the adequacy of its objective manifestation in overt actions and material vehicles in relation to its subjective purpose.

A. The Intensity of Love

In intensity love ranges between zero and the highest point, arbitrarily denoted as infinity. The zero point is neither love nor hate. Below the zero point is hate (which has a similar intensity dimension). We all know this range of love intensity. When we observe a person who preaches love but does not practice it, we know that the intensity of his love is near the zero point; when preaching of love is used to mask selfish and hateful actions of hypocrites, actions fall below the zero point and become hateful actions of various intensities. An action such as offering a seat to another person on a streetcar is an action of love, though of low intensity. Actions by which a person freely gives to others his greatest values—"health, life, soul"—are love actions of the highest possible intensity. Between zero and the highest points of love intensity there are many intermediary degrees. As a whole, the range of love intensity is not scalar. Yet we can often see clearly *which intensity is really high and which low*. Thus, other conditions being equal, the act of merely offering the seat in a streetcar will be appraised by practically all normal beings as an action of much lower love intensity than the action of saving a life at the risk of sacrifice of one's own. Although by and large love intensity is not scalar, this, however, does not hinder us from seeing the greatly different intensities of various love actions; nor even from roughly measuring in numerical units these intensities.

B. The Extensity of Love

The extensity of love ranges from the zero point of love of oneself only, up to the love of all mankind, all living creatures and the whole universe. Between these minimal degrees lies a vast scale of extensities: love of one's own family, or a few friends, or love of all the groups one belongs to—one's clan, tribe, nationality, nation; religious, occupational, political, and other groups and associations. The zero point of love extensity is love of oneself only. The maximal point of intensity is the love of the whole universe.

C. The Duration of Love

The duration of love may range from the shortest possible moment to years throughout the whole life of an individual or of a group. Love actions of low intensity as well as many of the highest intensity may last but a short time; on the other hand, love actions of low as well as high intensity may endure for a long period, perhaps throughout the life of an individual.

D. The Purity of Love

The purity of love ranges from the love motivated by love alone— without the taint of a motive of utility, pleasure, advantage, or profit, down to the "soiled love" where love is but a means to utilitarian, hedonistic or other end. "I love Thee, Lord," says a hymn ascribed to St. Francis Xavier, "yet not because I hope for Heaven thereby; nor yet since they who love Thee not, must burn eternally . . . not seeking a reward; but as Thyself has loved me, O ever loving Lord." This is a striking expression of the purest love. Pure love is always for love's sake. The quoted statements of Jesus, St. Paul, and Aristotle tell the same thing.

E. The Adequacy of Love

The adequacy of the subjective goal of love to its objective manifestation ranges from a complete discrepancy between the subjective goal of love actions and its objective consequences, up to their identity. *Inadequacy may have two different forms:* (a) love experience may be subjectively genuine in the loving person, but the objective consequences of his love actions may be very different from, even opposite to, the love goal; (b) a person may have no love experience or intentions subjectively, yet the objective consequences of his actions, though motivated by something else than love, may be most beneficial for others, similar to the effects of genuine love. The first sort of love experience and activity is altruistic subjectively but not objectively. The second sort of experience and action is not altruistic subjectively but is altruistic objectively.

Let us briefly consider each of these two forms of *inadequate love*. An extreme case of such discrepancy is that in which a loving person, anxious to help a loved one, by mistake gives him poison instead of medicine. Such a discrepant love action is *inadequate, unwise, misled, ignorant, or blind love*. The necessary wisdom lacking, blind love miscarries in its objective manifestations and destroys itself; instead of benefiting the beloved person, it often harms him.

This form of subjective love action-reaction ranges upward in a series of ever-decreasing discrepancies, until we have adequate love, where the subjective aims of love and its objective consequences become identical.

In a purely *objective love* action a person may have no love motives in his activities, yet the objective consequences may be identical with those of genuine love actions of the highest intensity and purity. Many great creators of art values—Bach or Mozart, Beethoven or Shakespeare, Raphael or Michelangelo—were motivated in their creative activities not so much by love of goodness as by love of beauty, by a creative urge, or by even prosaic motives (money, fame, popularity, etc.). Objectively (though not always subjectively) they became by their achievements great benefactors; not only intellectual or aesthetic, but also moral educators of humanity.

The inadequacy of such "objective but not subjective" love actions ranges upward from those extreme cases where no motive of love is present to those highest instances where the love motive becomes dominant and finds its adequate expression in overt activities and achievements. These *objectively altruistic actions are possible mainly through the indivisible unity of goodness, truth, and beauty, and the possibility of their mutual transformation into one another.* If in their ontological nature they are inseparable—though distinct in their individuality—anyone who truly creates in one of these fields indirectly creates in the other two: genuine goodness is always true and beautiful; genuine beauty is always good and true; and genuine truth is always good and beautiful.

F. The Theoretical and Practical Significance of the Five-Dimensional System of Love

Because it is manageable and not too complex, this five-dimensional system of love serves us in many theoretical and practical ways.

First, it allows us to "grade" roughly the total, five-dimensional magnitude of love. Such grading is not a strict measurement, because each dimension is not strictly scalar. Yet when we are confronted with an unquestionably contrasting "small love" and "great love," we can use a rough numerical indicator as a shorthand symbol of obviously different magnitudes of love.[7] If we arbitrarily designate various values to each of the five ordinates by figures from 0 to 100, we may use them as indicators for notably different magnitudes of the total, five-dimensional love.

The greatest altruists, like Jesus, Buddha, St. Francis, would occupy the highest possible place, denoted by 100 in all five dimensions. Persons who are neither loving nor hating would occupy a position near zero. Others would find a place somewhere between these points, some higher, and some lower than the others. In this way a rough numerical denotation may be used to indicate obviously contrasting magnitudes of love.

Second, the five-dimensional system allows us to compare and concisely denote various forms of love. For instance, if we take only the dimensions of *intensity* and *extensity* of love, we can at once distinguish several types.

1. There are many persons whose love is very intense toward a small ingroup (their family, their friends, their clique or sect or faction), but whose love for anybody beyond this universe is nonexistent. The extensity of their love is thus very low.

2. There are many persons who profess to love the whole of humanity. The extensity of their love is thus enormous. But their love of humanity rarely goes beyond speech-reactional declarations, and shows little in their deeds. This is love of low intensity combined with vast extensity.

3. There are persons who most intensely love their little ingroup, then love *but in a decreasing degree of intensity* various larger groups: their neighbors, their village or town, their occupational or political or religious or national or state groups, then all of humanity. This type of love decreases in intensity as it increases in extensity.

4. We all know love actions of the *highest intensity* but of *very short*

duration. A soldier impulsively risking his life to save his comrade on a battlefield is such a case.

5. There are persons *who love for a long time but with a low intensity.* Persons who for years contribute their reasonable donation to a community fund are examples of this type.

6. There are persons who love intensely, and for an indefinitely long time, either a small or an extensive human universe.

7. We have love activities in which *high purity* is combined with high or low intensity, small or vast extensity, short or long duration, low or high adequacy; and similar combinations of *low purity* with other dimensional values. Which of these combinations is more frequent in an ordinary human universe remains unknown.

All this shows that our dimensional system permits us to classify the types of love activities and of loving persons, and to learn which types and combinations are more frequent in a given human universe.

The third service of our system is that it permits us to set forth and study the meaningful-causal relationships among the dimension variables. Are they clearly connected with one another? If so, how? Positively? Negatively? Which dimension variable with which? How closely?

At present our knowledge of these relationships is rather meager. We need far more study before our knowledge of the problem can begin to be useful. With this reservation, a few tentative uniformities in this field may be pointed out.

III. Uniformities in the Causal-Meaningful Relationships of Love's Dimensional Variables

A. Self-Evident Uniformity

The greater the five-dimensional magnitude of love, the less frequent it is in the empirical sociocultural world. The great altruists like Jesus, Buddha, St. Francis, and Gandhi are as rare as the greatest genius in the field of truth or beauty.

B. Less Self-Evident Uniformities

1. *Uniformities Between Intensity and Extensity.* Other conditions being equal, *the intensity of love tends to decrease with an increase of its extensity or the size of the universe of love.* Insofar as the empirical love of a person or a group is an energy of *limited magnitude,* the larger the

love universe, the thinner its spread. If a given reservoir of love supplies only three persons, its intensity is many times greater than if it supplies three thousand or three million persons. Herein lies the explanation of why frequently professed love of all humanity is so feeble in its intensity and rarely goes beyond a mere verbal declaration. If we assume that love is not energy or that its magnitude is unlimited, then the formulated uniformity becomes questionable.

As a variation of this uniformity, we have a *decreasing intensity of love (of the individual or group) with the passing from a small group dearest to them to ever larger groups that are socioculturally more distant from them.* The logical reason for this is the same as that just pointed out for the main uniformity.

Whether we take our own behavior or observe the behavior of other persons and groups, we see uniformly that our most intense love (in overt actions) applies only to a very limited number of persons (members of the family, a few friends, and generally a small ingroup). Next comes a socially more remote circle, which we still love tangibly but less intensely. The larger and more distant the group becomes, the feebler becomes our love in its intensity, until it becomes merely speech-reactional.

This uniformity is well corroborated by a few experimental studies. Here are the essentials of one of these:

In a study with children between the ages of three and five and high school children, the intensity of love or sociality was measured by the amount of work the subject did—carrying marbles and pails of sand from one corner of a garden to another, and other measurable forms of work: (a) for himself or herself; (b) for the dearest "pal" in the group; (c) for a member of the group he disliked or was indifferent toward. The results showed a decrease in the amount of work done by each child as we pass from the work "for himself or herself" to that for a "pal" and then for an indifferent or disliked member.

Similar results have been recorded in other experimental studies of the problem.[8]

2. *Uniformities Between Intensity and Duration of Love.* The relationship between these variables is little known. The subsequent uniformities are purely tentative.

(a) Assuming that the total magnitude of love energy in an individual is finite, *the intensity of love tends to decrease with an increase of duration, when the love expenditure of a given person is not correspondingly replenished by an inflow from other persons or other sources, empirical or transcendental.* And not only does the intensity decrease, but the more intensely love's reservoir is spent, the shorter becomes the period during which it is exhausted. Like any other limited amount of energy, love energy can be spent either very intensely in a short period or it can be spread more thinly over a longer time. *There are millions of heroes of love for a moment, but few for indefinitely long periods. And their number tends roughly to decrease as the duration increases.*

(b) *When an intense expenditure of love is reciprocated by love of others or is replenished by an inflow of love from external sources* [9]— whether this source be retroactive love, love generated by love actions themselves, public approval, popularity, fame, or other substitutes for love, or whether it be a love coming from mystical, little-known supraempirical sources—*the intensity of love does not necessarily decrease as its duration increases.* Since the expediture of love is either fully or partly compensated by its inflow from these sources, the intensest love can function for an indefinitely long time, as long, in fact, as the inflowing equivalent continues. *If this equivalent is greater than the expended love, its intensity can even grow in the course of time.*

To sum up: the secret of an undiminishing love intensity over long periods of time seems to lie in this inflow of love from outside the loving individual that replenishes his great expenditures of intense love energy.

3. *The Relationship Between the Intensity and the Purity of Love.* The basically nonscalar nature of these particular dimensions makes it especially difficult to define their qualitative relationship. *Nevertheless, all in all their interrelationships seem to be positive. Love becoming increasingly purer also increases in its intensity; and vice versa.* Only the purest love is capable of the greatest sacrifice, of being most intense, because from the standpoint of an impure love of utilitarian and hedonistic calculations, such sacrifice is disutilitarian, and antihedonistic. As such it is hardly possible. "Soiled love" is always fragile, weak, and short-lived. Hence it is of low intensity. And vice versa: the intensest love has to be the purest. It means a complete merging of the whole human ego (or egos) with those of the loved one: a complete identification of the intensely loving persons. Such an identification goes beyond any utilitarian-hedonistic motivations, which are inseparable from ego and egoism. Such a love is a "disinterested" love, free from "soiling ingredients."

These almost self-evident conclusions seem to be corroborated by all the data of observation and self-observation, however scarce they are. First, the love of the greatest apostles is simultaneously intense and pure.

The greatest sacrifice they made testifies to its intensity. The absence of all selfish—utilitarian and hedonistic—motives from their love activities testifies to its intensity. The absence of all selfish—utilitarian and hedonistic—motives from their love activities testifies to their purity. The love of Jesus, St. Paul, St. Francis of Assisi, Buddha, Dr. Theodore Haas, Serafim of Sarov, Damien the Leper, Gandhi, and of thousands of other apostles of love, had both these characteristics. On the other hand, millions of cases of love of low intensity invariably are a variety of "soiled love" in which selfish, utilitarian, and hedonistic motivations are conspicuous. Most such love relationships are not "familistic" but "contractual." By their very nature these are selfish and almost always are planned to get as much as possible for as little as possible.[10]

4. *The Relationship Between the Intensity and the Adequacy of Love.* Considering for a moment only the "subjective inadequacy" of love, its existence means that *the relationship between these variables is somewhat indeterminate and loose.* The love may be very intense and yet be utterly blind or inadequate in its objective manifestations—in overt actions and external instrumentalities. *Such instances are due mainly to a lack of knowledge or wisdom in the loving person, to a separation of love from truth and beauty.* Innumerable daily facts testify to the reality of this discrepancy. We all know persons who love intensely and make sacrifices for members of their family, for friends, or for others, which however make them objectively worse instead of better, and push them farther from the goals the blind love seeks to acomplish. In intergroup relationships a group with the most helpful intentions often hurts the other group instead of helping it. The destruction and death brought to Korea by the United Nations furnish a recent example. Facts of this kind are too numerous and too well known to need further corroboration.

On the other hand, *when the manifestations of intense love in its overt actions and instrumentalities are accompanied by wisdom and knowledge, then love intensity is positively connected with its adequacy.* This factor of sufficient wisdom or knowledge is essential if a loose or negative relationship of intensity and adequacy is to be turned into a positive one. Such wisdom or knowledge is not only the strictly "scientific" experience obtained through training, schooling, literacy, and that sort of education. In accordance with my theory of personality and the sources of knowledge (sensory, rational, and superconscious-institutional), such wisdom may be obtained through each of these channels, including intuition.[11] Insofar as love is ultimately connected with truth, intuitional wisdom operates fairly frequently. *When all these forms of cognition are considered, intensity, purity, and adequacy of love are somewhat more frequently associated positively than negatively or not at all.* Other conditions being equal, persons with intense love are likely to express it more adequately than persons with a low intensity of love.

In the relationship between love and the *objective consequences of creativity in the fields of truth and beauty*—creativity motivated otherwise than by love or goodness—we are confronted with the *phenomenon of transformation of the energy of truth or beauty into that of love or goodness, and vice versa.* Empirical facts and a careful analysis clearly show such transformation. *Real beauty,* whether in the form of great music, great literature, drama, painting, sculpture, or achitecture, simultaneously *purifies and ennobles us morally.* This transformation of beauty into goodness and love was observed, studied, and confirmed long ago. Mimesis and catharsis effected by a tragedy or other real art creation were indicated by Confucius, Pythagoras, Plato, Aristotle, as well as by recent thinkers and educators.[12] The morally ennobling educational effects of a genuine art creation are an axiom of contemporary educators as well as those of the past. Likewise, a legion of thinkers in the past, in recent times (like F. Nietzsche), and today have pointed out convincingly that *real beauty or art contains in itself cognitive elements which in their own way impart to us something of truth and knowledge.*[13]

That *real truth is beautiful and good* and transforms itself into beautiful and ethically good energies is nowadays an almost axiomatic proposition, questioned by hardly anyone. The aesthetic elegancy of a genuine mathematical, scientific, philosophical, or religious thought is obvious, as is its enormous role in aesthetic creativity itself; also obvious are its immeasurable benefits in enriching and ennobling the beauty realm of every one of us. The innumerable empirical facts of the most beneficial (altruistic) consequences of an important scientific discovery, constructive technological invention, enlightening philosophical thought, or genuine religious truth are well known and need not be demonstrated here.

On the other hand, *real goodness is always beautiful, in the noblest sense of the term.* If real beauty produces catharsis in us, then real love or goodness impresses us as the purest and noblest beauty. It is not incidental that the terms *love* and *beauty* are often used interchangeably as "lovely" and "beautiful." Likewise, real love or goodness contains in itself cognitive elements that enrich us with either intuitive, or rational, or even empirical cognition or truth. The ethical *summum bonum* has correctly been considered by Plato, Aristotle, and others as containing in itself also a true cognition. An analysis of the *value judgments as cognitive propositions* by past and contemporary thinkers is general evidence of the transformability of goodness into truth. Kant's "practical reason" is ethical as well as "cognitive reason." C. I. Lewis's recent work has adequately demonstrated the truth that value judgments are at the same time cognitive judgments.[14]

All this shows the transformability of truth-goodness-beauty into one another. This transformability explains why real creations in fine arts or discoveries in the cognitive field of truth have resulted in morally ennobling, beneficial effects for millions, though the creators of beauty and seekers of truth may not have been directly motivated in their activities by ethical or love impulses.

Transformability being certain, it does not preclude a difference in the efficiency of transformation. Even the transformation of the physical energies of heat, electricity, and motion into one another never reaches 100 per cent efficiency of transformation: a part of the energy is always wasted in radiation and other ways. Something similar occurs in the transformation of truth-love-beauty into one another. A part of the energy of beauty transformed into that of love is always partly "wasted," and always gives an efficiency of transformation below 100 per cent.

We do not know what factors govern this variation of the percentage of the efficient transformation; the problem has hardly even been investigated. Offhand, one can tentatively point out one or two conditions that seem important. One of these factors is the qualitative-quantitative magnitude of each energy in a given individual or group; *the intenser, purer, more extensive, durable, and adequate the given energy of truth or beauty is, the greater tends to be the percentage of its efficient transformation into goodness (love) energy; and vice versa.* The beauty of the great compositions of Bach, Mozart, and Beethoven seems to be much greater —intenser, purer, etc.—than, for instance, the beauty of third-class compositions or of the latest crooning or jazz "hit." The relevant facts seem to corroborate this expectation. The great art creations endure and continue to be transformed into goodness for generations, centuries, millennia. The splashy best sellers go into oblivion within a short time—a few months or a few years at the most.

5. *The Relationship Between the Extensity and the Adequacy of Love.* A very tentative uniformity appears to be that *with an increase in the extensity of love its inadequacy (subjective and objective) tends also to*

increase. There are several reasons for this tentative generalization. First, small groups are loved more genuinely, more intensely, and less hypocritically than large ones. Therefore the subjective motives of love are here more often genuine than when large groups are involved. Secondly, the adequacy or inadequacy of the objective consequences of love actions become apparent sooner and more clearly with a small group than with a large one. Whether one's love action hurts or helps the loved ones in a family, among friends, and in a face-to-face group shows itself clearly and quickly, whereas with vast groups the objective consequences of one's love actions rarely become apparent and clear, and still less rarely in a short time. This applies not only to the love actions of ordinary individuals, but also to the consequences of various laws enacted by supposedly competent legislators for the benefit of a nation, or a vast universal church, or a political party, or an international alliance. Practically all laws fall short of their expected results, and some even achieve results opposite those intended. The history of governments is full of examples of measures which, though enacted to establish peace, resulted in war, and vice versa; of measures enacted to increase prosperity that resulted in depression; of attempts at raising the birthrate that resulted in its decline; of reinforcements of order that produced disorders, and so on.

History is full of facts that illustrate this tragic discrepancy. If this happens persistently to legislators, rulers, and experts, it happens still more frequently to ordinary people.

6. *The Relationship Between the Duration and the Purity of Love.* Other conditions being equal, *the purer the love the more lasting it tends to be.* This follows from the very nature of pure love. Being love for the sake of love, it endures all ordeals, sufferings, disadvantages, and disutilities. It is not afraid of anything or anyone. Hence it can bear "all things," and by bearing them it lasts an indefinitely long time, often up to the death of the loving person and beyond. Impure love, motivated by utilitarian considerations, hedonistic expectations, and other selfish advantages, functions in a "soiled form" only as long as these utilities, pleasures, and advantages are forthcoming. As soon as they cease or are replaced by their opposites, such love dries up and dies.

Empirical observation corroborates this generalization. Heterosexual love motivated exclusively by sex pleasure lasts, as a rule, only as long as the libidinal pleasure continues. When it fades, or when erotic pleasure from copulation with another person becomes more attractive, such sexual love dies. Marriages based on it crumble; "romances" fade. Any love or alliance of persons or groups that is based on the hatred of a common foe is also short-lived. Once the common enemy has disappeared, that "love," "alliance," or "mutual aid" of the previously allied parties quickly dies out. Hitler, as a common enemy, cemented Communist and anti-Communist groups into an alliance, but as soon as Hitler and the Third Reich were defeated the alliance cracked and fell apart; previous comrades-in-arms became enemies. Similarly, Soviet Russia now cements the Western countries into one bloc; but if and when this common enemy disappears, the countries of the Western bloc may be fighting among themselves.

Again, any love among partners based on a profitable business cools fast whenever the partnership ceases to be profitable for one or for all the parties concerned. For the same reason many "brotherhood" communes, associations, and sects turn out to be short-lived as soon as the profits, pleasures, and advantages of their "love" and "brotherhood" fade. But the pure love of a married couple, of members of a family, of true friends, of members of a genuine religious sect, or a leader and his followers, of a teacher and his pupils, or of any totality of individuals, endures and is virtually immortal. The loved one departed from this life is neither forgotten nor loved less than in life. Suffering, pain, sorrow, disadvantage, are often incapable of breaking such a love.

7. *The Relationship Between the Duration and the Adequacy of Love.* For obvious reasons, *adequate love is likely to last longer than inadequate love.* From every standpoint, adequate love is more satisfactory for all persons involved. The unlovely and harmful consequences of an objectively inadequate love weaken and sometimes kill not only the love of the loved person, harmed by inadequate results, but even that of the loving person himself, made resentful by the "ingratitude" of the other party or shocked by the harmful results of his own love activities. As a rule, such "blind love" is quickly resented (repudiated, rejected, protested) by the other person, who suffers from its inadequate consequences; and this resentment cools or ends the love of the blindly loving person. The "ingratitude" of children toward their mother whose blind love has spoiled them; the "ingratitude" of many subjects of dependence toward their patrons, superiors, and other "blind benefactors"; the "ingratitude" of employees toward their employers for the latter's blind benevolence: these are all too well-known, perennial phenomena. They

demonstrate the tentative validity of our generalization when the inadequacy consists in a discrepancy between the objective consequences of love and those that were expected.

8. *The Relationship Between the Purity and the Adequacy of Love.* There appears to exist, on the whole, *a tangible, positive relationship between the purity and the adequacy of love.* Pure love contains an element of true wisdom or cognition as to the best means and ways of its manifestation. It implies a notable lack of emotional blindness, and a notable knowledge of the adequacy or inadequacy of its manifestation. *This association, however, does not need to be close.* In reality, we rarely find a strictly pure love; it almost always has some "soiling elements." Hence it is somewhat subject to emotional blindness in its manifestations. Then, too, the cognitive elements of even a pure love experience are always limited; pure love experience does not and cannot give all the necessary knowledge of the physical, biological, and psychological results of its manifestations. If such knowledge is not acquired by way of a cognitive experience, the objective manifestations of pure love may miscarry in its actual consequences.

These seem to be the main tentative uniformities in the relationship of the major dimensions of love.

NOTES

1. See M. Scheler, *Das Wesen und die Formen der Sympathie* (1929); N. Berdyaev, *Solitude and Society* (London, 1938), pp. 194 ff.; P. E. Johnson, *Christian Love* (New York, 1951). For other forms, see my *Society, Culture, Personality,* Chap. 5.
2. Aristotle, *The Nicomachean Ethics,* Bk. IX, 1166a; Bk. VIII, 1156a; Cicero, "On Friendship," Everyman's Library Edition, p. 179, *et passim.*
3. V. Solovyev, *The Meaning of Love,* pp. 22, 44, 53, 59, *et passim;* Berdyaev, *op. cit.,* p. 195. See a development of these ideas in Sri Aurobindo's *The Life Divine,* pp. 187 ff., 874, *et passim.*
4. See the data and literature in P. Sorokin, *Society, Culture, and Personality* (New York, 1947), p. 8 ff.; also P. Sorokin, *Altruistic Love: A Study of American "Good Neighbors" and Christian Saints* (Boston, 1950).
5. See E. Swedenborg, *De Divino Amore et de Divino Sapientia* (New York, 1890), pp. 96 ff.; Swami Vivekananda, *Karma-Yoga,* pp. 10–13.
6. See, on the life-span and longevity of various social organizations (states, business empires, political parties, educational institutions, religious organizations, and so on), my *Society Culture, and Personality,* Chaps. 34 and 47. Whereas the average duration of business empires is about 28 years, and that of empires built hastily through conquest is from a few years to a few centuries, the great religious organizations are the most long-lived of practically all social groups and cultural systems. They have already been living for one or several millennia.
7. Even Jesus used such a rough grading. *"Greater* love hath no man than this,

that a man lay down his life for his friends" (John 15:13). J. Bentham and other utilitarians do the same in their "moral arithmetics," though unfortunately they tend to look at their rough appraisal of various "utilities" as a real measurement; this is an error.

8. See J. B. Maller, *Cooperation and Competition: An Experimental Study in Motivation* (New York, 1929), Chap. 12. The somewhat different results obtained by B. A. Wright may be due to the fact that the choice of toys for friends and strangers was not actual but only imaginary and speech-reactional; and to several other conditions of the experiment. See B. A. Wright, *Selfishness, Guilt-Feeling and Social Distance;* and *Fairness and Generosity.* Both studies are unpublished theses (University of Iowa, 1940 and 1942).

9. This is somewhat similar to a "feedback" process. See N. Wiener, *Cybernetics* (New York, 1948), pp. 151 ff., *et passim.*

10. On familistic and contractual relationships, see my *Society, Culture, and Personality* (New York, 1947), Chap. 5.

11. See on this further my book *The Ways and Power of Love,* Chaps. 5 and 6; also my *Reconstruction of Humanity,* Chap. 13; and *Social and Cultural Dynamics,* Vol. IV, Chap. 16.

12. See the literature and quotations on this in my *Dynamics,* Vol. I, Chap. 12, *et passim;* H. Read, *Education Through Art* (London, 1943).

13. See on the "aesthetic component" and on art as a "pure intuition," F. S. C. Northrop, *The Meeting of East and West* (New York, 1946); Martin Johnson, *Art and Scientific Thought* (London, 1944); B. Croce, *Aesthetics* (London, 1909), pp. 385 ff. Nietzsche's fine arts as "a merry science," R. Wagner's theory of the fine arts as giving us the cognition of the ultimate reality, *"universalia ante rem,"* are but a few variations of this well-established fact of cognitive function of the fine arts.

14. See C. I. Lewis, *An Analysis of Knowledge and Valuation* (La Salle, 1947); see there also a history of this basic problem. Further see P. H. Furfey, *The Scope and Method of Sociology* (New York, 1953), Chap. 4; H. Hart, "Value-Judgments in Sociology," *Amer. Sociol. Rev.,* 3:862–867 (1938); H. Becker, "Supreme Values and the Sociologist," *Amer. Sociol. Rev.* 6:155–172 (1941); W. M. Urban. "Axiology," in D. D. Runes, ed., *Twentieth Century Philosophy* (New York, 1943); St. Thomas, *Summa Theologica,* I, q.5, a.6, and II-II, q.145, a.3.

21

Epilogue: Love—the Alpha and Omega

Herbert A. Otto

We are at a point in our development where a massive nourishing and flourishing of love has become a necessity if we are to survive as a species. How then are we to foster this massive nourishment and increased emergence of love in today's society? It is in this context that the contributions to *Love Today* become especially meaningful.

On reading the various essays it is once more clear that love and love relationships play a central and dynamic role from inception and birth until our death, and perhaps beyond. Since most people are surrounded by a loving and caring climate at their birth as well as at the time of their death, and since for most people the moment of conception is also a moment of love, love then can be said to be the beginning and the end, the alpha and omega of our being.

Within that context, personality growth and the actualizing of personal potential is our most engrossing lifelong adventure. Many of the contributors to this volume share insights, findings and conclusions *which are directly relevant to this task of expanding our own awareness and self-understanding.*

In turn, this increased self-awareness and understanding can be a means toward our becoming more loving beings. David Orlinsky's conclusion that "love relationships are . . . necessary links in the process of personal growth" is especially relevant. Alexander Lowen adds to this, "Love has the stabilizing element of the eternal. It is this quality in love that makes growth possible." To complete the picture David Jones finds that love and life goals are "inextricably woven together." The reaffirmation of the centrality of love by the contemporary behavioral scientists and thinkers who have contributed to this volume establishes a sound basis for a number of *action alternatives* which will be of special interest to those who believe the regeneration of love as a force in today's society should receive priority. One action alternative is the intensive study of love.

Specific chapters in this volume pose a variety of fascinating questions and furnish leads to inquiries which can more fully illuminate our understanding of love and its function. The work of the late Pitirim Sorokin, one of our profoundest contemporary students of the subject, invites us to explore the practical applications of his five-dimensional system of love to contemporary living. Alexander Lowen's contribution raises the whole question of the relationship between body motility and the capacity for love. How can we help people toward greater proficiency in the "practice of the love arts" as defined by David Jones—and are there other components of these arts yet to be discovered? Henry Winthrop invites us to focus attention on the relationship between the forms of love and companionship. In his essay on creativity and love Lowell Colston opens the door to a whole series of inquiries. Most intriguing to me are the questions "By what means can our love relationship become more of a bridge for the unfolding of our creative potential?" and "In what ways can we help our creative flow to nourish love and loving behavior in us?"

Other lines of inquiry which are suggested by the contributors are studies of the nonverbal communication of love, inquiries into the relationship between a healthy sensuality and sexuality and the capacity to give and receive love, etc.

I personally believe the phenomenon of "primary narcissism" offers one of the most promising lines of inquiry. Primary narcissism is the love of the infant for the mother, a very powerful undifferentiated emotion; undifferentiated because the infant loves himself, the mother *and* the world without separating one from the other. To the infant this love "encompasseth all things." This is a universal reservoir of goodwill, caring, affection, and perhaps the bedrock on which man's capacity to love is built. There is reason to believe that this reservoir of loving feelings can in some manner be reawakened so that this force will play a more active role in the total personality functioning. The Primal Sensory Experience * which I have developed for use in small groups and

* Herbert A. Otto, *Group Methods to Actualize Human Potential* (Holistic Press, 160 S. Robertson Blvd., Beverly Hills, Calif.), second edition, pp. 360–363.

field-tested over the past three years seems to be a step in the right direction. I am convinced that a whole range of techniques and methods can be devised and researched which will reawaken this primal love. This is a dynamic source, slumbering in every person, which can be tapped and utilized so that we will love ourselves more and be able to love our neighbor more.

The presence within our society of a considerable potential for violence and destruction is paralleled by the presence of an equal if not greater potential for caring and loving. There are many signs that young people especially are aware of this fact and are searching for life-affirmative directions. Significant segments of the younger generation in the United States especially and to a heretofore unsurpassed degree have chosen love and cultivation of loving behavior as a way of life. This appears to be an outgrowth of a strong spiritual thrust into the Eastern and Western religions, philosophy and mysticism which continues to gather momentum. Unfortunately, the media focus most attention on the bizarre and violent aspects of what has come to be called "the youth culture." The end result is the creation of an image which does not correspond to reality—young people emerge as bizarre types, prone to violence or committed to violent change. My association with young people, particularly during my study of the commune movement in this country in 1970, has convinced me *that the media's image effectively denies the most dynamic component of the youth culture—love.* Is it possible that our fear of love surpasses our fear of violence?

A concerted interdisciplinary approach to the study of love is urgently needed and at this point in man's development should be very much higher on the list of priorities than the innumerable inquiries into personality pathology and dysfunction which seem to preoccupy behavioral scientists and members of the helping professions and the mental health movement. The regeneration of love has broad preventive applications and can form the base for the development of a number of far-ranging preventive programs. Hopefully the mental health movement is now at a point in its evolution where there will be increasing recognition that more resources and effort need to be invested in the preventive area.

One action alternative is directly and indirectly suggested both by the nature of the contributions to this volume and some of the writers themselves. This is a multifaceted extensive research approach to the phenomenon of love utilizing the best tools, techniques and resources at our disposal. Adequate funding for such research is a prime requisite.

And hopefully this is a field in which private foundations will become interested, and to which the National Institute of Health will be more generous in giving support.

Underlying a concerted research approach would be the following basic questions: (1) What is the role of love in personality functioning and the actualizing of human potential? (2) What is the role of our social institutions vis-à-vis the emergence of caring and loving relationships between members of our society? (3) What generates fear of love and what prevents love from developing in man? (4) What means and approaches can we utilize and develop (including regeneration of our institutions) to help man today to become more of a loving and caring being?

The interdisciplinary team approach to the study of love needs to be particularly concerned with the key question, "How can two of our most powerful institutions—the schools and our religious organizations and churches—be helped to make love more functional in the lives of their members?" Certainly the school curriculum from grade school through college needs to be reexamined in the light of the above question. Where in the maze of classes, information giving and lectures do we explicitly foster the emergence and nurture of love as an ongoing part of the total educational experience? Similarly, sermonizing and the proscriptions and prescriptions from the pulpit utilized by so many religious organizations and institutions have not been very successful in fostering loving behavior in their members. Nor have these religious institutions been notably successful in helping their members to bring religious beliefs and value structures into close consonance with their daily lives and functioning. ("Living what we believe.")

Over the past decade, an increasing number of schools and religious institutions have used small group experiences as a means of coming to grips with man's estrangement from himself and his fellow man. T-group, sensitivity and encounter experiences have proliferated in many institutions. Unfortunately, over the past five years especially, an increasing number of institutions have been disillusioned with the sensitivity and encounter group approach. In most such instances, the many angry confrontations between group members and the consistent emphasis on problems and "hang-ups" has accounted for the strong backlash directed toward this type of group experience.

This ongoing angry, if not hostile, interaction is by no means characteristic of all encounter groups. A major variable here seems to be the facilitator's personality and leadership style which calls forth this consistent response. Institutions which are discontinuing the use of all small group approaches due to their negative experience with "sensitivity" or "encounter" are throwing out the baby with the bath water. A number of small group approaches exist which emphasize the development of a loving and caring climate. These approaches focus on the strengths and potentials of the participants. Problems are dealt with in this context and there is an emphasis on open communication, emotional honesty, and the development of empathy. Dr. Stewart B. Shapiro's program of positive experiencing * and the Developing Personal Potential program ** begun at the University of Utah in 1960 and currently offered by a number of universities and educational institutions are samples. The continued development of group experiences and programs which foster the emergence of love and caring in the participants and *making these or similar programs widely available to as many people as possible offers another major action alternative.*

A final action alternative is the organization of Love Team Centers and the initiation of Love Team Projects, a concept sparked by teacher Arleen Lorrance's program at Thomas Jefferson High School, Brooklyn, New York (see pp. 206–9). Love Team Centers and Projects can be a means of personal and social regeneration involving many segments and aspects of society including adolescents, college students, school children, minority groups, professionals, senior citizens, etc. Love Team Centers could be organized within schools, churches, clubs, and mental health clinics. These organizations would provide leadership and a physical meeting place for the Love Teams. The teams (with anywhere from five to twelve members) would have two major objectives—to create a loving and caring group climate which will enable participants to give to themselves and to each other and to formulate and carry out specific projects within the larger community expressing the spirit of giving, caring, and loving which has been created within the team.

The Love Team Center concept is based on the recognition that (a) to give love to others, it is best to begin by giving ourselves more love, (b) love is manifest through action, (c) to give and receive love is a means of developing respect for oneself and others, and (d) to give and receive love is a means of joyous and vital living and a way of communing with the essence of being and becoming.

---

* Stewart B. Shapiro, "Tradition Innovation," in *Encounter*, Arthur Burton, ed. (San Francisco, Jossey-Bass, Inc., 1969), p. 177.
** Herbert A. Otto, *op. cit.,* pp. 1–23.

Deep within some core of our being, most of us recognize that although we are led to believe we have only so much love to offer, *the more love we give, the more we have to give*. As Ashley Montagu so well expressed it during a Los Angeles address: "As a result of our misunderstanding of what we are on this earth for, we have brought ourselves very near to the edge of doom. I regard most people as dead, simply as creatures wandering around, having no realization of why they are on this earth. They have no idea that *the only reason for being on this earth is to live to love*." (Italics added.)

It is within our power to create a renaissance of love—a climate of sensitive caring which cradles each man in the recognition that his relatedness to the other is the means of growth, of becoming, of unfoldment. The shaping of this renaissance offers us an opportunity to join in an act of creation unparalleled in history: fostering the flowering of love in man and utilizing everything we have learned to date in the process, including the resources of our science and technology. In this particular period of explosive social change, our massive investment in the regeneration of love will create optimum conditions for the evolutionary process in which we are engaged. *It is by a massive investment in the regeneration of love that rapid social evolution will fail to turn into the violence of disintegrative revolution.*

If we examine our situation clearly, it becomes very evident that the renaissance of love and the regeneration of our social institutions are different faces of the same coin and are in fact inseparable. It is only when we shape our social institutions so that they will allow for the unfoldment and foster the development of love and deep caring of one human being for another that man's best qualities and deeper powers will make their appearance. It is only then that man begins to be in a position to realize his full potential. Paradoxically, the process of institutional regeneration begins with our own regeneration.

The renaissance of love is not a utopian dream. There exists a large array of facts, approaches and techniques which can bring about a rebirth of love, and the research suggested previously will add immeasurably to what we already have. The means are at hand for each man to transform himself into a more caring, loving human being.

Love is the most powerful agent for the transformation of man and his institutions. By learning to let love flow freely we gain both new dimensions of freedom and new responsibility (response-ability) in relation to ourselves and the world we live in. At this turning point in our history the renaissance of love can bring to this living entity we call earth a new health, beauty and oneness—the preconditions for the next step in man's growth.

Appendix

GROWTH CENTERS

The Human Potential Movement represents one of the most recent efforts to release and extend the power of love in the life of the individual. The list of such Centers presented here is by no means complete, and inclusion here does not necessarily imply an endorsement by the editor or contributors represented in this volume. The listing is included to inform the reader about organizations presently known for their work in this highly significant new field.

NEW ENGLAND

Associates for Human Resources
387 Sudbury Road
Concord, Mass. 01742

Boston Tea Party
55 Berkeley Street
Boston, Mass. 02116

Cumbres
Box C
Dublin, N. H. 03444

Foundation for Gifted and Creative Children
395 Diamond Hill Road
Warwick, R. I. 02866

Human Relations Center
Boston University
270 Bay State Road
Boston, Mass. 02215

Human Resources Development
Hidden Springs
South Acworth, N. H. 03607

Institute for Experimental Education
Box 446
Lexington, Mass. 02173

Lifwyn Foundation
52 South Morningside Drive
Westport, Conn. 06880

New England Center for Personal and Organizational Development
Box 575
Amherst, Mass. 01002

Number Nine
266 State Street
New Haven, Conn. 06511

Sky Farm Institute
Maple Corner
Calais, Vt. 05648

275

MIDDLE ATLANTIC

Anthos
24 East 22nd Street
New York, N. Y. 10010

Athena Center for Creative Living
2308 Smith Avenue
Aliquippa, Pa. 15001

Awosting Retreat
315 West 57th Street
New York, N. Y. 10019

Bucks County Seminar House
Erwinna, Pa. 18920

Center for Human Development
217 North Craig Street
Pittsburgh, Pa. 15213

Center for the Whole Person
1633 Race Street
Philadelphia, Pa. 19103

Community Consultation Services
285 Central Park West
New York, N. Y. 10024

Dialogue House Associates
45 West 10th Street
New York, N. Y. 10011

Encounters: Workshops in Personal
and Professional Growth
5225 Connecticut Avenue, NW
Suite 209
Washington, D.C. 20015

Groups for Meaningful Communication
645 West End Avenue
New York, N. Y. 10025

G.R.O.W.
312 West 82nd Street
New York, N. Y. 10024

Human Dimensions Institute
4380 Main Street
Buffalo, N. Y. 14226

Human Resources Institute
Box 3296
Baltimore, Md. 21228

Humanist Society of Greater New
York
2109 Broadway at 73rd Street
New York, N. Y. 10023

Instad—Institute for Training and
Development
625 Stanwix Street, Suite 2306
Pittsburgh, Pa. 15222

Institute for Living
300 South 19th Street
Philadelphia, Pa. 19103

Institute for Rational Living
45 East 65th Street
New York, N. Y. 10021

Institute for Research into Personal
Freedom
327 Sixth Avenue
New York, N. Y. 10014

Institute of Applied Psychotherapy
251 West 92nd Street
New York, N. Y. 10025

Interface, Inc.
Park Plaza #534
1629 Columbia Road, NW
Washington, D.C. 20015

Ithaca Seed Company
Box 651
Ithaca, New York 14850

Kirkridge
Bangor, Pa. 18013

Laboratory for Applied Behavioral
Science
Newark State College
Union, N. J. 07083

Mid-Atlantic Institute of Christian
Education
Suite 325
1500 Massachusetts Ave., NW
Washington, D.C. 20005

New York Institute for the Achievement of Human Potential
36 East 36th Street
New York, N. Y. 10016

N.T.L. Institute for Applied Behavioral Science
1201 Sixteenth Street, N.W.
Washington, D.C. 20036

Orizon Institute
2710 – 36th Street, NW
Washington, D.C. 20007

Pendle Hill
Wallingford, Pa. 19086

Personal Growth Laboratories
112 Hunter Lane
North Wales, Pa. 19454

Plainfield Consultation Center
831 Madison Avenue
Plainfield, N. J. 07060

Princeton Associates for Human
Resources
341 Nassau Street
Princeton, N. J. 08540

Quest
3000 Connecticut Avenue, NW
Washington, D.C. 20008

Relationship Development Center
P.O. Box 23; Gedney Station
White Plains, N. Y. 10605

Sensitivity Training for Educational
Personnel
Herbert H. Lehman College
Bedford Park Boulevard West
Bronx, N. Y. 10468

Sentio
247 West 72nd Street
New York, N. Y. 10023

Spruce Institute
1828 Spruce Street
Philadelphia, Pa. 19103

Tao House
522 Eastbrook Road
Ridgewood, N. J. 07450

Tarrytown House
Box 222
Tarrytown, N. Y. 10592

Training for Living Institute
80 Fifth Avenue
New York, N. Y. 10011

Wainwright House
Milton Point
Rye, N. Y. 10580

W.I.L.L. (Workshop Institute for
Living-Learning)
333 Central Park West
New York, N. Y. 10025

SOUTH

Adanta
3379 Peachtree Road, NE
Suite 250
Atlanta, Ga. 30326

Atlanta Workshop for Living-Learning
3167 Rilman Road, N.W.
Atlanta, Ga. 30327

The Center
Box 157
Syria, Va. 22743

The Center of Man
Micanopy, Fla. 32667

Espiritu
1214 Miramar
Houston, Tex. 77006

The Family Relations Institute
3509 Farm Hill Drive
Annandale, Va. 22044

The Han Institute
% Denis O'Donovan
Executive Suite N
Weir Plaza Building
855 South Federal Highway
Boca Raton, Fla. 33432

Hara, Inc.
7322 Blairview
Dallas, Tex. 75230

Heliotrope
Box 9041
Fort Lauderdale, Fla. 33312

Keystone Experience
West Georgia College
Psychology Department
Carrollton, Ga. 30117

The Laos House: Southwest Center
for Human Potential
700 West 19th
Austin, Tex. 78701

Maitreyan Foundation
220 SW 2nd Street
Boca Raton, Fla. 33432

Omega Institute
Box 263
Merrifield, Va. 22116

The Piedmont Program
Box 6129
Winston-Salem, N. C. 27109

S.I.P.O.D.
2606 East Grove
Houston, Tex. 77027

Southwest Motivation Center, Inc.
Cambridge Tower
1801 Lavaca
Austin, Tex. 78701

MIDDLE WEST

Alverna Retreat House
8140 Spring Mill Road
Indianapolis, Ind. 46260

Amare: The Institute of Human
Relatedness
Box 108
Bowling Green, Ohio 43402

Antioch Group for Human Relations
Antioch College
Yellow Springs, Ohio 45387

Cambridge House
1900 North Cambridge Avenue
Milwaukee, Wis. 53202

Center for Creative Interchange
602 Center Street
Des Moines, Ia. 50309

Communication Center No. 1
1001 Union Boulevard
St. Louis, Mo. 63113

Domus
2722 Park Avenue
Minneapolis, Minn. 55407

Forest Growth Center
555 Wilson Lane
Des Plaines, Ill. 60016

Gestalt Institute of Cleveland
12921 Euclid Avenue
Cleveland, Ohio 44112

Greenerfields Unlimited
1740 Waukegan Road
Glenview, Ill. 60025

Human Resource of Developers
520 North Michigan, #520
Chicago, Ill. 60611

Inscape
2845 Comfort
Birmingham, Mich. 48010

Kopavi
Box 16
Wayzata, Minn. 55391

Midwest Personal Growth Center
200 South Hanley Road
Clayton, Mo. 63105

Mobius, Inc.
Box 445
Menomonie, Wis. 54751

Oasis: Midwest Center for Human
Potential
20 East Harrison
Chicago, Ill. 60605

Omega Center
Unity Village, Mo. 64063

Ontos, Inc.
40 South Clay
Hindsdale, Ill. 60521

Outreach
University of Michigan

Psychology Department
Ann Arbor, Mich. 48104

People
4340 Campbell
Kansas City, Mo. 64110

Seminars for Group Studies
Center for Continuing Education
University of Chicago
1307 East 60th Street
Chicago, Ill. 60637

Shadybrook House
Rural Route 1
Mentor, Ohio 44060

University Associates
Box 24402
Indianapolis, Ind. 46224

University Associates
Box 615
Iowa City, Ia. 52240

Northwest

Northwest Family Therapy Institute
Box 94278
Tacoma, Wash. 98494

Seminars in Group Process
8475 S.W. Bohmann Parkway
Portland, Ore. 97223

Senoi Institute, Inc.
Route 2, Box 259
Eugene, Ore. 97401

Star Weather Ranch Institute
Box 923
Hailey, Ida. 8333

Mountain

Arizona Training Laboratories for
Applied Behavioral Science
Box 26660
Tempe, Ariz. 85281

Evergreen Institute
3831 West Wagon Trail Drive
Littleton, Col. 80120

Institute of General Semantics
University of Denver
Denver, Col. 80210

Rocky Mountain Behavioral Institute
12086 West Green Mountain Drive
Denver, Col. 80228

Vida
Ventures in Developing Awareness
1934 East Charleston
Las Vegas, Nev. 89104

Yogi Academy Foundation
3209 Burton Avenue, SE
Albuquerque, N. M. 87107

CALIFORNIA

Analysis Institute
1394 Westwood Boulevard
Los Angeles, Calif. 90024

Berkeley Center for Human Interaction
1820 Scenic
Berkeley, Calif. 94709

Berkeley Institute for Training in
Group Therapy & Psychodrama
1868 San Juan Avenue
Berkeley, Calif. 94707

Berkeley Movers
4919 Clarke Street
Oakland, Calif. 94609

Bindrim, Paul & Associates
2000 Cantata Drive
Los Angeles, Calif. 90028

Blue Mountain Center of Meditation
1960 San Antonio
Berkeley, Calif. 94707

Bridge Mountain Foundation
2011 Alba Road
Ben Lomand, Calif. 95005

Casaelya
2266 Union Street
San Francisco, Calif. 94123

The Center
Box 3014
Stanford, Calif. 94305

The Center for Creativity and
Growth
599 College Avenue
Palo Alto, Calif. 94306

Center for Human Communication
120 Oak Meadow Drive
Los Gatos, Calif. 95030

Center for Interpersonal Development
3127 Eastern Avenue
Sacramento, Calif. 95821

Center for Studies of the Person
1125 Torrey Pines Road
La Jolla, Calif. 92037

Counseling Associates
30 South El Camino Real
San Mateo, Calif. 94401

Counseling Associates
6275 Shadygrove Court
San Jose, Calif. 95129

Dialogue House Associates
Box 877
San Jacinto, Calif. 92383

Edmucko
P.O. Box 216
Ben Lomond, Calif. 95005

Elysium Institute
5436 Fernwood Avenue
Los Angeles, Calif. 90027

Emotional Studies Institute
775 Camino del Sur C-2
Goleta, Calif. 93017

Esalen Institute
Big Sur, Calif. 93920

Esalen Institute
1776 Union Street
San Francisco, Calif. 94123

Esalen Institute
Stanford University
Stanford, Calif. 94305

Eureka Center for Communication
and Encounter
4300 Crest View Drive
Eureka, Calif. 95501

Explorations Institute
Box 1254
Berkeley, Calif. 94701

Foundation for Human Achievement
291 Geary Street
San Francisco, Calif. 94102

Gestalt Therapy Institute of Los Angeles
337 South Beverly Drive
Suite 206
Beverly Hills, Calif. 90212

Gestalt Therapy Institute of San Diego
7255 Girard Avenue, Suite 27
La Jolla, Calif. 92037

Gestalt Therapy Institute of Southern California
1029 Second Street
Santa Monica, Calif. 90403

Guild for Psychological Studies
2230 Divisadero Street
San Francisco, Calif. 94115

High Point Foundation
1001 East Rosecrans Avenue
Compton, Calif. 90221

Human Dynamics Workshop
Box 342
Boulder Creek, Calif. 95006

Human Potential Institute
2550 Via Tejon
Palos Verdes Estates, Calif. 90274

Human Resources Institute
1745 South Imperial Avenue
El Centro, Calif. 92243

Human Resources Institute
7946 Ivanhoe Avenue
La Jolla, Calif. 92037

Humanist Institute
1430 Masonic Street
San Francisco, Calif. 94117

Institute for Creative and Artistic Development
5935 Manchester Drive
Oakland, Calif. 94618

Institute for Group and Family Studies
347 Alma
Palo Alto, Calif. 94301

Institute for Growth
3627 Sacramento Street
San Francisco, Calif. 94118

Institute for Integrative Psychology
School of Social Sciences
University of California
Irvine, Calif. 92664

Institute for Multiple Psychotherapy
3701 Sacramento Street
San Francisco, Calif. 94118

Institute of Ability
P.O. Box 798
Lucerne Valley, Calif. 92356

Institue of Behavioral Dynamics
9000 Sunset Boulevard
Los Angeles, Calif. 90069

Institute of Human Abilities
80 Hamilton Place
Oakland, Calif. 94612

International Cooperation Council
17819 Roscoe Boulevard
Northridge, Calif. 93124

Kairos–Los Angeles
P.O. Box 75426
Los Angeles, Calif. 90005

Kemery Institute
304 Parkway
Chula Vista, Calif. 92010

Lafayette Center for Counseling and Education
Brook Dewing Medical Building
914 Dewing Street
Lafayette, Calif. 94549

National Center for the Exploration of Human Potential
8080 El Paseo Grande
La Jolla, Calif. 92037

New Consciousness Program
Old Student Union; Room 142
University of California
Santa Barbara, Calif. 93101

Pacific Training Associates
3516 Sacramento Street
San Francisco, Calif. 94118

Palo Alto Venture
P.O. Box 11802
Palo Alto, Calif. 94306

Personal Exploration Groups
2400 Bancroft Way
Stiles Hall
Berkeley, Calif. 94704

San Francisco Gestalt Therapy Institute
1719 Union Street
San Francisco, Calif. 94123

San Francisco Venture
584 Page Street
San Francisco, Calif. 94117

Schiffman, Muriel, Communication
& Self Therapy Workshops
340 Santa Monica Avenue
Menlo Park, Calif. 94025

S.E.L.F. Institute
40 Hawthorne Avenue
Los Altos, Calif. 94022

Self-Other Systems Institute
Maple Street
Redwood City, Calif. 94063

Society for Comparative Philosophy, Inc.
Box 857
Sausalito, Calif. 94965

Sweet's Mill
Auberry, Calif. 93602

Tahoe Institute
Box DD
South Lake Tahoe, Calif. 95705

Thomas Jefferson Research Center
1143 North Lake Avenue
Pasadena, Calif. 91104

Topanga Center for Human Development
2247 Topanga Canyon Road
Topanga, Calif. 90290

Viewpoints Institute
833 North Kings Road
Los Angeles, Calif. 90069

Well-Springs
2003 Alba Road
Ben Lomond, Calif. 95005

Western Center Consultants
9400 Culver Boulevard
Suite 206
Culver City, Calif. 90230

HAWAII

Human Explorations Program
P.O. Box 1145
Kanehoe, Hawaii 96744

CANADA

Claremont Experiment
P.O. Box 123
Weston, Ont.

Cold Mountain Institute
P.O. Box 2884
Vancouver, B.C.

Cold Mountain Institute
P.O. Box 4362
Edmonton 60, Alba.

Dynacom
2955 Fendall
Montreal 250, Que.

The Gestalt Training Institute of
Canada
Lake Cowichan, Box 39
Vancouver, B.C.

Human Development Association
P.O. Box 811, Station B
Montreal, Que.

Shalal
750 West Broadway
Vancouver, B.C.

Strathmere
North Gower, Ont.

Synergia
P.O. Box 1685, Station B
Montreal 2, Que.

Toronto Growth Centre
Box 11
Downsview, Ont.

FOREIGN

Apartado Postal 85
San Miguel de Allende
Guanajuato, Mexico

Esalen-in-Chile
% Claudio Naranjo
1413 Allston Way
Berkeley, Calif. 94702

John C. Lilly
% Oscar Ichazo
Casilla 614
Arika, Chile

Tarango-Centro de Desarrollo Humano
Norte 59 #896
Industrial Vallejo
Mexico 16, D.F.

Yoloti
Sierra Vertientes 365
Mexico D.F. 10, Mexico

Australian Institute of Human Relations
12 Webb Street
Altona, Australia

Human Interaction Seminars
Box 4984
G.P.O. Sydney 2001 NSW
Australia

Center House
10-A Airlie Gardens
Kensington, London W8, England

Centre for Applied Social Research
The Tavistock Institute
Belzise Lane
London NW 3, England

M. Ferdinand Cuvelier
179 Passtraat
Geel, Belgium

Diipf
Box 900280, Schloss Straase 29
6 Frankfurt 90, Germany

Quaesitor
Vernon Road
Sutton, Surrey, England

Notes on Contributors

JOE K. ADAMS, Ph.D. taught at Bryn Mawr College (assistant professor and chairman), also has worked as clinical psychologist in a clinic and in private practice. Among Dr. Adams' publications are articles in *Journal of Humanistic Psychology, Psychological Review, Psychological Bulletin* and *Psychedelic Review.* Books by Dr. Adams include *Basic Statistical Concepts* (McGraw-Hill, 1955), and *Secrets of the Trade* (Viking Press, 1971).

THEODORE H. BLAU, Ph.D. Independent practice of clinical psychology. Adjunct Professor of Behavioral Science, University of South Florida. Member, board of directors, American Psychological Association. Dr. Blau has published articles in *Journal of Abnormal and Social Psychology, American Psychologist, Journal of Consulting Psychology,* and *Journal of Projective Techniques.* Dr. Blau has written *Private Practice in Clinical Psychology* (New York, Appleton-Century-Crofts, Inc., 1951).

LOWELL G. COLSTON, Ph.D. is professor of Pastoral Care, Christian Theological Seminary, Indianapolis, Ind. Dr. Colston's articles have appeared in *Pastoral Psychology* and in *Christian Herald.* Books by Dr. Colston include *The Context of Pastoral Counseling,* with Seward Hiltner (Abingdon Press, 1961); *Wake Up, Self* (Christian Board of Publication, 1969); "Pastoral Theology and Clinical Training," in *The New Shape in Pastoral Theology* (Abingdon Press, 1969); *Judgment in Pastoral Counseling* (Abingdon Press, 1969); *Personality and Christian Faith,* with Paul E. Johnson (Abingdon Press, Spring, 1972).

DAVID G. JONES, Ph.D., Ed.D. President, David G. Jones, Inc. and formerly executive vice-president, Jones and Byrd, Inc.; on faculty of Boston University and Tufts University; training officer, Episcopal Executive Council. Dr. Jones has written *Communication: The Seven C's of Family Communication* (Jones and Byrd, Inc. 1970), and *A Planning Guide for Church Renewal* (David G. Jones, Inc., 1971).

284

SIDNEY M. JOURARD, Ph.D. has a part-time private practice in consulting psychology and is on the board of advisors of several "growth centers." He is also a Veterans Administration consultant. Among Dr. Jourard's publications are articles in *Mental Hygiene, Scientific American,* and *Psychological Report.* Dr. Jourard has written *Personal Adjustment: An Approach Through the Study of Healthy Personality* (New York, Macmillan, 1958); *The Transparent Self: Disclosure and Well-Being* (Princeton, Van Nostrand, 1964), and *Disclosing Man to Himself* (Princeton, Van Nostrand, 1968).

CARL D. LEVETT, Ph.D. is a clinical psychologist. He has conducted a private practice in psychotherapy and marriage counseling since 1953 and was formerly director of the Westchester County Family Relations Center, a private resource for the treatment of family problems. He has also served as a free-lance group leader for groups seeking to develop human potentialities. Dr. Levett has written articles for *New Frontiers* and is one of the contributors to *The Family in Search of a Future* (New York, Appleton-Century-Crofts, 1970).

AL LEWIS, Ph.D. is executive director, National Center for the Exploration of Human Potential, La Jolla, Calif. His special field of interest is the impact of the industrial environment on social structure.

ROSALIND LORING, M.A. is director of the Department of Daytime Programs and Special Projects at UCLA, and chairman, AEA National Convention in Los Angeles, 1971. She organized and was the first chairman of the Adult Educators of Greater Los Angeles (1969–70).

ALEXANDER LOWEN, M.D. is executive director of the Institute for Bio-energetic Analysis and is a practicing psychiatrist in New York City and New Canaan, Conn. Books by Dr. Lowen include: *Physical Dynamics of Character Structure* (Grune & Stratton, 1958); *Love and Orgasm* (Signet, 1965); *The Betrayal of the Body* (Collier Books, 1967), and *Pleasure: A Creative Approach to Life* (Coward-McCann, 1970).

PAUL MARIAH, M.A. is founder and co-editor of *ManRoot* magazine and was poetry editor for *Van Guard* and *Vector* magazines. He has had poetry published in *Van Guard, The Ladder, The Berkeley Tribe, Aldebaran Review, Poetry* and others. Works by Mr. Mariah include *Diana,* a folio of 16 poems (Goliards Press, 1968).

DEL MARTIN, is a founder of the Daughters of Bilitis, a homophile organization in San Francisco, and is presently a member of the Task Force on Homosexuality for the San Francisco Mental Health Association. Ms. Martin has written articles for *The Ladder, motive, Sisters,* and *Vector.* Ms. Martin is the author of chapters in the following books: *Sexual Latitude: For and Against* (Hart Publishing, New York, 1971); *Is Gay Good? Ethics, Theology and Homosexuality* (Westminster Press, Philadelphia, 1971), and *The New Women* (Bobbs-Merrill, 1970).

DAVID E. ORLINSKY, Ph.D. is Associate Professor of Psychology and Social Sciences, University of Chicago. Dr. Orlinsky has published papers in *The Journal of Abnormal Psychology, The Journal of Consulting and Clinical Psychology, Annual Review of Psychology, Archives of General Psychiatry,* and *Psychotherapy: Theory, Research and Practice.* His book *Varieties of Psychotherapeutic Experience* (co-authored with Kenneth Howard) will be published by Teachers College Press, Columbia University.

HERBERT A. OTTO, Ph.D. is professor, Counseling, San Diego State College, and president, National Center for the Exploration of Human Potential, La Jolla, Calif. His articles have appeared in *Saturday Review, Marriage and Family Living, International Journal of Social Psychiatry, Group Psychotherapy, Social Casework,* and *Psychiatric Quarterly.* Editor of *The Family in Search of a Future* (Appleton-Century-Crofts, New York, 1970); *The New Sexuality* (Science and Behavior Press, Palo Alto, Calif., 1971); and author of *Guide to Developing Your Potential* (Charles Scribner's Sons, New York, 1967) and *Group Methods Designed to Actualize Human Potential: A Handbook* (Holistic Press, Beverly Hills, Calif. 1968).

BILLY B. SHARP, Ed. D. was formerly executive director, W. Clement and Jessie V. Stone Foundation, Chicago, Illinois. He is presently president, Combined Education Motivation Systems, Chicago, Ill. Books by Dr. Sharp include: *Choose Success* (Hawthorn Books, New York, 1970) and *Learning: The Rhythm of Risk* (Combined Motivation Education Systems, Chicago, 1971).

EVERETT L. SHOSTROM, Ph.D. is director, Institute of Therapeutic Psychology and Chairman, Division of Clinical Psychology, San Diego, Calif. Dr. Shostrom has written articles for *Journal of Consulting Psychotherapy, American Journal of Psychotherapy, Journal of Consulting and Clinical Psychology,* and *Psychology Today,* among others. His books include *Man, the Manipulator* (New York, Abingdon Press, 1967); *The Manipulator and the Church,* with Dunnam, M. and Herbertson, G. (New York, Abingdon Press, 1968); *Therapeutic Psychology; Fundamentals of Actualization Counseling and Psychotherapy,* with L.M. Brammer (Englewood Cliffs, N. J., Prentice-Hall, 1968), and *Between Man and Woman,* with James Kavanaugh, Ph.D. (Los Angeles, Nash Publishing, 1971).

PITIRIM A. SOROKIN (1889–1968), Dr. Sociology. Emeritus Professor, Sociology, Harvard University. Director, the Research Center for Creative Altruism, Cambridge, Mass. Published numerous articles in professional and scientific journals and former president, the American Sociological Association. Among his best known books are: *Altruistic Cove* (Beacon Press,

1950), *Explorations in Altruistic Love and Behavior* (Beacon Press, Boston, 1950); *The Ways and Power of Love* (Beacon Press, Boston, 1954); and *Power and Morality* (Sargent, Boston, 1958).

CLIFFORD H. SWENSEN, Ph.D. is professor of Psychology, Purdue University, Lafayette, Indiana. Dr. Swensen has written articles for *American Psychologist, Psychological Bulletin, Journal of Clinical and Consulting Psychology, Journal of Counseling Psychology,* and *Psychotherapy: Theory, Research and Practice.* He is the author of *An Approach to Case Conceptualization* (Houghton-Mifflin, Boston, 1968).

COLIN WILSON. Widely published novelist and essayist and one of the original English "Angry Young Men." Among his best known books are *The Outsider* (Houghton-Mifflin, Boston, 1956); *Poetry and Mysticism* (San Francisco, City Lights, 1969); and *Voyage to a Beginning: An Intellectual Autobiography* (New York, Crown, 1969).

HENRY WINTHROP, Ph.D. is Professor, Department of Interdisciplinary Social Sciences, University of South Florida at Tampa, Fla. His extensive publications have appeared in various professional journals, chiefly in the behavioral and social sciences, philosophy, the humanities and education.